BECOMING VEGETARIAN

The Complete Guide to Adopting a Healthy Vegetarian Diet

Vesanto Melina, R.D.

Brenda Davis, R.D.

Victoria Harrison, R.D.

MACMILLAN CANADA
TORONTO

Canadian Cataloguing in Publication Data
Davis, Brenda, 1959–
        Becoming vegetarian
Includes index.
ISBN 0-7715-9045-8

1. Vegetarianism.   2. Vegetarian cookery.   I. Harrison, Victoria, 1941–   .
II. Melina, Vesanto, 1942–   . III Title.

TX392.D38   1994   613.2'62   C94-930816-1

Macmillan Canada wishes to thank the Canada Council, the Ontario Ministry of Culture and Communications and the Ontario Arts Council for supporting its publishing program.

A complete list of references for this book is available upon request from the authors. Please contact Macmillan Canada's editorial department for further details.

Design and text production: Counterpunch
Cover illustration: Helen D'Souza

Macmillan Canada
A Division of Canada Publishing Corporation
Toronto, Ontario

6 7 8 9 10 TRI 02 01 00 99 98

Printed in Canada

To our children,

Chris and Kavyo;
Leena and Cory;
Richard, Christina and Rachel.

May each day of your life fill you with the inspiration
and courage to stand for what you believe.

SELECTED REFERENCES

American Dietetic Association. 1993. Position of the American Dietetic Association: Vegetarian diets. *J. Am. Diet. Assoc.* Vol. 93:1317–1319.

Bourne, G.H. *Nutritional Value of Cereal Products, Beans and Starches.* Basel, Switzerland: Karger, 1989.

Brown, M.L. *Present Knowledge in Nutrition.* Washington, D.C.: International Life Sciences Institute, Nutrition Foundation, 1990.

Chow, C.K., ed. *Fatty Acids in Foods and their Health Implications.* New York. Marcel Kekker Inc., 1993.

Committee on Diet and Health, Food and Nutrition Board, Commission on Life Sciences, National Research Council. *Diet and Health.* Washington, D.C.: National Academy Press, 1989.

Draper, A., Lewis, J., Malhota, N. et al. 1993. The energy and nutrient intakes of different types of vegetarian: a case for supplements? *Brit. J. Nutr.* 69:3–19.

Dwyer, J.T. Nutritional consequences of vegetarianism. 1991. *Annu. Rev. Nutr.* 11:61–91.

Erdman, J.W. and Fordyce, E.J. 1989. Soy products and the human diet. *Am. J. Clin. Nutr.* 49:725–737.

Hallas, T.J. and Walker, A.F., eds. Vegetarianism: the healthy alternative? pp. 210–247 in Walker, A.F. and Rolls, B., eds. *Issues in Nutritional Toxicology.* New York: Elsevier Applied Science, 1992.

Harland, B.F. 1989. Dietary fiber and mineral bioavailability. *Nutr. Res. Rev.* 2:133–147.

Health and Welfare Canada. *Nutrition Recommendations: The Report of the Scientific Review Committee.* Ottawa: Supply and Services Canada, 1990.

Heaney, R. P., 1993. Protein Intake and the Calcium Economy. *J. Am. Diet. Assoc.* Commentary Vol. 93: 1250–1260.

Lee, K., Oilce Y., and Kanazawa T., eds. *The Third International Conference on Nutrition in Cardiovascular Diseases.* Annals New York Acd. Sci. Vol. 676, 1993.

Mangels, A.R. 1992. Vegetarian infants and children: a review of recent research. *Issues in Vegetarian Dietetics.* Vol. 1, No. 2: 4–6.

O'Connell, J.M., Dibley, M.J., Sierra, J. et al 1989. Growth of vegetarian children: the farm study. *Pediatrics.* Vol. 84, No. 3: 475–481.

Panel on Dietary Reference Values of the Committee on Medical Aspects of Food Policy. *Dietary Reference Values for Food Energy and Nutrients for the United Kingdom.* London: H.M.S.O., 1991.

Pennington, J.A. *Bowes and Church's Food Values of Portions Commonly Used.* 16th ed. Philadelphia: Lippincott Company, 1993.

Sanders, T.A.B. 1988. Growth and development of British vegan children. *Am. J. Clin. Nutr.* 48:822–825.

Young, V. R. 1991. Soy Protein in Relation to Human Nutrition and Amino Acid Nutrition. *J.Am. Diet. Assoc.* 91: 828–835.

World Health Organization Study Group on Diet, Nutrition and Prevention of Noncommunicable Diseases. *Diet, Nutrition and Prevention of Chronic Diseases.* Geneva, Switzerland: Technical Report Series No. 797. World Health Organization, 1991.

CONTENTS

ACKNOWLEDGEMENTS

To every person who made this book possible, through their unfailing enthusiasm, support, patience and advice, we offer our gratitude. We are especially indebted to the following people:

Our deepest thanks to:
Dr. Paul Harrison for relentless hours of literature searches, dedication, encouragement and sound judgement. Paul Davis for valuable courier services, unfailing patience and advice. David Melina for his thoughtful review of the manuscript and unique perspective and his example. Kirsten Hanson, our editor, whose guidance, skill and clarity were central to the completion of this work. Louise Lambert-Lagacé for her inspiration, careful analysis of the manuscript and her suggestions. Karin Litzeke, RDN, for ongoing support and excellent advice and insight. Susan Denton for her thorough work on recipe analysis and figure confirmations. Kedong Yin for his assistance in preparing tables and figures. Lara Victoria for recipe illustrations.

Many thanks to our professional reviewers and advisors for their assistance, support and advice:
Dial-a-Dietitian Staff: Kathleen Quinn, RDN, Susan Ferris, RDN, Jane Swalling, RDN and Jean Fremont, RDN; Dr. Joseph Leichter; Dr. Susan Barr; Dr. R.G. Ackman; British Columbia's Children's Hospital dietitians: Hugette Cloutier, RDN, Barbara Cheng, RDN, and Vikki Lalari, RDN; Healthiest Babies dietitians: Jeannie Dickie and Shefali Raja; Ketti Goudey, RD; Gerry Kasten, RDN; Sherry Ogasawara, RDN; Cheri Kutynik, RDN; Linda Watts, RDN; Fiona Smith, RDN; Kyra Bartlett; Laurie Hunter; Patty Pasinyk, RDN; Dr. Tai C. Chen; Dr. Vernon Young; Dr. Connie Weaver; and the British Columbia Dietitians and Nutritionists Association.

Sincere thanks to friends and acquaintances who provided thoughtful chapter reviews and hours of undaunted recipe testing:
Joseph Forest, chef Michael Fisher, Ruth Sebastian; Ken and Susan Collerman, Sandra Lindstrom; Lynn Berowski, and Pam Grover. Thanks also to Sunrise Tofu Company for providing samples used in recipe testing.

We also offer our heartfelt appreciation to:
Dr. E.S. Goranson (Vesanto's father) and John and Doreen Charbonneau (Brenda's parents) and Jean Harman (Victoria's mother) for setting the high standards by which we live and work, and for giving us the inspiration to follow our hearts.

FOREWORD

Vegetarianism has been practiced for centuries in much of the world for many different reasons. No one can deny that over the past several decades vegetarianism has become trendy in North America. Still, it remains an enigma or a risky diet in the minds of many consumers and health professionals. No wonder, since the term "vegetarian" can have different meanings, and since meatless meals, which can easily be very nutritious, are so often inadequate.

A few weeks ago I had at my nutrition clinic a teenager who wanted to become a vegetarian but could not; she was in tears, but her parents refused as they did not think she could become vegetarian without jeopardizing her growth and health. Other days I see young adults who have opted for a meatless diet but who suddenly develop daily sugar cravings; they have replaced meat with greens or beautiful vegetables, but have not included adequate proteins at every meal. I also see new vegetarians who lack iron in their blood after months without red meats, having switched to cheese as their mainstay. My advice in such cases is not a return to meat protein but a better selection of good plant protein and iron sources. Vegetarian menus can be very healthy, but sound, reliable and accurate information is badly needed to plan them.

Becoming Vegetarian fills the void.

Vesanto Melina, Brenda Davis and Victoria Harrison have done a superb job with this challenging topic. These three dedicated dietitians have worked for many months finding the most recent data, developing practical eating guides and testing delicious recipes. They provide complete answers to all your worries, such as finding and preparing good plant proteins, including iron-rich foods, replacing milk products if desired, feeding a vegetarian child or teen, dining out or entertaining without meat or poultry, planning menus for picnics or box lunches. Another important aspect of their contribution is that they practice what they preach. Their book reflects their beliefs and eating habits.

I am honored to have the possibility to publicly endorse *Becoming Vegetarian*. I am sure you will find it user-friendly!

Louise Lambert-Lagacé
Consulting dietitian and author of *The Nutrition Challenge for Women*

INTRODUCTION

Becoming Vegetarian is an invitation to explore nutrition options that could well change the way you look at food. It is for the many people who find themselves adopting or moving toward a plant-based diet. Whether you are just beginning the transition, or are a vegan, this book will help to answer your most challenging questions.

You may wonder why three dietitians would write a book that encourages people to eliminate meat from their menu. We are often asked if we have been vegetarians all our lives. To the contrary: Vesanto followed the lead of her daughter some 15 years ago; Brenda has been a vegetarian for four years; Victoria for two. All three of us were raised in traditional homes where meat was the focus of our meals. We went through mainstream universities and taught nutrition using the trusted four-food-group method. We told people to eat their meat for high-quality protein and iron, and drink their milk for calcium. But it became harder to ignore the evidence implicating the typical North American diet in chronic disease. We became aware of the powerful connection between our food choices, the environment, and world hunger. We began to take a good look at the way our food arrives on the table, and were deeply saddened by the conditions in which the animals people consume live and die. For us, the decision to become vegetarian was not difficult: it was the only option.

If you too find yourself moving in this direction, rest assured that you are not alone. Every year, more than a million North Americans become vegetarian, and many others take giant strides in that direction, so you are not alone. But if you grew up on meat, you may feel at a loss as to what to do with tofu. You may be unsure of how to plan a meatless menu with a full complement of necessary nutrients. And you may wonder if this way of eating is healthy for your children. As nutrition professionals, we understand these concerns and have committed ourselves to easing your transition. During our years as vegetarians we have gained valuable insight from many people in the world who maintain excellent health without any significant reliance on meat or milk. Our experience has taught us that vegetarian eating can not only be healthy, but interesting and delicious.

Becoming Vegetarian will give you new confidence in your ability to put together wonderfully nutritious meals, and provide guidance and encouragement as you make choices that support a healthier world.

Vesanto Melina, R.D.
Brenda Davis, R.D.
Victoria Harrison, R.D.
1994

WHAT IS A VEGETARIAN?

Over 14 million North Americans consider themselves "vegetarians." Of these, about a third completely eliminate meat, poultry and fish from their diets. The others generally include poultry or fish, but avoid red meat. It may strike you as rather odd that so many people who eat meat choose to identify themselves as vegetarians. Perhaps it is an indication that vegetarianism is now being viewed as a positive step by many people.

Although vegetarians are by no means a homogeneous group, there are certain characteristics that are more prevalent in this population than in the rest of society. Perhaps the most obvious is a strong interest in health. They often select minimally processed foods, and tend to use less salt, sugar and caffeine. Some prefer organically grown foods and avoid artificial colors, preservatives and additives.

But while vegetarians often share an interest in health and ecology, there is tremendous variety among their ranks, not only in their individual diets, but also in their reasons for becoming vegetarian. For some people vegetarianism is a way of achieving better health, while for others it is a matter of ethics, religion, ecology or animal rights. Indeed, some find themselves facing rather difficult questions regarding their degree of commitment to vegetarianism; questions such as: Do real vegetarians eat marshmallows? Am I still a vegetarian if I eat turkey at Christmas? But these kinds of issues are not important. It matters far more how comfortable you are with your choices and how well they fit into your life. Each one of us will make the transition towards vegetarianism in our own way and in our own time; one way is not necessarily any better than another.

TYPES OF VEGETARIAN DIETS

Vegetarians are generally described according to the foods that they include in their diets. These categories serve to make communication a little less complicated, and they can reduce the need for lengthy explanations about what foods one is or is not willing to eat. Food consumption patterns rarely fall into neat categories; they are a blend of culture, preferences and beliefs that reflect our individuality.

Those who include both plants and animals in their diets are called "omnivores." In contrast "vegetarians" completely avoid animal flesh, whether it comes from cows, chickens or fish. When people become vegetarian for reasons of health, there may be some flexibility in their use of animal foods. When the choice is made on the basis of ethics or religion, there is a greater tendency towards complete adherence to the diet.

LACTO-OVO VEGETARIAN

Lacto-ovo vegetarians avoid all animal flesh, but continue to use eggs (ovo) and dairy products (lacto). Approximately 90–95 percent of vegetarians in North America include dairy and/or eggs in their diets. Lacto vegetarians exclude animal flesh and eggs, but continue to use dairy products, and ovo vegetarians use eggs, but avoid dairy products.

PURE VEGETARIAN OR VEGAN

The pure (total) vegetarian or vegan avoids all foods of animal origin, including eggs, dairy foods, gelatin and honey (the product of bees). Although the terms vegan and pure vegetarian are generally used interchangeably, some experts make a distinction between the two. Vegans usually go beyond diet, avoiding as much as possible products derived from animals. They may shun leather goods, wool and silk, tallow soaps and standard photography that requires gelatin. (Gelatin, used in making marshmallows, Jell-O and other confections, is made from the bones and connective tissue of animals.)

There are many variations within each "category" depending on religion, culture, and beliefs about food and nutrition. Some choose to eat only raw foods; others choose to eat only that which has been organically grown. One of the more restrictive vegetarian patterns is:

MACROBIOTIC

The macrobiotic diet was first popularized in the West in the 1940s and 1950s, and the system is intended to promote longevity. The principles of macrobiotics are based on the conventional Chinese concepts of "yin" and "yang."

George Ohsawa, the founder of macrobiotics, classified foods according to where they would fall on a yin and yang continuum. Alcohol, sugar and fruits were considered the furthest extreme of yin (expansiveness), while meats and salt were on the furthest extreme of yang (contractiveness). Foods classified on the extreme ends of the spectrum are less desirable than those falling closer to the center. Brown rice is considered the most balanced single food, as it falls precisely half-way in between. The macrobiotic diet is based on a system in which there are ten progressively more restrictive regimes. The least restrictive includes small amounts of fish and some dairy products, but excludes soda pop, coffee, refined grains, sugar, canned and frozen foods, hot spices and irradiated foods. The most restrictive level includes only brown rice and water. Fluid restriction is recommended at all ten levels to varying degrees. The top levels are void of all animal products.

The potential advantages to the macrobiotic diet include less obesity, lower blood cholesterol levels and lower blood pressure. These advantages, however, are quickly negated when the level of food restrictions rises, as the diet becomes increasingly deficient in essential nutrients and there is insufficient fluid intake.

Several of the criticisms of vegetarianism as a whole have been based on studies of macrobiotic communities. Severe nutritional deficiencies and growth retardation have been reported on numerous occasions in macrobiotic children. A special word of caution is warranted regarding Kokoh, the traditional weaning milk that is made from beans, grains and seeds. This "milk" has been found to contain inadequate levels of several vitamins and minerals. The mixture is sometimes over-diluted which can also make it deficient in calories and protein.

Others Choosing a Plant-Based Diet

There are many individuals who are "in transition" toward vegetarianism and are slowly reducing their consumption of animal foods. Others, although consciously reducing their intakes of animal foods, have little intention of ever completely eliminating animal flesh from their diet. Many such individuals are making dietary changes in an effort to improve health. Some are moved to reduce the consumption of animal foods for ecological reasons. Whatever their reason for moving toward a plant-based diet, we lack a suitable adjective to define this group. The following terms are sometimes used, though these may be inappropriate, particularly for those individuals who have no desire to ever become "vegetarian."

PESCO-VEGETARIANS

Pesco-vegetarians include those people who have chosen to eliminate red meat and fowl, but continue to use fish and seafood.

SEMI- OR PARTIAL-VEGETARIANS

Semi- or partial-vegetarians use some poultry and fish, but eat primarily vegetarian fare. These individuals generally avoid red meat.

REASONS WHY PEOPLE BECOME VEGETARIAN

The reasoning that moves a person toward a vegetarian diet includes matters of both the heart and the head. Many believe that a vegetarian diet is more healthful. Many also believe that killing animals for food is wrong, particularly when the animals are mistreated during their lives. Almost 70 percent of North American vegetarians still cite one of these as being their primary reason for becoming vegetarian. The connection between the food that we choose and the state of the environment, human hunger and economics also moves people toward a plant-based diet.

The decision to become vegetarian is not one that is taken lightly, for it is a decision that is contrary to our culture, our tradition and what most of us grew up believing. Regardless of the hurdles, every year more and more people are making the switch, and others are beginning to sit up and take notice. Some of the more common reasons why include:

Health

Health is the number one reason people become vegetarian. There is a strong consensus that a vegetarian diet is healthier than a diet that includes, and particularly emphasizes, animal foods. The points most frequently cited are:

- A vegetarian diet reduces one's risk of chronic, degenerative diseases such as heart disease, cancer, diabetes, obesity, osteoporosis, gallbladder disease and hypertension.
- A plant-based diet more commonly meets the current recommendations for percentages of fat, carbohydrate and protein than an omnivorous diet. We are told to cut back on fat, especially saturated fat, to

emphasize grains, fruits and vegetables and to increase fiber. This is a fairly simple task for a vegetarian.

• There is less chance of contracting a bacterial infection such as *E. coli, Camphylobacter* or *Salmonella* on a meat-free diet.

• Vegetarian diets generally contain fewer pesticides. Many of these substances accumulate as we move up the food chain. Some pesticides are fat soluble, thus when animals eat contaminated plants, the pesticide can become concentrated in their fat. When we eat the animals these pesticides are deposited in our fat.

• Diseases such as bovine spongiform encephalopathy (BSE), bovine leukemia virus (BLV) and bovine immunodeficiency virus (BIV) found in aminals could potentially affect human health.

Ethics and Animal Rights

For many people vegetarianism is a statement against violence and cruelty. There is a feeling that taking the life of another creature is fundamentally wrong. Every year in the United States and Canada more than seven billion animals (not including fish) are slaughtered for food. People who choose to be vegetarian as a means of protest express their concerns as follows:

• Animals are feeling creatures with complex behavioral patterns and intense bonds to their offspring.

• Today's system of animal agriculture treats animals like inanimate objects. As our population and our food needs grow, incidences of overcrowding, confinement, isolation and brutality increase. The animals are often robbed of the opportunity to behave in instinctive ways and can be driven insane.

• Animals are transported to slaughter in appalling conditions, often without food or water for extended periods of time. Millions of animals die each year en route to slaughter as a result of such conditions.

• The actual slaughter is inhumane, primitive and violent. Stunning methods are sometimes unreliable, and many animals move in pain along the disassembly line toward becoming our food.

The Environment

There is an unprecedented reaction by our society to the state of the environment. People are beginning to realize that we cannot continue to consume the earth's resources at this rate if there is to be any hope for future generations. They make the choice to become vegetarian as a way of further reducing environmental destruction. Their arguments are as follows:

• The raising of livestock is a major contributor to desertification (loss of topsoil, and drying-out of the land to such an extent that it cannot support the growth of any vegetation) and deforestation (loss of trees in many settings, including those of the precious rain forest).

• Animal agriculture demands tremendous amounts of fresh water. For example, it takes about 25 gallons (110 litres) of water to produce a pound of wheat and 390 gallons (1,700 litres) to produce a pound of beef. It takes less water to produce the food that a pure vegetarian needs for one year than to produce the food that a meat eater needs for a month.

• The earth's topsoil, which is essential for growth of plants, is being depleted more quickly than it is being formed. Animal agriculture contributes significantly to this critical situation.

• Animals raised for food require intensive use of fossil fuels. Fuel is needed to transport animal feed (grains and legumes), to heat animal shelters (often large buildings), and to transport animals to slaughter, meat packing plants and grocery stores. This heavy requirement for fossil fuels and, to a lesser extent, methane production by animals, contribute to global warming.

• Large amounts of pesticides, herbicides and fertilizers used to grow feed for animals contribute to pollution when they make their way onto the land and into the water supply, with far-reaching effects.

• The destruction of natural habitats to make room for animal agriculture contributes to the rapid rate of extinction of many plants and animals.

Human Hunger

World hunger is a problem of enormous proportion. Nearly one-quarter of the human population does not get enough to eat. Of these, 40–60 million die of starvation and related diseases each year. Many people who choose a vegetarian diet do so, at least in part, to make some contribution to the reduction of world hunger. Their rationales include the following:

• Animal agriculture is a very inefficient use of our food resources. It requires tremendous energy, and produces little usable food, in comparison to plant yields.

• The demand for meat among the rich people of the world takes precedence over the need for grain and legume production among the poor in developing countries. Land owners frequently opt to grow or raise whatever brings in the greatest profit. That often means choosing to grow beef for the rich rather than beans for the hungry. The land, labor and resources of the poor are often exploited in the process.

• In developing countries, land desperately needed to grow indigenous foods is used to grow cash crops, animal feed and fodder, and livestock for export in order to service international debts.

• Two-thirds of the grain exported from North America to other countries goes to feed livestock. This livestock in turn goes to feed only those people who can afford it.

• One quarter of the world's population uses 80–86 percent of the non-renewable resources and 34–53 percent of the food. In the United States, 230 lbs (103 kg) of animals are consumed by each man, woman and child per year, while in India animal consumption is less than 5 lbs (2 kg) per person.

Economics

Many of the world's people exist on vegetarian or near-vegetarian diets simply because they cannot afford meat. Economics can mold political decisions and dictate food choices. For some people economics is yet another driving force toward a vegetarian diet. The arguments that they use to support this decision include:

• In many affluent countries meat is affordable only because it is subsidized by government. Without such subsidies, meat would be far less affordable and more people would have to base their diets on grains and vegetables. These subsidies on meat make little economic sense when the very foods that are being subsidized are the primary contributors to the excesses that are linked to many chronic degenerative diseases. Our governments are in fact subsidizing the cost of the meat three times over: first for its production, second for its environmental cost, and third for the increase in health care costs.

• If farming policies favored grains and vegetables, the use of land would shift and populations could be fed more cheaply and efficiently.

• A plant-based diet is generally more affordable than a diet which is based on animal foods, even when meat subsidies are considered.

Religion

Although it is important to mention religion as a reason why people become vegetarian, in most cases the rationale for a church recommending this dietary regime is based on health issues or a belief that killing is inherently wrong.

• Some Christian groups, including both the Trappist monks of the Catholic Church and the Seventh-day Adventist Church, encourage a vegetarian diet.

• Many religions of the east, including Buddhism, Hinduism, Brahmanism and Jainism, adhere to a philosophy that promotes reverence for life and harmony with nature. The slaughter of animals is limited or prohibited within their following.

VEGETARIANISM STANDS THE TEST OF TIME

Vegetarianism has been a dietary option since the dawn of recorded time. Its origins remain somewhat of a mystery, though the mythologies of many cultures tell of a beginning without violence, where people lived off the plants of the earth. One of the most widely recognized records is that found in the Old Testament where Adam and Eve are told what is to be their food:

> And God said, behold, I have given you every herb-bearing seed, which is upon the face of all the earth, and every tree, in the which is the fruit of a tree yielding seed; to you it shall be for meat.
> *Genesis 1:29*

Throughout history, vegetarianism has been woven into cultures around the world. Many of the world's greatest philosophers and intellects refused meat in times when such a choice was contrary to dictates of the ruling class.

In the west, the first of these was Pythagoras, who is often considered "the father of vegetarianism." Until the late 19th century, when the word "vegetarian" was coined, people who lived on a meatless diet were referred to as "Pythagoreans." Pythagoras, born in approximately 580 B.C., was credited with the discovery of the Pythagorean theorem, many other mathematical and geometrical findings, the idea of planetary motion and the speculation that the earth moves around the sun. He also founded a society that pursued wisdom, believed in the transmigration of souls and practiced meditation. Among the Pythagoreans, materialism and meat-eating were taboo. Contrary to the general view of the time, women were considered equal to men. Pythagoras also believed that one's maximum philosophical potential could be reached only when the body was an efficient instrument. Thus, a strict exercise regime including gymnastics, running and wrestling was practiced.

Following Pythagoras, many influential thinkers through the centuries refused to eat meat:

> I have from an early age abjured the use of meat, and the time will come when men such as I will look on the murder of animals as they now look on the murder of men.
> *Leonardo da Vinci, 1452–1519*

My refusing to eat flesh occasioned an inconvenience, and I was frequently chided for my singularity, but with this lighter repast I made the greater progress, from greater clearness of head and quicker comprehension.

Ben Franklin, 1706–1790

Flesh foods are not the best nourishment for human beings and were not the food of our primitive ancestors. There is nothing necessary or desirable for human nutrition to be found in meats or flesh foods which is not found in and derived from plant foods.

Dr. J. H. Kellogg, 1852–1943

It ill becomes us to invoke in our daily prayers the blessings of God, the compassionate, if we in turn will not practice elementary compassion toward our fellow creatures.

Mahatma Gandhi, 1869–1948

Whenever I injure any kind of life, I must be quite certain that it is necessary. I must never go beyond the unavoidable, not even in apparently insignificant things. That man is truly ethical who shatters no ice crystal as it sparkles in the sun, tears no leaf from a tree . . .

Albert Schweitzer, 1875–1965

Nothing will benefit human health and increase the chances for survival of life on earth as much as the evolution to a vegetarian diet.

Albert Einstein, 1879–1955

The list goes on – Plato, Socrates, Plotinus, Plutarch, Newton, Voltaire, Shelley, Darwin, Emerson and Shaw, to name a few. It took great courage for these people to become advocates of vegetarianism in their times.

George Bernard Shaw (1856–1950) describes the reaction of his physician when he announced his choice to remove meat from his diet. His physician cautioned the young Shaw that if he continued to insist on this meat-free diet, he would surely die of malnutrition in short order. Shaw replied that he would sooner die than consume a "corpse." It's rather ironic when you read the words of Shaw as he approached his 85th year:

The average age of a meat eater is 63. I am on the verge of 85 and still work as hard as ever. I have lived quite long enough and I am trying to die; but I simply cannot do it. A single beef steak would finish me; but I cannot bring myself to swallow it. I am oppressed with a dread of living forever. That is the only disadvantage of vegetarianism.

In 19th-century England, the influence of those individuals with a compassion for all living things affected many people. They began to draw together for discussion and support. The modern world's first vegetarian society, formed in England in 1847, was followed by similar societies in many European countries and the United States. The growth in vegetarianism was slow. During the first half of the 20th century movements were fueled by the ideals of health reformers and those defending the ethical principles of a vegetarian diet.

It is interesting to note that although meat was considered a symbol of social status and culture, it is only in the last century that anyone other than the very rich could afford to eat it in any quantity. Even in the 18th and 19th centuries well-to-do families of many European countries such as France and Holland could seldom afford to eat meat more than once a week. The truth is that the vast majority of the world's population has existed on a near-vegetarian diet and still does, though not necessarily by choice.

A New Era for Vegetarianism

The late 1960s and early 1970s brought a new era for vegetarianism. Peace-loving "counterculture" groups sprang up with a message of ecology and natural living. Vegetarianism became synonymous with the hippie movement to many people. Health professionals often viewed the vegetarian diet as a dangerous fad which led to nutritional deficiencies.

In 1971, Frances Moore Lappé's book *Diet for A Small Planet* gave a tremendous boost to the vegetarian cause. Her work drew many supporters toward a vegetarian diet with a strong argument for the environment and world hunger issues.

John Robbins further strengthened the vegetarian movement with his books, *Diet for a New America*, 1987, and *May All Be Fed*, 1992. Robbins' arguments are based on issues that appeal to a mainstream audience – the environment, world hunger and the degenerative diseases of affluence. He also presents a strong voice for animal rights which has profoundly touched people as an idea whose time has come.

The 1980s also saw a push for vegetarianism from members of the health community. Dr. Colin Campbell spearheaded a huge epidemiological study of 6,500 Chinese. Dr. Dean Ornish presented evidence for the reversal of atherosclerosis through diet. Both made a case for vegetarianism. The Physicians' Committee for Responsible Medicine, headed by Dr. Neal Barnard, although under fire by more conventional health professionals, also encourages a vegetarian diet. Many other outspoken physician-writers, including Dr. Michael

Klaper, Dr. John McDougall and Dr. Benjamin Spock, have persuaded people to remove meat and milk from their diets.

THE FUTURE IS BRIGHT!

The old stereotype of the vegetarian flower-child is finally being laid to rest. Today we see people of every age and from every walk of life choosing vegetarianism, and fewer people condemning that choice.

Although the diversity among vegetarians is considerable, there also seems to be a common bond that creates kinship among those who opt to exclude animal flesh from their diets. People are making this choice out of concern for health – the health of human beings, of the earth and of the animals with which we share this planet. As these concerns increase, the vegetarian alternative offers hope for a brighter future.

The growth in the vegetarian movement today is greater than at any other time in history. In response to this growth, vegetarian options are sprouting up everywhere: vegetarian convenience foods, meatless restaurant options, vegetarian magazines and books, and even vegetarian spas. Conferences, workshops, newsletters and journals for health professionals often feature materials on vegetarianism. There is no doubt that the dietary shift toward vegetarian foods is gaining momentum and there's no indication that it's going to slow down any time soon. The impact of these trends is potentially enormous. Perhaps someday soon veggie burgers will be a regular option on the menus in hospitals, school cafeterias and fast food restaurants. Perhaps the day will come that the sales of veggie burgers outnumber hamburgers at McDonald's.

THE EVIDENCE IS IN

oday's consumers are bombarded with messages that sell health through promises of good nutrition. Retailers no longer promote cooking oil on the basis of its performance or taste; rather we are sold on the product's lack of cholesterol or high concentration of poly- or mono-unsaturated fats. This emphasis on the nutritional value of food is a reflection of the interest, on the part of many consumers, in the relationship between the foods we eat and disease. Everywhere we turn, there is another headline associating diet and disease. That association has created a dramatic shift in the way people view food. A well-marbled steak is less highly esteemed in our society than it once was. Instead, we are turning to pasta and broccoli.

In this chapter we examine the evidence that links diet to disease. Why are people moving away from a diet centered on animal foods toward one centered on plant foods?

THE STANDARD NORTH AMERICAN DIET – GUILTY AS CHARGED?

The Standard North American Diet, which on occasion has been referred to as "SAD," has been "on trial" for its potential link to hundreds of millions of deaths in North America. Scientists have acted as lawyers for both the prosecution and the defense. They have produced tens of thousands of pages of research examining the connection between diet and chronic degenerative diseases. In order to assess the strength of this evidence the World Health Organization (WHO) commissioned a panel of nutrition experts from around the world. The result, a 200-page technical paper entitled "Diet, Nutrition and the Prevention of Chronic Diseases," was published in 1990 and an executive summary in 1991. They conclude:

> Medical and scientific research has established clear links between dietary factors and the risk of developing coronary heart disease, hypertension, stroke, several cancers, osteoporosis, diabetes, and other chronic diseases. This knowledge is now sufficiently strong to enable governments to assess national eating patterns, identify risks and then protect their populations through policies that make healthy food choices the easy choices.

The evidence is in and a verdict has been reached. The diet of affluence is found guilty as charged. The most fitting sentence, as seen by health authorities, is death by public education.

The Evolution of the "Affluent Diet"

In pre-agricultural, hunter-gatherer societies the human diet consisted of approximately 20 percent of total calories from fat, and a higher ratio of unsaturated to saturated fatty acids. Daily fiber intake was approximately 40 grams per day, calcium intake was an estimated 1500 mg per day (from plant sources – no dairy), and vitamin C intake was several times what it is today. Over many centuries, different populations varied the composition of this diet by consuming more or less plant and animal foods, depending largely on the availability of these items. In virtually all cases, plant foods were consumed in a fairly natural state, fats and sweets were minimal, and the animals that were consumed were far leaner than domestic animals.

The development of agricultural societies, which began about 10,000 years ago, meant a significant improvement in food security. Gradually, agricultural techniques became more sophisticated, and people began to have a choice in the foods that they wanted to consume. The real changes in terms of the amount of fat, sugar, and other nutrients that people received was surprisingly small. The most obvious changes were a slightly lower intake of fat, and higher intake of starchy foods.

About 200 years ago the industrial revolution brought about a more dramatic shift in our food supply. With technological advances, production, processing, storage and distribution improved, and the population began to climb. As more people moved to urban centers, the pressure on the agricultural industry to produce a safe and adequate food supply intensified.

By the 1930s, governments were placing a greater emphasis on public health, and nutrition became recognized as a significant contributor to the overall health of the population. The elimination of deficiency diseases emerged as the nutritional challenge of the day. Animal products carried special weight as foods rich in protein and minerals. Early studies showed that diets emphasizing animal foods reduced the risk of malnutrition, as evidenced by feeding trials on children. Governments responded by offering special incentives to increase the production of meat and milk, and by educating the public about the importance of such foods in the diet.

In earlier days meat was generally found as an ingredient in stews, casseroles and soups. Now meat took center stage on our dinner plates. The changes in our diets were more radical than they had ever been. Compared to the agriculturalists of 200 years ago, we now consume double the fat, half the carbohydrate and half the fiber. However, diseases of nutritional deficiences were rapidly diminishing, and it appeared as though the job of improving the health of the nation through nutrition had been well accomplished.

But by the late 1940s a new health picture emerged, with heart disease and cancer at the helm. These disorders presented a real challenge to researchers who could uncover no bacteria or virus on which to blame the latest "plagues." Scientists began to ponder the possibility of an environmental influence, and a massive investigation was underway.

Scientists had some good leads, based on laboratory research. As far back as 1913, Russian researchers Anitschkow and Chalatow noted a possible connection between dietary cholesterol and heart disease. Numerous studies of varying sizes and designs were initiated in an attempt to determine the extent of the link between the foods we eat, and the diseases from which we suffer.

HEART DISEASE

Many North Americans have come to think of heart disease as a fact of life. After all, there aren't too many things that we can count on more than our odds of dying of heart disease. It may seem as though it's just the luck of the draw, but in reality heart disease is far from being a random killer. It preys on those who haven't built an adequate defense. Fortunately, people are beginning to realize that changes as simple as a morning walk and a bowl of porridge can go a long way to helping build that defense.

Cardiovascular disease has been on the downward swing since the 1960s, when it accounted for over half the deaths in North America. Although some of the credit must go to advancements in medical care, we can't underestimate the value of our positive lifestyle changes. People are making a conscious effort to cut back on fat and increase dietary fiber. As a result, blood cholesterol levels are starting to come down. But don't start doing a victory dance quite yet.

Heart disease still manages to claim more lives than any other cause of death in North America.

It is important to realize that heart disease is not the work of a single villain, but rather of a whole gang of offenders. The more evidence that accumulates, the more it becomes apparent that diet is a ring leader. The three primary controllable risk factors for heart disease are high blood cholesterol levels, high blood pressure and smoking. Both blood pressure and blood cholesterol levels are closely linked to dietary choices. Blood cholesterol is the factor most closely associated to diet, and for every 1 percent increase in blood cholesterol, we have a 2 percent increase in our risk of heart disease.

Evidence Linking Diet and Heart Disease

Epidemiological studies allow researchers to compare people living in one area with people living in another. They may study two or more groups of people within a single country, or people from different countries. The rates of disease are generally examined, as well as the environment and lifestyle factors that could be contributing to the disease. Scientists may also follow people that move from a country with a low incidence of a particular disease to a country with a high incidence, and evaluate the effects of the newly adopted lifestyle on the rates of the disease in these people.

Although epidemiological studies can help to provide clues as to what might be responsible for a particular disease, they don't establish a definitive cause and effect relationship.

STUDIES BETWEEN POPULATIONS

International comparisons of various populations have provided compelling evidence for a direct link between the food we eat and our risk of heart disease. A classic work is Keys' Seven Countries Study (Keys, 1970), which followed over 12,000 men for 20 years. The participants were from 16 different regions of seven countries: Finland, United States, Netherlands, Italy, Greece, Yugoslavia and Japan (listed according to their incidence of coronary heart disease [CHD] from highest to lowest). Those countries with the highest intake of saturated fat also had the highest blood cholesterol levels and the highest incidence of heart disease. These results provided a powerful incentive to delve more deeply into the connection between the foods that we eat and our risk for heart disease.

Since Keys' study numerous works have further confirmed these findings.

MIGRATION STUDIES

Although studies between countries provided some convincing evidence, researchers wondered how much of these findings could be due to variations in the constitutions of different ethnic groups. If indeed the people of a given culture are blessed with a great resistance to heart disease, changes in lifestyle practices should have little impact on their overall risk for the disease. In order to assess these possibilities, migration studies were carried out. These studies looked at groups who were moving to another country and adopting a new way of life.

The most widely recognized of the migration studies include those that took place between 1973 and 1975 looking at Japanese men who moved from Japan to Hawaii and San Francisco. As they gave up their traditional low-fat eating patterns in favor of the high-fat American diet, they experienced progressively greater increases in their blood cholesterol, and their incidence of heart disease became indistinguishable from that of Americans.

Good genes can offer considerable protection against heart disease, but it seems as though the average person can neutralize their good genes by choosing a bad diet.

STUDIES WITHIN A SINGLE POPULATION

Within a given country interesting differences in risk have been noted according to lifestyle practices.

In 1949, a landmark study began in Framingham, Massachusetts. Over 5,000 participants were followed for more than 30 years. The results provided powerful evidence for a link between heart disease and high blood cholesterol levels. This study showed that people with an average cholesterol level of 6.7 mmol/l (260 mg/dl)★ suffered heart attacks three to five times more often than people with levels below 5.0 (195). Blood cholesterol levels of 5.7 to 6.2 (220 to 240), which were considered normal by most North American physicians, were also found to increase the risk for heart disease. No one in the study who had a cholesterol level below 3.9 (150) suffered a heart attack. It is interesting to note that the average blood cholesterol level of vegans is about 3.2 (125).

A second important study, the Multiple Risk Factor Intervention Trial, followed 356,222 men from 1973 to 1985. This study demonstrated that the risk for heart disease is increased even with blood cholesterol levels as low as 4.7 (182). Study participants with higher levels experienced increases in fatal heart attacks (MI) as described in Table 2.1.

★People often refer to their cholesterol levels with just a number. But the number is in fact a measure of cholesterol concentration in mmol/l (the Canadian measure) or mg/dl (the U.S. measure).

Table 2.1: Risk for Fatal Heart Attacks with Increasing Blood Cholesterol Levels

Blood Cholesterol Level (mg/dl)/(mmol/l)	% Increase in Fatal MI
182-202 / 4.7-5.2	29%
203-220 / 5.2-5.6	73%
221-244 / 5.6-6.2	121%
over 245 / 6.2+	242%

Numerous epidemiological studies comparing groups of people have demonstrated that vegetarians, and particularly vegans, have lower blood cholesterol levels and are at a lower risk for heart disease than the general population. One of the largest studies followed 25,000 vegetarian and omnivorous male Seventh-day Adventists for over 20 years. Participants consuming meat four or more times per week had a fourfold increase in their risk of dying from heart disease in their 40s, and double the risk in their 60s. These figures included adjustment for smoking habits and activity levels.

WHAT WE LEARNED FROM THE EPIDEMIOLOGICAL STUDIES

These studies have served to present a powerful case regarding the relationship between dietary fat, blood cholesterol levels and heart disease. The primary hypothesis from these investigations was that a diet high in total fat, saturated fat and cholesterol raises blood cholesterol levels, thereby increasing one's risk for heart disease. The challenge that remained for researchers was to prove a cause and effect relationship between specific dietary components and heart disease.

Clinical studies, sometimes referred to as intervention or controlled trials, help to confirm a hypothesis, or prove a cause and effect relationship between a factor or group of factors and a disease. In these studies two or more groups of participants are compared. One receives a treatment (such as a specific diet or lifestyle change), and the other goes untreated or receives a placebo. Clinical studies are generally done on a smaller scale than epidemiological studies.

Many clinical studies have been carried out to help determine those dietary factors that have the potential to either increase or decrease blood cholesterol levels. Scientists have found that certain dietary components are powerful cholesterol-raising agents, while other dietary components actually lower our blood cholesterol levels.

DIETARY FACTORS THAT INCREASE
BLOOD CHOLESTEROL LEVELS

Total fat and saturated fat

Significant cholesterol-lowering effects of diets with reduced total fat and saturated fat have been demonstrated consistently by many studies. The findings are so conclusive that the reduction of total fat and saturated fat in the diet is now recognized as the most effective dietary means of reducing blood cholesterol levels (Dayton, 1969; Hjermann, 1981; Mattson and Grundy, 1985).

While some saturated fats are powerful cholesterol-raising agents, several studies have demonstrated that not all saturated fats have this effect. (See Chapter 6 for more details.)

Cholesterol

Dietary cholesterol raises blood cholesterol levels, regardless of dietary fat consumption (Stamler and Shekelle, 1988). It has been estimated that for every 100 mg of cholesterol consumed per 1000 calories, there is an average increase in plasma cholesterol of approximately 12 mg/dl. If an average person, eating 2000–2500 calories and 600–750 mg cholesterol a day, reduced their intake of cholesterol by 400–500 mg per day, they would reduce their overall heart disease risk by almost 50 percent. In real terms, it would mean eating no more than 200–250 mg of cholesterol per day (the amount in one egg or 3 oz (90 g) of cheese plus 3 cups (750 mL) of whole milk).

Although the influence of dietary cholesterol on blood cholesterol levels is very significant, many scientists feel that saturated fat has a greater overall influence on blood cholesterol levels than does cholesterol itself (McNamara 1987; Bowman, 1988).

Animal protein

Animal protein has been shown to increase blood cholesterol levels, while plant protein reduces blood cholesterol levels. It has been estimated that animal protein can increase blood cholesterol levels by 5–20 percent, depending on the quantity of protein consumed (Carroll, 1991).

WHAT WE LEARNED FROM THESE CLINICAL STUDIES

Many large, well-controlled studies have confirmed that saturated fat and cholesterol raise blood cholesterol levels. Cholesterol is found only in animal foods. It is highest in eggs and organ meats, but it is also found in significant quantities in other meat, poultry, seafood and dairy products. Saturated fat is also found primarily in animal products, although vegetable oils can be turned into saturated fats by hydrogenation (the process used to make shortenings and most margarines). The main vegetable sources of saturated fats are tropical oils such as coconut and palm oil. Animal protein also raises blood cholesterol, although its effects are less significant than saturated fat.

Dietary Factors that Reduce Blood Cholesterol Levels

Polyunsaturated fat

Since the early 1950s, scientists have suspected that by replacing saturated fats with polyunsaturated oils, we could lower blood cholesterol. Numerous studies have confirmed their suspicions. Polyunsaturated fats lower LDL cholesterol (a lipoprotein that carries cholesterol and increases the risk of heart disease – sometimes referred to as "bad cholesterol"). For every 1 percent increase in polyunsaturated fat, it is estimated that a decrease of approximately 1.4 mg/dl total cholesterol can be expected (Keys, 1965).

The effects of polyunsaturated fats on HDL cholesterol (a lipoprotein that decreases the risk of heart disease – sometimes referred to as "good cholesterol") are not as clear. Some researchers have found that polyunsaturated fats lower HDL, while others have observed little or no effect on HDL. Studies have shown that saturated fats are about twice as effective at raising blood cholesterol levels as polyunsaturated fats are at lowering them.

Monounsaturated fat

For many years monounsaturated fats were thought to be fairly neutral in their effects on blood cholesterol levels. In 1985, Grundy and Mattson demonstrated that monounsaturated fats can be equally as effective as polyunsaturated fats at reducing LDL cholesterol. They may be even more beneficial than polyunsaturated fats in that they either raise or have no effect on "good" HDL cholesterol. Since then several other studies have confirmed these findings. The new information on monounsaturated fats has helped to explain why the people of southern Italy and Greece, who consume a high-fat diet, have low blood cholesterol levels and a relatively low incidence of heart disease. The saving grace for these people appears to be their reliance on olive oil and olives which are excellent sources of monounsaturated fats.

Fiber

Fiber, particularly soluble fiber (see Chapter 7), can also have a significant impact on blood cholesterol levels. Dr. James Anderson sparked considerable interest in this area in the 1970s, when he published studies that examined the effects of fiber on health. This work demonstrated that giving individuals with high levels of blood cholesterol (greater than 260 mg/dl or 6.8 mmol/l) approximately 17 grams of soluble fiber each day could produce a reduction in blood cholesterol of about 20 percent. Seventeen grams of fiber can be found in about 7 cups (1.75 L) of cooked oatbran (2⅓ cups/575 mL uncooked), or one bowl of oatbran, seven or eight servings of fruits and vegetables, ½ cup (125 mL) of cooked beans plus five or six servings of whole grains. Although the cholesterol-lowering effects of soluble fiber are not as dramatic in people with normal blood cholesterol levels, the addition of 17 grams of soluble fiber per day can be expected to lower cholesterol levels about 6 percent.

WHAT WE LEARNED FROM THESE CLINICAL STUDIES

Studies that have examined dietary factors which can lower blood cholesterol levels have taught us that reducing total fat is the most important step. The specific types of fat we choose also affect blood cholesterol levels. Both poly-unsaturated and monounsaturated fats have been shown to lower blood cholesterol levels. Polyunsaturated fats are found primarily in plant foods such as safflower, sunflower, soy and corn oil, as well as nuts, seeds, soy beans and tofu. Monounsaturated fats are found mainly in olive, canola and peanut oil, avocados and olives. Soluble fiber has also been found to reduce blood cholesterol levels. Fiber is not found in animal foods. It is found in plant foods, and soluble fiber in particular is found in oats, legumes, fruits and vegetables.

STUDIES SHOWING REVERSAL OF HEART DISEASE

Although scientists had proof of the beneficial effects of diet changes on blood cholesterol levels, they did not know if it was possible to produce a regression or reversal of atherosclerosis (the build-up of cholesterol and other fatty substances in the walls of the blood vessels). Exciting research from the late 1980s and early 1990s has demonstrated that when the reduction in blood cholesterol levels is profound, a regression of atherosclerosis can be achieved.

Dr. Blankenhorn divided 162 patients into a study group and a control group. The study group used a combination of a low-fat, low-cholesterol diet (less than 22 percent of calories from fat, less than 125 mg cholesterol per day), regular exercise (20–30 minutes at 80 percent of maximum heart rate at least three times per week) and cholesterol lowering drugs. The control group received a less-rigid diet and a placebo. The study group experienced an average 43 percent reduction in LDL cholesterol and a 37 percent rise in HDL (protective) cholesterol. The control group showed improvements of no more than 5 percent. About 16 percent of the study group actually experienced regression of atherosclerosis (Blankenhorn et al., 1988).

Dr. Dean Ornish produced more profound regression of atherosclerosis using a strict vegetarian diet of 75 percent complex carbohydrate, 15 percent protein, 10 percent fat, less than 5 mg cholesterol per day, no caffeine, minimal egg white and skim milk. The experimental group also performed relaxation techniques and did 20–30 minutes of exercise every day. A control group followed a "heart healthy" diet containing no more than 30 percent of calories from fat. Overall, 82 percent of the experimental group experienced significant regression or reversal of atherosclerosis, while 53 percent of the control group experienced a progression or worsening of their disease (Ornish, 1990).

The message regarding heart disease is crystal clear. If you center your diet on high-fat, fiber-free animal foods such as meat and milk, your chances of dying of heart disease are very good. On the other hand, if you totally eliminate animal foods from your diet, your odds of dying of heart disease are fairly slim.

Many people aren't willing to completely eliminate animal foods, and they naturally question the extent to which one must go to reap reasonable benefits. The answer is not a simple one. It depends largely on individual constitution. Some people can get away with eating more fatty foods than others. In general, if we are to have any real impact on the incidence of heart disease, we must shift from a meat-centered diet to a plant-centered diet. In real terms that means eating oatmeal instead of eggs for breakfast, fresh strawberries instead of a strawberry sundae for a snack, and a bean burrito and salad instead of a cheeseburger and chips for dinner.

For people with high blood cholesterol levels, the implications are enormous. Many people can turn to diet rather than drugs for effective results in lowering blood cholesterol levels. Diet has one major advantage over drugs – the side effects are pleasant. When you begin eating a low-fat, low-cholesterol plant-centered diet, you can anticipate some weight loss, improved energy, and possibly a reduction in other ailments such as arthritis. It certainly beats stomach aches, diarrhea, flushing, nausea and liver damage which many people experience on cholesterol-lowering drugs.

CANCER

One in four individuals in North America can expect to die of cancer. It is estimated that of these cancers, some 30–40 percent are diet-related in men, and as many as 60 percent are diet-related in women. The cancers that are most often associated with diet are cancer of the mouth, pharynx, larynx, esophagus, stomach, colon, liver, pancreas, lung, breast, uterus and prostate. Although we are beginning to understand the links between diet and certain forms of cancer, there are many questions yet unanswered. The one thing that we do know is that, unlike heart disease, mortality rates from cancer show no signs of abating.

Vegetarians experience a lower death rate from all forms of cancer than do non-vegetarians. Studies comparing vegetarian Seventh-day Adventists with similar non-vegetarian Seventh-day Adventists have reported 50 percent less cancer in the vegetarian group. In comparison to the general population, Seventh-day Adventist vegetarians suffer 59 percent less cancer of all kinds, and 97 percent less colon cancer. Other studies have reported similar benefits from vegetarian diets.

Throughout the world, people in developed countries experience significantly higher cancer rates than those of people in developing countries. The World Health Organization's executive summary on the relationship between diet and chronic disease attempts to explain this difference:

> Diets high in plant foods, especially green and yellow vegetables and citrus fruits, are associated with a lower occurrence of cancers of the lung, colon, esophagus and stomach. Although the mechanisms underlying these effects are not fully understood, such diets are usually low in saturated fat and high in starches and fiber as well as in some vitamins and minerals, including beta-carotene and vitamin A.

Although it is not entirely clear why people consuming plant-based diets are at a reduced risk for cancer, there are many interesting clues in the scientific literature.

Food Components that May Protect Against Cancer

DIETARY FIBER

Considerable evidence exists for the protective effects of dietary fiber, particularly with reference to insoluble fiber and colon cancer (see Chapter 7 for specific mechanisms involved). Numerous epidemiological studies have assessed the relationship between dietary fiber and colon cancer. Many have found that an inverse association exists. Some researchers have suggested that it may be other components in fiber-rich foods that offer protection rather than the fiber itself.

Cancer of the colon is significantly lower in vegetarians than in non-vegetarians, and the difference is even more pronounced in vegans. The reasons for the reduced incidence of colon cancer in vegetarian populations is believed to be owing, at least in part, to the high fiber content of the diet.

VITAMINS AND MINERALS

Vitamin A and carotenoids

Studies indicate a beneficial effect of vitamin A, and specifically carotenoids, on reducing cancer risk, particularly cancers of the lung, colon, skin and esophagus. Carotenoids include over 500 compounds found primarily in dark green, orange and deep yellow vegetables as well as tomatoes and other fruits. About 10 percent of these carotenoids can be converted to vitamin A in the body, and of these beta-carotene converts to vitamin A the most readily. The question facing scientists was whether the protective effect of vitamin A is mainly from the pre-formed vitamin (found in animal foods such as milk and liver), from specific carotenoids such as beta-carotene, or from other carotenoids with less or no vitamin A activity. The bulk of the evidence to date strongly suggests that carotenoids, including beta-carotenes, exert the greatest influence on cancer incidence in humans. Researchers remain uncertain whether these effects are due solely to the carotenoids or other substances found in vegetables and fruits that are high in carotenoids. For this reason, experts recommend that we eat our vegetables instead of relying on supplements.

Vitamin C

Vitamin C is an antioxidant and thus may have a positive effect in reducing the formation of carcinogens (cancer-causing compounds). Diets low in vitamin C may be associated with a greater incidence of cancer of the stomach, esophagus and mouth.

Nevertheless, there is little evidence to suggest that megadoses (supplements containing nutrients at a level of at least 10 times the RDA or RNI) of vitamin C either prevent or cure cancer. In the *Nurse's Health Study* (Willet, 1992) researchers found no relationship between vitamin C megadoses and breast cancer incidence even when the large doses were taken over periods of ten years or more.

Other vitamins and minerals

Several studies are underway to clarify the role of vitamins, including vitamin D, vitamin E and folic acid, and minerals including selenium, calcium, iron, zinc, copper, molybenum and iodine, in cancer prevention. Each of these nutrients has shown promise as a potential protective agent. In some cases, it appears that a lack of the nutrient is the critical factor in promoting cancer, rather than large quantities reducing cancer activity.

At this point, there is little justification for taking megadoses of any of these nutrients in an attempt to reduce cancer risk. In some cases, megadoses may do just the opposite.

PHYTOCHEMICALS IN PLANTS

Phytochemicals include a broad range of chemicals, naturally present in plants. These chemicals protect the plants from stresses such as harsh climates, infections and destruction by animals and insects. Many of these chemicals have been shown to have some potential for protecting people against cancer, but this is a very new area of research and we are only beginning to understand how these beneficial chemicals work. At the present time, we have little hard data on just how effective phytochemicals are for people. Scientists expect that during the next decade we will be hearing much more about these substances. Some of the protective substances which have been studied are listed in Table 2.2. The primary mechanisms through which these chemicals act are:

- blocking prostaglandin E2 ("PG") tumor promotion activity. Prostaglandin E2 is a hormone-like substance that is essential for normal body functioning, although in excess, it can concentrate in cancerous tissues, promoting their growth. This effect is indicated in Table 2.2 as "↓ PG."
- increasing the estrogen estradiol 2-OH, which can reduce the activity of the more potent and potentially harmful estrogen, estradiol 16-OH. This is indicated in Table 2.2 as "↓ E."
- helping the body reduce the toxicity of harmful chemicals, and to excrete them from the body. This is indicated in Table 2.2 as "↓ toxins."

One obvious question that comes up is whether or not the cancer inhibiting substances that we find in food have the potential to slow or cure cancer in humans. At present, there isn't enough information to answer this question, although we can expect some interesting research to appear in the coming years. In the meantime, it wouldn't hurt to eat more grapefruit, sprinkle ground flax on your cereal, and eat plenty of colorful vegetables.

Food Substances that May Increase Cancer Risk

FAT

A high-fat diet has been implicated in cancer of the colon, breast and prostate. Evidence from population studies suggests that the greatest link is for total fat, and in some cases, for saturated fat.

The strongest evidence regarding the connection between fat and cancer is for colon cancer. Numerous studies have demonstrated a positive association between total fat consumption and the incidence of colon cancer. Although most studies have not differentiated between total fat, animal fat, and other specific types of fat, two large epidemiological studies have shown a strong positive relationship between animal fat and colon cancer. It is generally believed that dietary fat acts as a promoter of colon cancer rather than as an initiator of the disease.

Table 2.2 Phytochemicals in Food

Anticarcinogenic Plant Constituent	Activity of this Chemical	Common Sources
Dithiolthiones and isocyanates	↓ PG	cruciferous vegetables (e.g. cabbage, brussels sprouts, broccoli and cauliflower)
Indoles	↓ E	cruciferous vegetables
Allium (sulfur containing) compounds	inhibits the conversion of nitrate to nitrite ↓ PG	allium vegetables (e.g. garlic, onions and chives)
Coumarins	↓ toxins	umbelliferous vegetables (e.g. carrots, parsley, parsnips and celery), citrus fruits
Flavonoids	antioxidant ↓ E	umbelliferous vegetables, citrus fruits
Limonene	↓ toxins	citrus fruit (bitter principles of grapefruit)
Isoflavones	↓ E	legumes (especially soy products)
Triterpenoids	↓ toxins	licorice root, legumes
Lignans	prevents the conversion of cholesterol to estradiol	flaxseeds, fruits and vegetables
Saponins	reduces cell proliferation in the colon	legumes

TOTAL ENERGY

Excessive energy (calorie) intake leading to obesity may be related to cancer of the breast, prostate, colon, rectum and female reproductive organs. Numerous studies have confirmed that a low energy intake decreases both the initiation and promotion of tumors, although in human populations it is difficult to know whether these effects are owing to low calorie intake or low fat intake.

Not all cancers seem to be negatively affected by too many calories, and certain cancers, including those of the stomach, lung and bladder, may actually increase with lower body weight. (One suspects that these statistics could be slanted by thin smokers who are at greater risk for these types of cancers.) The consensus, though, is that a relatively low energy intake and low body weight reduces overall cancer risk. This effect is not as significant as when total dietary fat is reduced.

NATURALLY OCCURRING CARCINOGENS

Some food molds produce highly carcinogenic toxins called *mycotoxins*. These toxins occur mainly in crops that are grown and stored in a moist, warm environment. One of the more widely recognized of the dangerous mycotoxins, *aflotoxin,* is found in mainly brazil nuts, pistachios, peanuts, peanut butter and corn, although it can contaminate almost any grain, fruit or vegetable. Aflotoxin is a potent promoter of liver cancer, and populations that inadvertently consume significant quantities of aflotoxin experience a greater incidence of this disease. To minimize exposure to these toxins, never eat nuts that look off-color, smell or taste bad, are moldy or are of questionable quality. Throw out grains, including bread, that have become moldy, and remove mold from cheese and fruits before eating. Don't give up these foods; just buy the freshest possible, and store them appropriately (see Chapter 12 for guidelines on storing foods).

Other chemicals in foods have been found to be carcinogenic. Examples include piperine, safrole and terpenes in black pepper, solanine in the green skin and sprouts of potatoes, and safrole in some spices. The message here is that we must remember to be moderate in our intake of all foods, and to select wholesome and fresh-looking food.

CARCINOGENS ADDED IN GROWING OR PROCESSING FOODS

Pesticides
The impact of pesticides on our risk for cancer is a matter of tremendous debate. Pesticides vary considerably in their potential for causing cancer. Those pesticides that have been found to pose the greatest threat, including DDT and other chlorinated hydrocarbons, are no longer used in most developed countries, although they remain in use in many developing nations. The question is whether or not human exposure to pesticides is sufficient to make this a real issue in terms of cancer risk, particularly for the average (non-farming) person whose exposure to these chemicals is limited to their normal diet.

When we consider pesticide residues with respect to food, we think fruits, vegetables and other plant foods, but in fact many pesticide residues are present in even higher amounts in animals. Grains grown for animals are often heavily treated with pesticides. The animals consume the grains, and the fat-soluble pesticide residues become concentrated in the fat of the animals. As fat is marbled throughout the meat (although it may be hard to see at times), it is impossible to consume the meat without eating some fat.

At present, we do not have enough information to quantify the risk of cancer caused by pesticides. We do know that the risk is disproportionately higher for children, who have smaller bodies and therefore a reduced capacity to handle toxic substances. The Natural Defense Resource Council (NRDC) published the 1989 report "Intolerable Risk: Pesticides in Our Children's Food," which concluded that 55 percent of a person's lifetime cancer risk stems from carcinogens ingested prior to the age of six.

Considering what we do know, it makes sense to reduce our exposure to pesticide residues in foods. We can begin by selecting foods that are lower on the food chain, washing fruits and vegetables well before eating them, buying produce that has been grown organically (without the use of pesticides) when possible, and growing our own.

Food additives
The public has long been under the impression that food additives are the most potent of food carcinogens, although their relative importance to overall cancer risk is probably far less than is generally perceived.

Preservatives commonly used in the industrialized world include antioxidants such as BHT and BHA, mold inhibitors such as sodium benzoate and calcium or sodium propionate, sulfites and nitrites. Of these substances, the only one which has been positively associated with cancer promotion is nitrites. Indeed, scientists have found that some chemical preservatives, particularly the antioxidants may play a favorable role in cancer prevention.

Nitrites can interact with substances in the stomach to form nitrosamines, which have been associated with cancer of the stomach and esophagus. Dietary nitrites come mainly from cured meats (nitrites have proven to be the safest, most acceptable way of preserving these foods). Vitamin C is now commonly used in meat curing to help minimize the conversion of these nitrites to nitrosamines.

Another chemical called *nitrate* can be converted to nitrite in our gastrointestinal system. Our exposure to nitrates comes mainly from our own saliva, in some drinking water and in vegetables. The vitamin C naturally present in vegetables helps minimize the conversion of nitrates to nitrites.

Many other food additives, including artificial sweeteners, artificial fats, colors and flavors are used on a regular basis in our food supply. In the past, some of these substances, consumed at very high doses, have been linked to cancer in laboratory animals, and have subsequently been restricted or removed from the food supply. Regardless, it is wise to select whole foods whenever possible rather than heavily processed foods which contain food additives. The whole foods are not only free of additives, but they are generally higher in nutrients and fiber.

Chemical changes that occur in food preparation
A number of cooking and food preparation methods can increase the formation of cancer-causing substances. Those which have received the most attention include smoking, barbecuing, charcoal broiling and frying. These cooking methods can result in formation of mutagens (substances that cause changes in the genetic material of cells), and the deposition of carcinogens on foods that are cooked. The higher the fat content of the food and the greater the temperature reached in cooking, the more these substances are produced. In North America, these cooking methods are used primarily for cooking meat.

Based on our present state of knowledge, it is relatively easy to make recommendations which could very likely have a significant impact on the overall incidence of cancer in developed countries, including the United States and Canada. The prescription sounds a lot like it does for heart disease. Center your diet on plants instead of animals. Choose foods that are not highly processed. Stew, bake or boil your food; avoid frying, barbecuing or broiling. Eat less fat and more fiber, whole grains, fruits and vegetables.

THE LINK BETWEEN DIET AND DISEASE: A CALL FOR ACTION

The debate about whether or not diet plays a role in chronic degenerative disease is over. There presently exists enough information to make recommendations that could vastly improve the health of our population. National governments are recognizing the value of this information, and are making changes in federal nutrition policies which more accurately reflect the current state of knowledge.

Actions such as new food guides and revised nutrition recommendations have been central to the disease reduction that we have seen, particularly with reference to heart disease. However, the priority given to these kinds of efforts is rarely sufficient to produce the level of disease reduction that one would hope for. The World Health Organization Study Group on diet and the prevention of chronic diseases provides the following commentary:

When food policies are acknowledged to have an impact on the consumer's choice of food, it becomes extremely important to consider whether these policies are encouraging consumers to choose foods conducive to good health. With diet now linked to the major chronic diseases, such considerations take on special urgency. As the health component of most food policies remains rigidly aligned with the dietary requirements set out 50 years ago to prevent deficiency diseases, adaptation to protect populations from dietary excesses will not be easy. Efforts to prevent chronic diseases through dietary intervention have not been given high priority by any government. Most governments have yet to realize that policies aligned with current medical views on diet and health can bring economic advantages. A very large proportion of international trade in cereals is for animal feed. If policies viewed high fat content in meat carcasses as a hazard rather than a standard for defining high quality and price, farmers would no longer have to follow the intensive feeding practices needed to produce fatty meat carcasses. Farming policies that do not require intensive animal production systems would reduce the world demand for cereals. Use of land could be reappraised, since cereal production for direct consumption by the population is much more efficient and cheaper than dedicating large areas to growing feed for meat production and dairying.

We can see these kinds of issues coming into play as we consider the shifts that have occurred in the recommendations for healthy eating within countries such as Canada and the United States. The national nutrition recommendations and food guides have clearly shifted toward an emphasis on grains, vegetables and fruits. We might assume that, in making this shift, the new guides would encourage a reduction in our consumption of animal foods, and the use of the appropriate plant foods in their place. Interestingly, the emphasis has been on choosing leaner meats and lower-fat dairy products rather than on reducing the quantity of such foods used.

The challenge that faces national governments is to make healthy choices the easy choices. In so doing, they need not concern themselves with establishing distinct sets of recommendations for each degenerative disease. The reality is that the same dietary factors are implicated in most of these diseases.

Nutrition Recommendations for the Prevention of Chronic Diseases *

1. Center your diet on a wide variety of plant foods.
Plant foods should be the foundation of your diet. Animal foods, if used,

---

* These recommendations are appropriate for people over 2 years of age.

should be accompaniments to meals rather than the central theme.

To obtain the maximum benefit, include a wide variety of grains, vegetables and fruits. Follow the vegetarian food guide (Chapter 8) to be sure to obtain adequate quantities of these foods.

Increase your use of legumes. These foods are ideal replacements for meat. They are low in fat, contain no cholesterol and are excellent sources of fiber. They are also rich sources of several protective phytochemicals.

2. Limit your use of fats, especially saturated fats.
Over-consumption of fat is risky business. Limit all fats, particularly saturated fats. Saturated fats are found in animal foods, coconut oil, palm oil, and hydrogenated vegetable fats.

It is quite possible for a person consuming a plant-centered diet to overdo fat, especially if full-fat dairy products, eggs, fried foods, and sweet baked goods such as pies and cakes are regularly consumed.

Your fat intake should not exceed 20 to 30% of calories for healthy adults and 15 to 20% of calories for those with elevated blood cholesterol levels. For children, fat should not exceed 30 to 35% of calories.

3. Include a source of omega 3 fatty acids in the daily diet.
Omega 3 fatty acids are important in helping to maintain health and prevent disease. Plant foods that are rich in omega 3 fatty acids include flaxseeds, walnuts, pumpkin seeds, leafy vegetables, wheat germ, canola oil and soy products.

Be sure that these foods are fresh when purchased, and store in refrigerator or freezer.

4. Choose whole grain rather than refined products.
Whole grain foods offer fiber in addition to many valuable vitamins and minerals. The soluble and insoluble fiber found in these foods provides protection against disease.

5. Achieve and maintain a healthy body weight.
Both overweight and underweight can increase the risk of degenerative disease. The safest way to maintain a healthy body weight is to eat a varied, balanced diet, and to exercise regularly.

6. Use salty foods in moderation.
Excessive consumption of salty foods may contribute to hypertension and some forms of cancer. Heavily salted foods include salty snack foods, many commercially prepared foods (such as soups, canned pasta products, frozen entrees,

packaged pasta and rice mixes), pickles and condiments. Many of these foods contribute relatively little to our overall nutrient needs and should therefore be used in moderation.

7. Limit your use of smoked, charred and cured foods.
These methods of food preparation and preservation can increase our exposure to carcinogens, and therefore should be minimized.

8. Use grains, legumes, fruits, vegetables, nuts and seeds grown without the use of pesticides whenever possible.
Some pesticide residues on foods can contribute to cancer, and can be particularly hazardous for children. Try to select foods that have been grown without pesticides, or with minimal use of pesticides.

9. Alcohol, if consumed, should be used in moderation.
Excessive consumption of alcohol displaces valuable nutrients, and contributes to degenerative disease.

The Diet of Choice: Mainly Plants

The evidence points directly to a vegetarian or near-vegetarian diet as the diet of choice in the prevention of chronic degenerative disease. Considering the track record of such diseases, vegetarianism can be a real health advantage. This advantage has not gone unnoticed.

The American Dietetic Association, in their position paper on vegetarian diets, concludes:

> A considerable body of scientific data suggests positive relationships between vegetarian lifestyles and risk reduction for several chronic diseases, such as obesity, coronary artery disease, hypertension, diabetes mellitus, colon cancer and others.

The National Institute of Nutrition in Canada acknowledges similar benefits:

> In recent years, vegetarianism has been associated with decreased risk of obesity, atonic constipation, lung cancer and alcoholism. Furthermore, vegetarianism may be associated with reduced risk for hypertension, coronary artery disease, non-insulin dependent diabetes and gallstones. Some evidence exists that a vegetarian diet may reduce risk for breast cancer, diverticular disease, colon cancer, calcium-containing kidney stones, osteoporosis and dental caries.

The evidence regarding the potential for vegetarian diets in preventing, and perhaps even in treating, chronic degenerative disease, is strong. Regardless of these benefits, many people are skeptical when they hear reports of vegan infants who are suffering from malnutrition or adults who have developed vitamin B$_{12}$ deficiency. The big question that arises is: do concerns regarding the adequacy of vegetarian diets outweigh their potential benefits?

THE ADEQUACY OF THE VEGETARIAN DIET

To assess the nutritional adequacy of a vegetarian diet, we will look at the evidence that has been provided by groups who have been living on a plant food diet for generations, and by some of the new vegetarians who have been experimenting with different patterns of diet.

GENERATIONS OF VEGETARIANS

Many cultures have existed for generations on vegetarian or near-vegetarian diets. These people enjoy the advantage of knowing what works and what doesn't work. From such groups come many important lessons.

The Sherpas, living in the eastern Himalayas, have long been admired for their incredible endurance on mountain expeditions. Their diet consists largely of rice and lentils with vegetables, barley, wheat, millet, and milk from yaks and goats. Meat is eaten only on occasion, and the stricter Buddhists of the group avoid it completely.

Numerous developing countries can attest to the adequacy of a varied plant-based diet. In many areas of the world meat is scarce, and the average family cannot afford to include it, except on rare occasions. When the native diet is varied and abundant, these groups are generally well nourished. Problems arise when the mainstay of the diet is a thin gruel of oats or corn, or another starchy food with relatively low nutritional value. When legumes, fruits and vegetables are added, these problems are generally resolved.

In North America, the group of vegetarians that has been most extensively studied is the vegetarian Seventh-day Adventists. In the early 1950s, Drs. Hardinge and Stare from Harvard University did the first extensive study on the nutritional status of this group. About half of the study participants were high-risk individuals such as pregnant women and teens. This study provided the evidence necessary to establish that the adequacy of a well-planned vegetarian diet is beyond dispute. Since this time, numerous studies have further examined the health status of Seventh-day Adventist vegetarians. These studies have consistently demonstrated that lacto-ovo vegetarian children can grow normally and maintain excellent health throughout adult life. Indeed, the average vegetarian Adventist lives four to five years longer than otherwise similar non-vegetarian Adventists.

All of these groups, and many more, have succeeded in creating wonderfully healthful vegetarian diets. The key is in variety. When a wide range of wholesome plant foods are used, necessary nutrients are amply provided.

THE NEW VEGETARIANS: A CAUSE FOR CONCERN?

The new vegetarians include a diverse group of people who have, for a variety of reasons, become disenchanted with our present way of eating. Not only are they choosing to cut down on, or completely cut out, foods of animal origin, but they often also reduce or eliminate other foods, such as processed products, concentrated fats and sugar. These people are, in some ways, pioneers, testing new ways of making vegetarian nutrition work. Some put together patterns that work very well, while others experience a few hitches in their plan. The more foods that are eliminated from the diet, without being replaced by plant foods that provide comparable nutrients, the more difficult it becomes to achieve a suitable balance. However, scientific studies have confirmed the adequacy of balanced vegetarian diets for people of all ages. These studies assess the nutritional status of participants in one or more of three ways: anthropometric assessment (age, height and weight), biochemical assessment (blood values of nutrients) and dietary assessment (analysis of foods eaten).

In 1989, a French study by Millet assessed the vitamin status of 37 vegetarians using both biochemical and dietary assessment. Results were compared to non-vegetarian controls. The vegetarians had higher intakes of thiamin, riboflavin, and vitamins C, A and E. The two nutrients which were found to be lower in the diets of the vegetarians were vitamin B_{12} and vitamin D. Low blood levels of vitamin D were found in 38 percent of the vegetarians, as compared to 27 percent of the non-vegetarians. Vitamin B_{12} was low in 6 percent of the male vegetarians and 17 percent of the female vegetarians. Numerous similar works have been carried out, with comparable results. Most experts agree that a lacto-ovo vegetarian diet can provide completely adequate nutrition. The consensus is somewhat weaker for the diets which go one step further and eliminate all animal foods.

SCIENTIFIC STUDIES ASSESSING
THE ADEQUACY OF VEGAN DIETS

Among the first research to address the nutritional adequacy of all plant diets was Hardinge and Stare's classic U.S. study, in 1954, of the diets of 27 vegans. These diets were generally well balanced, with only a few subjects having less protein, calcium and riboflavin than the recommended allowances. These vegan diets were rich in iron, thiamin, and vitamins A and C.

In 1962, Guggenheim, Weiss and Fostick studied the diets of 119 vegans from Jerusalem. Detailed dietary assessments were carried out, and the only nutrient which was present in inadequate amounts in the diets was riboflavin. Even without milk, the calcium content of the diet averaged 825 mg per person per day.

Dr. Ellis and colleagues carried out a number of investigations looking at the nutritional adequacy of vegan diets between 1966 and 1978. The studies examined the health of small groups of British vegans (less than forty participants per study). The subjects were from professional and middle classes, and were well informed regarding the vegan diet. Most of the study participants used a vitamin B_{12} supplement. Detailed medical examinations were carried out, including both physical assessments and blood work. Ellis's work showed that vegans were lighter in weight than omnivores, had lower blood cholesterol levels, and lower serum vitamin B_{12} levels, although signs of B_{12} deficiency were rare. Although Ellis did include some children in these studies, the numbers were not large enough to draw any significant conclusions.

In 1981, a small Swedish study examined the nutritive value of vegan diets using a technique that determined the nutritional value of foods by chemical analysis rather than using food composition tables. In addition, each subject was evaluated for clinical (blood pressure, height, weight and visual assessment) and biochemical (blood tests) parameters. Although the diets were low in protein (these vegans deliberately limited their intake of protein-rich foods), iodine, zinc and vitamin B_{12}, the clinical and biochemical data showed no signs of nutritional deficiencies. All other nutrients were well within recommended levels.

Overall, the studies assessing the nutritional status of vegan adults have provided reassurance that a well-planned vegan diet can supply adequate nutrition, provided that a source of vitamin B_{12} is present in the diet. The real acid test regarding the nutritional quality of a vegan diet comes when it is fed to the most vulnerable of our species – infants and children.

In 1988, T.A.B. Sanders reported on a longitudinal study of British vegan children. In this study the majority of children grew and developed normally, although they tended to be slightly smaller than children in the general population. Intakes for calcium, vitamin D and energy were generally below the recommended intakes. Most of the children were given vitamin B_{12} supplements. Overall, the health of these children was good, and the author concludes that, provided sufficient care is taken, a vegan diet can support normal growth and development in infants and young children.

The largest study on vegan children was done in 1989 on "The Farm" in Summertown, U.S.A. In this classic work, 404 vegetarian children between the ages of 4 months and 10 years were compared to U.S. reference patterns for age, weight and height. By the age of 10 years, children from The Farm averaged 0.7 cm and 1.1 kg less than the average U.S. child. This study concluded that a vegan diet can support normal growth in infants and young children.

Other studies have revealed less reassuring pictures. Restrictive vegan diets have produced gross malnutrition in vegan infants and children. Shinwell and Gorodischer, in 1982, published a report of 72 infants from a community of Black Americans living in Israel. These children suffered from multiple nutritional deficiencies, including protein-calorie malnutrition, iron-deficiency anemia, vitamin B_{12} deficiency, rickets, zinc deficiency and growth retardation. P.C. Dagnalie published 15 studies between 1988 and 1992 looking at the nutritional status of infants and children in macrobiotic communities in the Netherlands. Protein-energy malnutrition, growth retardation, and several nutrient deficiencies were reported in a significant proportion of the children assessed. The common denominator for these sad tales is that the chosen patterns were restricted in more than just animal foods. In some cases fat, protein and energy were limited as well. Parents often used unfortified home-prepared soy or nut "milks" as the main dietary constituent for these children. Fortified and other commercial products were denied, and nutritional supplements often avoided. Although these kinds of reports are rather discouraging, they are not the inevitable result of a vegan diet.

The lesson we learn from the reports regarding the health of vegan infants and children is to proceed with caution. Parents must educate themselves regarding the potential pitfalls of this type of diet, and do what is necessary to avoid them.

THE BOTTOM LINE

Both vegetarian and vegan diets can provide completely adequate nutrition and foster good health. There is nothing inherently wrong with either one. If you choose to eliminate only meat from your diet, you must find suitable plant replacements for some nutrients. If you choose to eliminate dairy products as well, you need to consider a few more nutrients. When you eliminate all foods of animal origin, there is still one more nutrient that deserves special attention. The next chapters will guide you through the science of vegetarian nutrition, and help you to translate that science into a healthful, practical and enjoyable way of eating.

Without Meat – Exploding the Myths

The typical North American diet is often referred to as a "meat-based diet," reflecting deeply held beliefs that animal foods outrank plant foods in value. To the question, "What's for supper tonight?" the answer is rarely "broccoli" or "potatoes." It's usually "hamburgers" or "roast pork." For many people, it's hard to imagine Thanksgiving dinner without the turkey. This focus on animal foods extends to the very heart of our relationship with food.

Three powerful myths have led many of us to believe that a plant-based diet is nutritionally inferior to a meat-centered diet:

Myth 1: A diet without meat cannot easily provide enough protein for good health.

Myth 2: The quality of plant protein is inadequate to meet our needs.

Myth 3: Iron deficiency anemia is a likely outcome of the switch to a vegetarian diet.

None of these statements is true; each is based on research and thinking from a bygone era. In fact, *there are no nutrients essential to human life found in meat that are not also found in plant foods.* As we look down the food chain, we see that all of the nutrients that are used to build animal and human bodies come from plants. Protein and iron required for the muscles and blood of even such large herbivores as elephants are derived from grains, legumes and vegetables. The bones and the milk of cows contain calcium, which comes only from plants.

Even vitamin B_{12}, sometimes thought of as the nutrient we must get from animal foods, actually originates from the bacteria that grow in or on animals *and* plants. (Because modern agriculture and food production methods result in less bacterial production of vitamin B_{12}, we do not have reliable sources of vitamin B_{12} in plant foods. Thus, vegans must rely on fortified foods or nutritional supplements to be certain of their intake of this essential nutrient.)

In this chapter we will examine the truth about our needs for protein, iron and zinc, and look at plant sources for these nutrients. In later chapters we will explore sources of calcium, vitamin B_{12} and other important nutrients in diets without dairy products.

Whether you are beginning to cut down on the amount of meat in your diet, or have made a complete shift from meat, fish, poultry and other animal foods, you need to pay special attention to three nutrients: protein, iron and zinc. We begin with protein, that essential part of all plant and animal cells, and a myth about the need for animal protein.

PROTEIN

Myth 1: A diet without meat cannot easily provide enough protein for good health.

Vegetarians are often asked, "How will you get enough protein?" For a variety of reasons this concern has been overemphasized. During the first half of the twentieth century, there was considerable emphasis on the elimination of deficiency diseases, including protein-energy malnutrition. In North America, meat was seen as the saving grace, and governments began to encourage a growth in animal agriculture by subsidizing farmers. This resulted in a substantial increase in the use of animal foods. While the average protein intake of people in developing countries is about 60 grams per day, those of us in developed countries ingest, on average, over 100 grams of protein. This means that for many in the West, over 15 percent of our calories comes from protein. The result of excessive protein consumption is not simply bigger muscles, as we might like to believe. According to the World Health Organization (WHO):

> There are no known advantages from increasing the proportion of energy derived from protein (above 15 percent of total calories) and high intakes may have harmful effects in promoting excessive losses of body calcium and perhaps in accelerating age-related decline in renal function.

It appears that the somewhat lower protein contents found in vegetarian diets may turn out to be a health advantage.

To further quote the WHO Study Group:

> Many epidemiological studies have linked a low intake of animal protein to high childhood mortality, morbidity and growth failure. For many years, this evidence was interpreted as meaning that the amino acids present in animal proteins were necessary to complement the amino acids in plant foods. . . . Progressively, it was recognized that even in totally vegetarian diets containing a diversity of foods, plant sources tended to complement one another in amino acid supply. . . . If the energy needs of the child or adult are met by these diets – then so are the amino acid needs.

Protein is present in most foods, with the notable exceptions of sugar, fats and oils. In fact, diets which provide enough calories and are based on an assortment of plant foods will easily meet and exceed protein requirements. Evidence has supported the adequacy of protein intake from plant-based diets since the classic study by Hardinge and Stare in the 1950s. Figure 3.1 shows the comparison of intakes of protein (plant and animal) of male and female lacto-ovo vegetarians, vegans and omnivores. On this chart, the protein intakes are expressed as percentage of recommended intake, which is set at 100 percent. *For all groups, the average protein intake was more than one third higher than the recommended intake.*

In the diets of the omnivores shown here, approximately two-thirds of the protein was of animal origin and one third of the protein was from plant sources; this ratio reflects a pattern similar to the overall protein intake of people in North America and Europe.

Recommended Protein Intakes

How much protein do you really need for good health?

The exact amount of protein you require depends on your age, body size and to some extent on the composition of your diet. Protein needs are greater than average for some athletes (for example, while building muscle mass) and for people recovering from certain illnesses. Scientists have established recommended intakes which include a minimum requirement and a *generous margin of safety* (because people differ metabolically, and because proteins differ in composition and digestibility).

Figure 3.1 Protein Intake on Various Diets

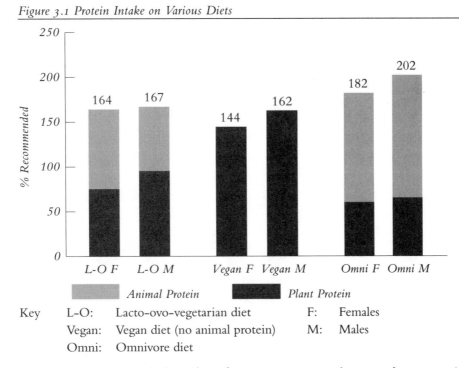

Key   L-O: Lacto-ovo-vegetarian diet   F: Females
        Vegan: Vegan diet (no animal protein)   M: Males
        Omni: Omnivore diet

The recommended intake of protein assumes that people are getting enough total calories. If they are not (for reasons of economics, illness, extreme weight loss diets or anorexia nervosa), protein will be used to meet energy needs rather than being spared for its roles in building body proteins and regulating the manner in which cells function. During pregnancy and other stages of growth, protein needs are increased and thus recommended intakes are higher (see Chapter 9 and Appendix 2).

RECOMMENDED PROTEIN INTAKE
ON THE BASIS OF BODY WEIGHT

The recommended intakes for most nutrients vary slightly between countries, depending on the interpretation of data by scientific committees, and on other factors, such as the food sources that are commonly used in each country. In the United States the amount of protein recommended for healthy adults is 0.8 grams protein per kilogram of body weight. In Canada the figure is 0.86 grams per kilogram. Let's see how much protein this works out to be, for people of different body weights:

Table 3.1 Examples of Recommended Daily Protein Intakes for Adults

Body Weight	American Recommended Intake	Canadian Recommended Intake
130 pounds (59 kg)	0.8 x 59 kg=47 g protein	0.86 x 59=51 g protein
170 pounds (77 kg)	0.8 x 77 kg=62 g protein	0.86 x 77=66 g protein

RECOMMENDED PROTEIN INTAKE
AS A PERCENTAGE OF TOTAL CALORIES

Another way of looking at protein recommendations is to consider the percentages of total calories coming from the three nutrients: protein, carbohydrate and fat. Carbohydrate and protein provide approximately 4 calories per gram, whereas fat, a concentrated form of energy, provides 9 calories per gram. The current recommendation by the WHO Study Group for dividing the caloric intake of adults among these three nutrients is given in Table 3.2

Table 3.2 Recommended Distribution of Calories

Protein	Fat	Carbohydrate
10 to 15%	15 to 30%★	55 to 75%

★ The upper limit of 30% is an interim goal; the group states that further benefits would be expected by reducing fat intake toward 15% of total energy.

Protein in Various Menus

But what does all this mean when it comes to the food on your plate? On the next few pages are typical one-day menus for people who have chosen different ways to eat:

> *Menu No. 1* Omnivore (including all animal and plant foods)

> *Menu No. 2* Lacto-Ovo-Vegetarian (with high dairy and egg)

> *Menu No. 3* Lacto-Ovo-Vegetarian (with less dairy and egg)

> *Menu No. 4* Vegan (plant foods only)

Each menu provides approximately 2200 calories and more than enough protein for a person weighing 130 pounds (59 kilos). It becomes clear that even at somewhat lower calorie intakes, protein needs can be easily achieved on the full spectrum of these diets. Below each menu are foods that might be added for a 170 pound (77 kilos) person, to give a total caloric intake of 2800-2900 calories for the day. These four menus will be referred to throughout the book to illustrate the sources of different minerals and vitamins in animal- and plant-based diets.

MENU NO. 1: OMNIVORE

Our omnivore has adopted some "healthy eating" measures. He or she
- follows recommended intakes from the food groups
- uses lean meats
- avoids the skin on chicken
- chooses low-fat yogurt and 2% milk

Table 3.3 Menu No. 1 Omnivore

		Protein (grams)	
Breakfast	Orange juice, ½ cup (125 mL)	0.9	
	Cornflakes, 1 cup (250 mL)	2.2	
	Milk, 2%, 1 cup (250 mL)	8.1	
	Toast, whole wheat, 1 slice (21 g)	2.6	
	Butter, 1 pat (5 mL)	0	
	Non caloric beverage	0	
	Breakfast total	13.8	(401 calories)
Lunch	Roast beef sandwich:		
	Bread, white, 2 slices (25 g)	4.0	
	Beef, round lean, 2½ oz (70 g)	20.7	
	Margarine, 2 pats (10 g)	0.1	
	Mayonnaise, 1 tsp (5 g)	0.1	
	Lettuce, 1 leaf (14 g)	0.2	
	Carrot, 1 medium	0.7	
	Low-fat fruit yogurt, ¾ cup (170 mL)	7.0	
	Apple, 1 medium	0.3	
	Non-caloric beverage	0	
	Lunch total	33.1	(683 calories)
Supper	Chicken, roasted 3.5 oz (100 g)	28.9	
	Potato, scalloped, ½ cup (125 mL)	3.7	
	Green peas, ½ cup (125 mL)	4.4	
	Dinner roll, white (1 small)	3.3	
	Butter, 1 pat (5 mL)	0	
	Non-caloric beverage	0	
	Supper total	40.3	(545 calories)
Snacks and Desserts	Cheesecake, ¹⁄₁₀ pie	7.7	
	Strawberries, 4 large	0.4	
	Apple juice, 1 cup (250 mL)	0.2	
	Snacks total	8.3	(567 calories)

Day's total protein for 130-pound (59 kilo) omnivore: 95.5 grams (2196 calories). The recommended protein intake for someone of this weight is approximately 50 grams. The totals of iron and zinc in this menu are 16.3 mg iron and 12.0 mg zinc.

For a 170-pound person, we add the following foods to the preceding menu:

Breakfast:	Toast with butter, 1 slice
Lunch:	Sandwich, ½
Supper:	Chicken, 2 oz (60 g)
Snack:	Muffins, 2

Day's total protein for 170-pound (77 kilo) omnivore: 139 grams (2880 calories). The recommended protein intake for someone of this weight is approximately 65 grams. The totals of iron and zinc in this menu are 20.8 mg iron and 15.0 mg zinc.

COMMENTS ON THE OMNIVORE'S DIET

Protein

Athough animal foods are often looked upon as the essential protein foods while plant foods are considered to be insignificant sources, in this menu, plant foods contributed 20 grams of protein. With the addition of the animal foods, which are concentrated protein sources, the final total is approximately *twice* the recommended intake for protein.

Calorie Distribution in Menu No. 1

Percentage of calories from

Protein	17%
Fat	33%
Carbohydrate	50%
Cholesterol	374 milligrams

A lowered intake of fat would be possible with non-fat dairy products and low-fat fish, but the proportion of protein would still be high. It would be beneficial to shift some of the calories from protein and fat to carbohydrate.

Fat

You may think that a fat intake of 33 percent is high. In fact, the fat intake in this menu is significantly *lower* than the average North American intake of 37-38 percent.

MENU NO. 2: LACTO-OVO VEGETARIAN

The second menu is for a vegetarian who is essentially replacing the meat, fish and poultry with eggs and dairy products.

Table 3.4 Menu No. 2: Lacto-Ovo Vegetarian (Dairy & Egg Emphasis)

		Protein (grams)	
Breakfast	Orange juice, ½ cup (125 mL)	0.9	
	Oatmeal, 1 cup (250 mL)	6.4	
	Milk, 2%, 1 cup (250 mL)	8.1	
	Whole wheat toast, 1 slice (21 g)	2.6	
	Butter, 1 pat (5 mL)	0	
	Non-caloric beverage	0	
	Breakfast total	18.0	(443 calories)

Lunch	Egg salad sandwich:		
	Whole wheat bread, 2 slices (56 g)	5.2	
	Hard-boiled eggs, 2 small (80 g)	10.1	
	Margarine, 2 pats (10 mL)	0.1	
	Mayonnaise, 1 tsp (15 mL)	0.1	
	Lettuce, 1 leaf (14 g)	0.2	
	Carrot, 1 medium	0.7	
	Apple, 1 medium	0.3	
	Chocolate chip cookies, 2 small (26 g)	1.4	
	Non-caloric beverage	0	
	Lunch total	18.1	(649 calories)
Supper	Vegetarian lasagna (263 g)	32.9	
	Garlic bread:		
	French bread, 1 small slice (14 g)	1.3	
	Butter, 1 tsp (5 mL)	0	
	Green salad, 1 cup (250 mL)	1.8	
	Italian dressing, 1 tbsp (15 mL)	0	
	Non-caloric beverage	0	
	Supper total	36.0	(601 calories)
Snacks and	Cherry pie, ⅛ pie (118 g)	3.0	
Desserts	Banana, 1 medium	1.2	
	Apple juice, 1 cup (250 mL)	0.2	
	Snacks total	4.4	(537 calories)

Day's total protein for 130-pound (59 kilo) lacto-ovo vegetarian: 76.5 grams (2230 calories). The totals of iron and zinc in this menu are 16.9 mg iron and 8.5 mg zinc. The recommended protein intake for someone of this weight is approximately 50 grams.

Extra foods for a 170-pound (77 kilo) person:
Breakfast: Toast with butter, 1 slice
Lunch: Cookie, 1
Supper: ½ cup (125 mL) lasagna and slice of garlic bread
Snack: Blueberry muffin

Day's total protein for the 170-pound (77 kilo) lacto-ovo vegetarian: 100 grams (2830 calories). The totals of iron and zinc in this menu are 22.3 mg iron and 10.7 mg zinc.

COMMENTS ON LACTO-OVO VEGETARIAN MENU NO. 2

Protein
Without any meat, poultry or fish, the protein in this menu is *1 ½ times* the recommended intake; as a percentage of calories it is within the recommended

range of 10-15 percent of calories from protein. Although there is no emphasis on concentrated plant protein sources such as legumes or tofu in the menu,
half of the protein comes from plant foods.

Calorie Distribution
    Percentage of calories from
        Protein   13%
        Fat   34%
        Carbohydrate 53%
        Cholesterol   481 milligrams

Fat
Although this menu is vegetarian, it is high in total fat, saturated fat and
cholesterol.

MENU NO. 3: LACTO-OVO VEGETARIAN WITH LESS DAIRY AND EGG

Next we look at a vegetarian menu with a greater emphasis on plant foods,
although milk is used on cereal, and egg is used in baked goods. In this menu,
the plant foods alone provide enough protein to exceed the recommended
intake. A few of the protein sources may be new to you. For example, almond
butter (a spread similar to peanut butter) replaces butter on the toast, providing calcium, iron and zinc as well as protein.

Table 3.5 Menu No. 3 for Lacto-Ovo-Vegetarian (Lower in Egg and Dairy)

		Protein (grams)	
Breakfast	Orange juice, ½ cup (125 mL)	0.9	
	Oatmeal, 1 cup (250 mL)	6.4	
	Milk, 2%, 1 cup (250 mL)	8.1	
	Whole wheat toast, 1 slice (21 g)	2.6	
	Almond butter, 1 tbsp (15 mL)	2.4	
	Non-caloric beverage	0	
	Breakfast total:	20.4	(504 calories)
Lunch	Hummus, ½ cup (125 mL)	9.6	
	Pita bread, 1 (38 g)	4.0	
	Cherry tomatoes, 4	0.5	
	Carrot, 1 medium	0.7	
	Apple, 1 medium	0.3	
	Oatmeal raisin cookie, 1 large (23 g)	1.4	
	Non-caloric beverage	0	
	Lunch total	16.5	(589 calories)

Supper	Spaghetti, whole wheat,		
	1½ cups (375 mL)	11.4	
	Tomato-lentil sauce, 1¼ cups		
	(300 mL, recipe page 237)	10.9	
	Parmesan cheese, 2 tbsp (13 g)	4.2	
	Green salad, 1 cup (250 mL)	1.8	
	Italian dressing, 1 tbsp (15 mL)	0	
	Non-caloric beverage	0	
	Supper total	28.3	(632 calories)
Snacks and	Apple brown betty, ¾ cup (175 mL)	2.5	
Desserts	Banana, 1 medium	1.2	
	Cashews, ¼ cup (50 mL)	5.3	
	Snacks total	9.0	(545 calories)

Day's total protein for 130-pound (59 kilo) lacto-ovo vegetarian: 74.2 grams (2270 calories). The recommended protein intake for someone of this weight is approximately 50 grams. The totals of iron and zinc in this menu are 21.6 mg iron and 12.3 mg zinc.

Extra foods for a 170-pound (77 kilo) person:
Breakfast:　　1 slice toast with almond butter, ½ cup (125 mL) oatmeal
Lunch:　　　Cookie, 1 large
Supper:　　　Roll, 1 small
Snack:　　　　Muffin, 1

Day's total protein for a 170-pound (77 kilo) lacto-ovo vegetarian: 91.4 grams (2840 calories). The totals of iron and zinc in this menu are 26.1 mg iron and 15.2 mg zinc. The recommended protein intake for someone of this weight is approximately 65 grams.

COMMENTS ON LACTO-OVO VEGETARIAN DIET, LOWER IN EGG AND DAIRY

Protein
In this menu the protein intake is well above the recommended intake.

Calorie Distribution
　　　Percentage of calories from
　　　　　Protein　　　13%
　　　　　Fat　　　　　28%
　　　　　Carbohydrate　59%
　　　　　Cholesterol　　55 milligrams

The distribution of protein, fat and carbohydrate provided by this menu is more suited to today's health guidelines (see Table 3.2) than is the first lacto-ovo vegetarian option.

Fat

The fat content is below the 30 percent recommendation. As we can see from this menu, a shift in the direction of plant foods is a simple way to lower dietary fat and cholesterol.

MENU NO. 4: VEGAN

The vegan menu includes a number of less commonly used but highly nutritious foods. For example, tahini (a spread made from ground sesame seeds) and molasses on toast are rich sources of minerals.

Table 3.6 Menu No. 4 for Vegan

		Protein (grams)	
Breakfast	Orange, 1 medium	1.3	
	Red River cereal, 1 cup (250 mL)	7.0	
	Wheat germ, 2 tbsp (30 mL)	3.4	
	Soy milk, 1 cup (250 mL)	6.9	
	Whole wheat toast, 1 slice (21 g)	2.6	
	Tahini, 1 tbsp (15 mL)	2.7	
	Blackstrap molasses, 1 tsp (5 mL)	0	
	Non-caloric beverage	0	
	Breakfast total	23.9	(537 calories)
Lunch	Eggless egg sandwich made with nutritional yeast (recipe page 220)	12.7	
	Carrot, 1 medium	0.7	
	Apple, 1 medium	0.3	
	Muffin, 1 (100 g) (recipe page 247)	7.3	
	Non-caloric beverage	0	
	Lunch total	21.0	(681 calories)
Supper	Spiced lentils:		
	Lentils, 1 cup (250 mL)	17.9	
	Onions, ¼ cup (50 mL)	0.8	
	Oil, ½ tsp (2 mL)	0	
	Brown rice, 1 cup (250 mL)	4.9	
	Green salad		
	Kale, 1 cup (250 mL)	2.4	
	Romaine lettuce, 1 cup (250 mL)	1.0	
	Tahini salad dressing, 1 tbsp (15 mL, recipe page 227)	2.7	
	Non-caloric beverage	0	
	Supper total	29.7	(649 calories)

Snacks and	Trail mix, 3 tbsp (45 mL) walnuts, 3 figs	3.9	
Dessert	Carrot cake, small slice		
	(50 g, see recipe page 249)	2.4	
	Total snacks	6.3	(366 calories)

Day's total protein intake for 130-pound (59 kilo) vegan: 80.9 grams (2233 calories). The total iron and zinc in this menu are 29.1 mg iron and 15.5 mg zinc. The recommended protein intake for someone of this weight is approximately 50 grams.

Extra foods for a 170-pound (77 kilo) person:
Breakfast: ½ cup (125 mL) of cereal and slice of toast with tahini and molasses
Lunch: ½ sandwich
Supper: ½ cup (125 mL) of rice
Snacks: Banana and a small piece of carrot cake

Day's total protein for the 170-pound (77 kilo) vegan: 101 grams (2950 calories). The totals of iron and zinc in this menu are 36.1 mg iron and 17.2 mg zinc. The recommended protein intake for someone of this weight is approximately 65 grams.

COMMENTS ON MENU NO. 4 FOR VEGAN

Protein
Although there are no animal foods, the protein provided in this menu is over one and a half times the recommended protein intake. Even if the two most concentrated sources of protein were removed – the lentils and the tofu – this vegan menu easily exceeds recommended levels.

Calorie Distribution in Vegan Diet
    Percentage of calories from
        Protein   14%
        Fat   27%
        Carbohydrate 59%
        Cholesterol   0 milligrams

Fats
The fat content is below 30 percent and is virtually cholesterol-free since plants provide no significant amounts of cholesterol.

PROTEIN, FAT AND CARBOHYDRATE IN FOODS

Many of us are unaware of the substantial amounts of protein contributed by the plant foods in our diets. Although we generally think of meat and other animal foods as concentrated sources of protein, in fact, a plant-based diet can easily meet our protein needs. Table 3.7 shows the percentage of calories from protein, fat and carbohydrate in some common plant and animal foods. When we compare these with the recommended distribution for our total diet (shown at the bottom of Table 3.7), it becomes clear that a heavy reliance on animal foods has led to our North American dietary imbalance toward excessive protein and fat.

Table 3.7 Distribution of Calories from Protein, Fat and Carbohydrate in Foods

Percent Calories From:*	Protein	Fat	Carbohydrate
Animal Foods			
Cod	92%	8%	0%
Salmon, sockeye	52%	48%	0%
Beef, lean ground	37%	63%	0%
Beef, regular ground	33%	67%	0%
Eggs	32%	65%	3%
Cow's milk, 2%	27%	35%	38%
Cheddar cheese, medium	25%	74%	1%
Plant Foods			
Legumes and their products			
Tofu, firm	40%	49%	11%
Lentils	30%	3%	67%
Kidney beans	28%	1%	71%
Garbanzo beans (chickpeas)	21%	14%	65%
Vegetables			
Spinach	40%	11%	49%
Broccoli	32%	11%	57%
Carrots	8%	3%	89%
Nuts, seeds and their products			
Almonds	14%	74%	12%
Sesame butter (tahini)	11%	76%	13%
Grains			
Oatmeal	17%	16%	67%
Wheat	15%	5%	80%
Quinoa	13%	15%	72%
Millet	11%	7%	82%
Rice	9%	5%	86%

Fruits			
Orange	8%	1%	91%
Apples	1%	5%	94%
Recommended Distribution in Diet:	*10-15%*	*15-30%*	*55-75%*

★ Percentages were derived using the values 4 calories per gram for protein and carbohydrate, and 9 calories per gram for fats.

Which Plant Foods Give Us Protein?

GRAINS

Grains such as wheat, oats, millet and rice, which are not often thought of by Westerners as significant protein foods, provide almost half the world's protein. Certain grains, such as South American amaranth and quinoa, have amino acid patterns similar to those found in foods of animal origin. It is interesting to note that in grains, the percentage of calories provided by protein is in the neighborhood of 10 to 15 percent, the precise quantity recommended by health experts as a desired goal for our overall diet. As a bonus, whole grains are low in fat and provide iron, zinc and B vitamins.

LEGUMES

Legumes – plants which have seeds in pods – are the protein powerhouses of the plant kingdom, with approximately twice the protein content of cereal grains. There are more than 11,000 kinds of legumes, but many North Americans would have trouble naming five. Familiar legumes include peas, lentils, peanuts, soybeans and chickpeas. Like meat, legumes are good sources of iron and zinc. Legumes provide three distinct advantages over animal protein foods: they generally contain very little fat, and that which is present is primarily unsaturated; legumes are high in soluble and insoluble fiber; and they are sources of calcium. Legumes fit right into today's nutritional recommendations, and frequent consumption of legumes has been shown to reduce high blood-cholesterol levels and improve blood sugar control in diabetics.

Soybeans are unusual because they contain relatively high amounts of polyunsaturated oil, and have a protein quality comparable to animal foods. Tofu, a traditional product of soybeans, has been called "the cow of China": it provides protein and iron, as does meat, and when made with calcium it is a good source of this mineral as well. Tofu will take up the flavor of other ingredients in a dish, making it an extremely versatile food (see Chapter 12 for recipe ideas).

North American farmers are major producers of about 20 types of legumes or beans, and we can truly support our agricultural economy when we use these foods. Adding legumes to one's diet has elements of taking a world food tour – think of all the tasty dishes from home and around the globe. We may have a favorite family recipe for pea or lentil soup, enjoy chili at a Mexican restaurant, or have acquired a taste for Middle Eastern or East Indian dishes while traveling. Preparing ethnic foods at home is a wonderful way to begin incorporating more legumes into our diets.

NUTS AND SEEDS

Nuts, instead of being considered salty, high-fat snack foods, are looked upon as tasty sources of protein and other nutrients in the vegetarian diet. When we eliminate meat, and perhaps dairy products as well, our intake of fats (especially in the forms of saturated fats and cholesterol) drops substantially. Nuts and seeds provide valuable oils. For example, walnuts will contribute valuable omega-3 fatty acids to vegan diets. For growing children and for other vegetarians with high-energy needs, these high-calorie foods balance the low-fat levels of most other plant foods, and thus are important additions. Nuts and seeds also provide vitamins and the minerals calcium, iron and zinc. Tahini (made from ground sesame seeds) or almond butter may replace the butter and margarine on toast or breads. Seed butters form a flavorful base for salad dressings, replacing all or part of the oil to provide a highly nutritious addition to salads (see Chapter 12).

VEGETABLES

Vegetables provide just a little protein; however, the amino acids provided in vegetable protein help to complement the other amino acids in plant-based diets.

CONVENIENCE FOODS

In addition to simple grains, legumes and nuts, many new "fast" foods developed from these plant sources are available in the freezer, refrigerator and produce sections of supermarkets and health food stores. There are a wide variety of veggie burgers, tofu dogs and other meat "analogues." These products resemble meat in taste and texture and have its nutritional benefits without the saturated fat and cholesterol.

Now that we have debunked the first myth, that plant foods could not provide an adequate quantity of protein, let's look at the second great protein myth.

Myth 2: The quality of plant protein is inadequate to meet our needs.

When we consider the *quality* of dietary protein, we look at two factors: *digestibility* and the *relative amounts of the essential amino acids* present in the protein. We'll look first at digestibility.

PROTEIN DIGESTIBILITY

Proteins differ in the efficiency with which they are digested. Plant protein in its natural form is generally less easily absorbed than animal protein. Food preparation, especially wet cooking methods such as the boiling and simmering often used with grains and legumes, can increase the digestibility. Processing techniques can dramatically alter protein digestibility. For over 3,000 years, in the Orient, people have processed soybeans to create tofu and other products. The protein in tofu is similar in quality and in digestibility to that found in animal foods.

For a lacto-ovo vegetarian diet, the practical significance of differences in digestibility between plant and animal foods are considered to be slight and we do not need to adjust our recommended total protein intakes.

When a vegan diet is composed of many raw foods and coarse grains, the recommended protein intake may be increased by about 10 percent. (Expert opinions vary about whether this is necessary.) As you saw with the menus in this chapter, achieving a protein intake 10 percent higher than recommended levels is easily accomplished. For toddlers who have small stomachs and limited food capacity, it is important to include nut butters, seed butters and tofu in addition to breast milk or infant formula. All of these provide protein as well as concentrated calories in the form of oils. (For further recommendations for children, see Chapter 9.)

ESSENTIAL AMINO ACIDS AND PROTEIN COMPLEMENTATION

Proteins are composed of very long chains of smaller units called amino acids. There are 20 amino acids commonly found in nature. Amino acids are built by plants, from the air, soil and water. With a supply of amino acids, plants can then build proteins.

In humans, the process is a little different. To meet our protein building needs, we have two requirements:

1. We need to have nine of the amino acids supplied in our diets. These are called the *essential amino acids* and they originate from plant foods. We can also get these amino acids from animal foods, but their origin, for the animals as well, was plant foods. Each of the nine essential amino acids must be present in our diet in certain amounts.

2. We must have enough *total* protein in the diet. This protein includes the essential amino acids, as well as a variable assortment of the other (non–essential) amino acids.

The amino acids from dietary protein are the basic building materials for body proteins. During the process of digestion protein is broken down to form a common pool of amino acids. From this pool, we create our body proteins, whether for muscle, hair or other uses. These proteins are built to exacting specifications.

ESSENTIAL AMINO ACIDS: HOW MUCH DO ADULTS NEED?

The relative amounts of the essential amino acids which we require to build our body proteins are the subject of considerable research and discussion. The United Nations Provisional Pattern, Figure 3.2, shows the estimated requirements of these nine amino acids for adults. They are stated in milligrams of amino acid per gram of protein in the diet. The names of the nine essential amino acids are shown in the key.

Figure 3.2 Estimated Essential Amino Acids for Adults

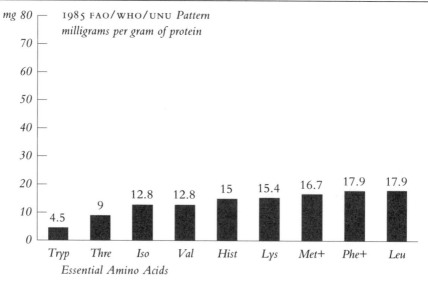

Key for Figures 3.2 to 3.4 – Essential Amino Acids

Tryp	Tryptophan	Lys	Lysine
Thre	Threonine	Met+	Methionine (plus Cystine)
Iso	Isoleucine	Phe+	Phenylalanine (plus Tyrosine)
Val	Valine	Leu	Leucine
Hist	Histidine		

We can use this Pattern as a gauge against which to measure the amino acids in specific foods and in our overall diets. Figure 3.3 shows the essential amino acids patterns of egg, tofu, wheat and quinoa (a South American grain). If you compare the patterns for tofu, quinoa or wheat with Figure 3.2, you can see that there is no essential amino acid lacking in these plant foods. Any of these foods alone easily meets the essential amino acid needs for adults in that the level of all the essential amino acids per gram of protein is higher than required.

Figure 3.3 Essential Amino Acids in Egg, Tofu, Wheat and Quinoa

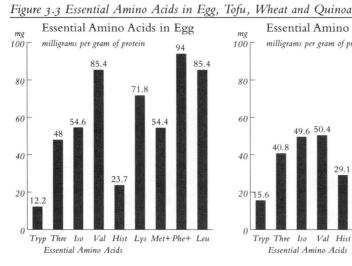

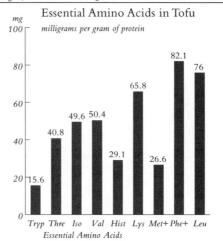

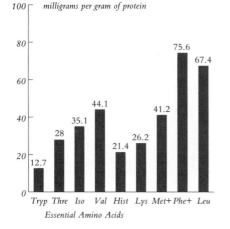

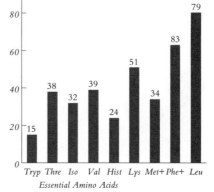

ESSENTIAL AMINO ACID NEEDS OF CHILDREN

From infancy to adulthood, our amino acid needs change. For example, the amino acid histidine is really only essential in infancy. After that, we appear to have the ability to make at least some of it ourselves. Plans similar to the one shown in Figure 3.2 have been developed for children of different ages. The United Nations Provisional Pattern for preschool children is shown in Figure 3.4. When we compare the two Patterns, it becomes apparent that *young children require more of the essential amino acids per gram of dietary protein* than do adults.

While adults can easily meet their amino acid and protein needs on a plant-based diet, it is more of a challenge to meet those needs in the growing years. For this reason we have given specific recommendations in Chapter 9 for each stage of development. These recommendations emphasize the foods with amino acid patterns similar to those needed by growing children: breast milk, soy based formula, tofu, grain and legume combinations. Lacto-ovo veg-etarians can add cow's milk and eggs. When these guidelines are followed, total protein intake and the intakes of essential amino acids are more than sufficient for vegetarian children, including vegan children.

Figure 3.4 Essential Amino Acids for the Preschool Child

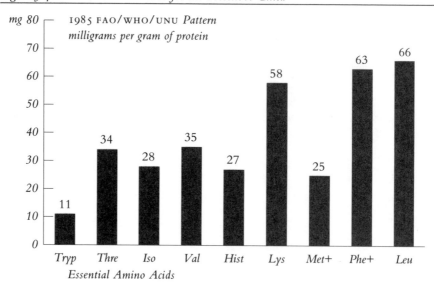

THE CONCEPT OF THE "LIMITING AMINO ACID"

As we have seen from Figure 3.3, the patterns of essential amino acids differ from food to food. When we compare the amino acid pattern for a single food to the Pattern for adults or for children, one amino acid may be present in rel-atively small amounts. For example, wheat is low in lysine, when you compare it to the Pattern for preschool children. Lysine is, in this situation, called the *limiting amino acid*. This is of great importance *when the total quantity of protein in the diet is barely adequate*, as is true for some children in developing countries. It would also be of great importance *if wheat were the only food available*.

However, other foods have different amino acid patterns, some provid-ing relatively large amounts of lysine. Legumes have more than enough lysine and can therefore balance the shortage of this amino acid in wheat. Soybeans are particularly rich in lysine, which makes tofu and other soy products valuable in vegetarian diets. The amino acid pattern of egg is closest to the Plan. Egg would provide enough, or more than enough, of the nine essential amino acids, even if it were the *only* source of protein in a diet which barely met protein requirements.

EARLY RESEARCH ON AMINO ACID REQUIREMENTS

In the first half of this century, when protein quality was originally studied in controlled laboratory situations, single foods were used as the sole protein source. The research focused on how well single plant or animal foods would support growth, often in rats. Baby rats grow very quickly, compared to humans; they double their birth weights in six days. To do this, they need somewhat more concentrated protein sources, such as those found in animal protein (like rat's milk or cow's milk). It was found that the amino acid in shortest supply in the plant foods had the effect of limiting protein production and thus limiting the growth of rats. The scientists who conducted the animal studies designated the proteins from certain plants as "incomplete proteins" because alone, the plant foods did not sustain the *very* fast growth in baby rats.

In fact plant proteins are not "incomplete"; *all* of the essential amino acids are present, although they are not provided in the concentrated amounts needed by baby rats. When the findings from animal studies were applied to humans, the value of the plant protein in our diets was underestimated.

These conclusions from animal studies have limited relevance because

1. single foods were used, rather than the combinations that would be freely chosen by either animals or humans;

2. the protein needs of baby rats are far different from those of humans at any age;

3. in many cases, foods were not prepared in ways to maximize digestibility.

Humans living on vegetarian or omnivorous diets derive proteins from not just one but from almost all of our foods. Each food has strengths and weaknesses in its amino acid pattern when it is compared to the patterns of amino acids that we require. For this reason, it is extremely important to include a variety of foods, as shown in the food guide in Chapter 8. When we eat foods from different food groups, we end up with the range of amino acids necessary for our protein-building needs.

COMPLEMENTATION AND TIMING

The book *Diet for a Small Planet* by Frances Moore Lappé, which introduced vegetarian nutrition to the North American general public in the early 1970s, stressed the need for complementing grains with legumes at the same meal.

Some people were left with the impression that one needed to spend hours with scales and calculator in hand, planning a vegetarian menu. Research since then has shown that amino acids from the foods eaten throughout the day form an amino acid pool in muscle and other body tissues and can be drawn on throughout the day. Lappé's more recent writings reflect the understanding that strict complementation does not have to be done at the same meal. Specific guidelines for vegan infants and children are given in Chapter 9.

It's nice to know that we don't have to worry about it, but the fact is that people generally *like* to eat combinations of grains with legumes or nuts, in which the amino acid patterns complement each other. In North America, ethnic dishes based on centuries-old combinations of grains and legumes, or grains and nuts, are becoming increasingly popular and available. Some of these combinations are shown in Table 3.8.

Table 3.8 Plant Food Combinations that Provide
Complementary Patterns of Essential Amino Acids

Grains plus Legumes	Cornbread and Boston baked beans (United States)
	Bread and split pea soup (Canada)
	Crackers and lentil soup (Middle East)
	Cereal with soy milk (North America)
	Rice and tofu (the Orient)
	Toast and peanut butter (North America)
	Cornmeal tortillas and vegetarian chili (Mexico)
	Bun with tofu burger (North America)
	Chapatis and dahl (India)
	Rice and red beans (United States)
	Pita bread and falafel (Middle East)
	Pita bread and hummus (Greece)
	Toast with scrambled tofu (North America)
	Sticky bun with black bean sauce (China)
	Muffins and soy milk (North America)
Grains plus Nuts	Toast and almond butter (North America)
	Granola or muesli with nuts (Switzerland)
	Pasta with pine nuts (Italy)
	Walnut cookies or muffins (England)
	Rice with cashew-vegetable stir-fry (China)

The complementation process does not stop here; for example, spinach adds enough of the amino acid threonine to further balance a grain and legume combination. In fact, the foods for meals and snacks will all contribute amino acids necessary for protein building, and protein complementation is not the difficult challenge it has long been perceived to be.

We can easily meet protein needs when we include legumes, nuts and seeds on a daily basis, eat a variety of whole grains, and limit the intake of foods high in sugar and fats. The usual dietary combinations of plant foods provide a complete range of the amino acids we need, in more than adequate quanitities. As we will see in the next sections, these foods also provide the valuable trace minerals iron and zinc.

IRON IN VEGETARIAN DIETS

After protein, iron seems to surface as the second major concern people have about a shift toward a plant-based diet. We often think of iron as the mineral from red meat, an association strengthened by the meat industry and by advertising. Athletes, in particular, have been conditioned to link their performance with diets featuring steaks and burgers. In this section we will examine facts about the iron in our bodies and in our food supply. In doing this, we will shed light on another myth.

> *Myth 3:* Iron deficiency anemia is a likely outcome of the switch to a vegetarian diet.

IRON DEFICIENCY ANEMIA

Although we have eliminated many deficiency diseases in the developed world, iron deficiency is one that remains for a small but significant number of people in specific age groups. The effects of iron deficiency include fatigue, a weakened immune system, and reduced ability to concentrate. Children, women in the child-bearing years, and the elderly sometimes have difficulty meeting their iron needs – these tend to be the most vulnerable groups. Iron deficiency anemia occurs in a small percentage of vegetarians and non-vegetarians alike. However, many studies looking at the nutritional status of vegetarians in North America and Western Europe show that long term vegetarians *do not* have a greater incidence of iron deficiency anemia than does the population at large.

When people stop eating red meat, they may replace it with poultry, fish and dairy products and not emphasize the good plant sources of iron. Whether you are near-vegetarian, lacto-ovo vegetarian or vegan, it is necessary to choose iron-rich foods (see Table 3.9) and to make sure that the iron in your diet will be well absorbed. There are many precautions that can be taken in food selection and preparation to help ensure that you get enough iron. Before we address this issue it is important to understand some of the workings of iron in our foods and in our bodies.

Types of Iron in the Diet

When we start to eat more plant foods and to eliminate meat, fish and poultry from our diet, we stop eating foods made of blood and muscle. We do not, however, need blood-containing foods to form our own hemoglobin, the iron-containing protein in our red blood cells. Iron, protein and folic acid, all of which are necessary for the formation of healthy blood, are present in plant foods. Iron from plant foods is absorbed quite differently from the iron found in meats. Other components of the diet eaten at the same time can have a big effect on the absorption of the iron from legumes, vegetables and grains. In other words, the composition of the rest of the diet is significant. It may be that the diets of health-oriented vegetarians maximize the effectiveness of their iron sources.

HEME AND NONHEME IRON

There are two forms of iron present in foods: heme iron and nonheme iron. Forty percent of the iron in meat, and a lesser amount in fish and poultry, is "heme iron." Heme iron is present in animal flesh in the form of muscle myoglobin, and blood hemoglobin. We usually absorb 15 to 35 percent of the heme iron from foods.

The remainder of the iron in meat and all of the iron in plant foods and eggs is called "nonheme iron." The proportion of nonheme iron that is absorbed varies from 2 to 20 percent, depending in part on other foods eaten at the same time. The absorption of the heme iron is not affected by accompanying foods in the same way. Vitamin C can enhance the solubility of nonheme iron, resulting in rates of absorption at the upper end of this range. Thus many vegetables and some fruits containing both iron and vitamin C have high iron availability. Studies have shown that iron absorption from cereal will be increased two to three times when a large orange or a glass of juice providing 75 to 100 mg of vitamin C is consumed at the same time. Smaller amounts of vitamin C in fruits and vegetables will enhance absorption proportionally. On the other hand, drinking black tea with breakfast can result in a *lower* rate of absorption of nonheme iron from your cereal.

When iron reaches our cells and is used to manufacture hemoglobin for the blood, it is *equally* well utilized whether it came from broccoli or a steak.

The Roles of Iron in the Body

Iron is best known for its role in transporting oxygen from the lungs to cells throughout the body via hemoglobin. Iron is also present in muscle tissue, where it helps to store oxygen for future use. Small amounts of iron help us regulate cell metabolism and resist infection. Our bodies efficiently recycle iron, but we need to replace the small amounts lost – less than 1.5 milligrams per day. Because we don't absorb all of the iron present in food, the recommended iron intakes for adults are in the range of 8 to 15 milligrams per day. Women need more iron than men, because iron is lost in blood each month during menstruation. Increased amounts of iron are needed during pregnancy, childbirth and lactation, during the growth spurts of childhood and adolescence and for endurance athletes.

The walls of our intestines are highly selective about how much iron they will allow to pass from our food supply into the bloodstream. The proportion absorbed from the overall diet varies, depending on a wide range of factors. For example, when our iron reserves are low, iron absorption from a meal may double.

Lab Tests and Supplements

Lab tests can give a complete picture of a person's iron status. As with protein, we are finding that more iron is not necessarily better. There are health risks linked to high intakes of iron and the overconsumption of iron supplements. For a small proportion of people who have a hereditary disorder, iron overload is a problem because of super-efficient iron absorption. If you're at all concerned about the adequacy of your iron intake, it is a good idea to have blood tests done reflecting red blood cell status (hematocrit and hemoglobin) and iron stores (ferritin).

In many cases, iron deficiency anemia is indicative of overall poor diet, including low intakes of vitamin C-rich fruits and vegetables. Since many nutrients are involved in the process of building healthy red blood cells, an overall improvement in diet, including vegetables, fruits and iron-rich foods, could prove effective in the long run.

Recommended Intakes of Iron

The recommended intakes of dietary iron for adults are given in Table 3.9. These are based on average requirements, with an additional safety factor. They are expressed on a daily basis, but should be regarded as the average recommended intake over a period of time, such as a week.

Table 3.9 Recommended Intakes of Iron

Age and sex	Canada	United States
Women, aged 19 to 49 (premenopausal)	13 mg	15 mg
Women, aged 50 and over	8 mg	10 mg
Men, aged 19 and over	9 mg	10 mg

Iron in the Menus in this Chapter

The total iron in the four menus shown earlier in this chapter are shown in Table 3.10.

Table 3.10 Iron Provided in Menu Nos. 1 to 4.

	For 130-pound (59 kilo) person	For 170-pound (77 kilo) person
1. Omnivore Menu	16.3 mg	20.8 mg
2. Lacto-Ovo Vegetarian Menu	16.9 mg	22.3 mg
3. Lacto Ovo Vegetarian Menu	21.6 mg	26.1 mg
4. Vegan Menu	29.1 mg	36.1 mg

Comparison with Recommended Intakes

All menus met and exceeded the recommended adult intakes of 8 to 15 milligrams for a day.

MENU NO. 1

Over 75 percent of the iron in this menu comes from plant sources. In this, as in the next two meal patterns, the orange juice at breakfast (with 40 to 60 mg vitamin C) increases the absorption of the iron from the accompanying cereal and toast. Fresh-squeezed juice gives more vitamin C than does canned or frozen. Total vitamin C: 131 mg.

MENU NO. 2

Ninety percent of the iron comes from plant sources in this menu, and 10 percent from egg. At supper, the 40 mg of vitamin C provided by tomato sauce, onions and salad helps iron absorption from tofu in the lasagne and from pasta and bread. Total vitamin C: 120 mg.

MENU NO. 3

The iron in this and the next menu was from plant sources. At lunch, the lemon used in the hummus recipe and the cherry tomatoes taste good together; they also increase the absorption of iron from garbanzo beans. At supper, 80 mg of vitamin C provided by green salads, tomato sauce and onions assists with the iron uptake from from lentils and pasta. Total vitamin C: 180 mg.

MENU NO. 4

Almost one third of the iron comes from tofu and lentils; additional iron comes in small amounts from *every* food eaten, with the exception of the small amount of cooking oil used in the lentil dish. The orange at breakfast (with 60 to 80 mg of vitamin C) helps iron uptake. A hearty salad and onions bring the vitamin C intake at supper to over 100 mg, enhancing iron absorption from all of the foods eaten. Total vitamin C: 191 mg.

Iron Intakes and Status of Vegetarians

Many studies in developed countries comparing the intakes of dietary iron of vegetarians with those of age-matched omnivores show the iron intakes of the vegetarians, including vegans, to be higher. Overall, the reported incidence of iron deficiency anemia is not greater than with omnivores. Vegetarians, including vegans, have been shown to consume more fruits and vegetables, and to have substantially greater intakes of vitamin C-rich foods, enhancing the iron absorption from plant foods. As with omnivores, some studies have shown that children and elderly women are at greater risk for iron deficiency. This situation could be improved by food preparation techniques which maximize iron absorption, and by ensuring that good sources of vitamin C are consumed at all meals with iron-rich foods.

Sources of Iron in Vegetarian Diets

Table 3.11 shows the iron contents of a range of foods.

There are other breakfast cereals and grain products, not shown in Table 3.11, that are enriched with iron, often providing 4 milligrams of iron per serving. Iron-fortified infant cereals can be added to porridge, pancakes and muffins for older children and for adults. Meat analogues, tofuburgers and similar products provide iron; for details, read package labels.

Table 3.11 Iron in Foods

	Volume*	Weight (g)	Iron Content (mg)
Legumes and Foods Made from Legumes			
Tofu, firm	½ cup (125 mL)	124	13.0**
Tofu, regular	½ cup (125 mL)	124	6.6**
Lentils, cooked	½ cup (125 mL)	100	3.3
Beans (kidney, garbanzo, pinto, white, blackeye), cooked	½ cup (125 mL)	85	2.2-2.6
Beans (adzuki), cooked	½ cup (125 mL)	115	2.3
Hummus	½ cup (125 mL)	123	1.9
Soy milk	1 cup (250 mL)	240	1.4 (or see label)
Split peas	½ cup (125 mL)	98	1.3
Nuts and seeds			
Tahini	2 tbsp (30 mL)	30	2.7
Almond butter	2 tbsp (30 mL)	32	1.2

Grains and cereal foods

Cream of wheat (fortified), cooked	¾ cup (185 mL)	179	9–11
Bran flakes with raisins	¾ cup (185 mL)	38	4.5
Quinoa, uncooked	¼ cup (60 mL)	42	3.9
Wheat germ	2 tbsp (30 mL)	14	1.3
Whole wheat bread	1 slice	25	0.9
Oatmeal, cooked	½ cup (125 mL)	130	0.8

Vegetables

Wax beans, canned or cooked	½ cup (125 mL)	119	3.1
Potato, with skin	1	202	2.8
Peas, raw, boiled or split, cooked	½ cup (125 mL)	80	1.2
Broccoli or bok choy, cooked	½ cup (125 mL)	80	0.9
Kale, cooked	½ cup (125 mL)	65	0.6
Tomato, whole	1	123	0.6

Seaweeds

Hijiki, dry	¼ cup (60 mL)	10	6.4
Nori, 1 sheet, dry		3	0.4

Fruits

Prunes, dried	10	84	2.1
Apricot halves, dried	10	35	1.7
Prune juice	½ cup (125 mL)	128	1.5

Other foods

Blackstrap molasses	1 tbsp (15 mL)	20	3.2
Egg	1 large	50	1.0

For purposes of comparison:

Beef hamburger, lean, cooked	2 oz	58g	1.2

★Throughout this book we follow common protocol for conversion of imperial to metric measures. Exceptions are made in Chapters 3 and 4 (Tables 3.11, 3.14, 4.2 and 4.6) where more exact metric conversions are used to reflect more accurately the nutrient contents of certain quantities of foods.

★★Note: there appears to be considerable variation in the iron content of tofu from different sources. For exact figures contact local suppliers.

Dietary Factors that Increase Iron Absorption

VITAMIN C

Foods rich in vitamin C work wonders with the iron from plants. Breakfast can be a great time to boost your iron intake. Fruit or juice will substantially increase the absorption of the iron from your cereal and toast. In one study, papaya was shown to increase iron absorption up to six times. Note that this contradicts popular ideas of "food combining" which dictate that fruits be eaten separately from other foods. If you want to do your hemoglobin a favor, eat fruits with iron sources. Fruits and vegetables provide the maximum amount of vitamin C when they are raw, although cooked foods, for example onion or tomatoes in a soup or casserole, can also be effective.

CAST IRON COOKWARE

Another sure way to increase iron intake is to use cast iron cookware. In one study of Brazilian infants, when cast iron utensils were used to prepare food, dietary iron was increased six times or more. This effect is especially significant when acidic foods such as tomato sauce are prepared using cast iron cookware.

Dietary Factors that Decrease Iron Absorption

While some factors help to increase iron absorption from foods, several factors decrease it. To get the most iron from the plant foods in your diet, it helps to eat and drink fewer of the things that block iron absorption at mealtime.

TANNIN-CONTAINING BEVERAGES

The primary culprit is tea, the second most widely consumed beverage in the world (next to water). Both black tea and oriental green tea, from the same plant, contain tannin. Tannin combines with iron to form an insoluble compound. For example, black tea with breakfast has been shown to cut the iron absorption in half. Coffee, containing similar compounds, seems to have a lesser effect. Most herbal teas do not contain tannin.

MILK AND CHEESE

A glass of milk (or a piece of cheese) has been shown to decrease iron availability by as much as 50 percent from accompanying foods.

OXALATES

Sorry, Popeye, but spinach isn't really the best source of iron, after all. Although his example was widely used to inspire children to eat their greens, the iron in spinach is bound with oxalates, making it largely unavailable. Oxalates are acids also found in rhubarb, Swiss chard and chocolate. On the other hand, broccoli, kale and oriental greens such as bok choy provide abundant *available* iron.

PHYTATES

Phytates are the storage form of phosphorus in seeds, and are associated with the fiber in raw whole grains and legumes. (For further discussion on phytates, fiber and minerals see Chapter 7.) Phytates, particularly in raw foods such as wheat bran, have been a concern because they can bind a portion of the iron, zinc and calcium, making the minerals unavailable for absorption. However, during specific food preparation processes such as soaking in water (as with legumes, oats and couscous), the yeast raising of bread doughs, and the sprouting of seeds and legumes, these phytates are destroyed by enzymes called phytases. The roasting of nuts also decreases phytate levels. Thus, food preparation methods developed over the centuries don't have the sole benefit of making the foods more tasty; these methods increase the mineral availability as well.

OTHER FOODS

Soy products such as tofu have some binding components, however their iron content is high. Include tofu as part of a meal with vegetables or fruit, for good iron availability. Tempeh and miso, which are fermented soy foods, and a very smooth product called silken tofu, have increased iron availability.

Challenges to Iron Out: Common Errors in Food Choices Leading to Low Iron Intakes, and Some Solutions

The following situations illustrate pitfalls which might occur for those shifting toward plant-based diets:

• A newly vegetarian teen may eat just the non-meat portion of family meals, and snack on fries and granola bars.

• A busy woman may find that cheese is a convenient source of protein and calcium and rely on it for many quick meals. Dairy products do have protein and calcium, but almost no iron.

• A man eating many refined foods may try to relieve constipation with special wheat bran supplements.

• Someone frequently eating at restaurants may order many pasta and cheese entrées, and drink tea with meals.

In these situations, the amount of iron eaten and absorbed could be low and, after a prolonged period of time, the person's energy level may drop. Each might think that a vegetarian diet is inadequate to meet his or her nutritional needs, and that it is necessary to reintroduce meat. Simple changes in the diet could solve these problems:

• The teen can make a big batch of hummus. Other fast options for teens are veggie burgers and tofu hot dogs, served with a sliced tomato. Families who have members with different dietary patterns can enjoy tacos together, with optional meat chili or vegetarian chili cooked in a cast iron pot.

• The busy woman may prepare a delicious tofu dish in minutes after work, and use the leftovers for next day's sandwich (see the recipe for Tofu Fingers on page 240). Instead of butter or margarine, she can spread her toast with almond butter, or with tahini and molasses. She can pick up a bean salad from a health food delicatessen, and stock her freezer with quick vegetarian entrées based on beans, tofu and grains.

• The man using refined foods can include more whole grains, vegetables and fruits. In doing this, he increases his iron intake and gets more fiber from whole foods rather than from fiber supplements (see Chapter 7).

• The restaurant eater may order oriental tofu dishes, a lentil or split pea soup, a bean curry or bean burritos with a salad; the accompanying vegetables will increase iron absorption. If traveling out of town, he or she could check through the Yellow Pages for vegetarian or ethnic restaurants. It is also a wise idea to drink tannin-containing teas between meals (rather than with your iron sources). With meals, drink juice, water or tannin-free herbal teas.

Iron-Clad Rules

Getting enough iron in your plant-based diet is not really so difficult.

1. Eat iron-rich foods every day (see Table 3.11). Following the food guide in Chapter 8, you can obtain iron from every one of the food groups. Don't waste calories on junk foods (high in fat, high in sugar, lacking in iron).

2. Help your body absorb the iron you do take in. Eat vitamin C-rich fruits and vegetables at meals. Avoid consuming black tea, other tannin-containing beverages, and raw wheat bran with your iron sources. Use foods that are yeasted (such as bread), sprouted, (such as bean sprouts), roasted (such as nuts) and fermented (such as tempeh).

3. Use cast iron cookware.

4. Have your iron status checked to see how you're doing while you get used to a new "plant food" way of eating.

ZINC

Whereas much concern has been focused on protein and iron, relatively little attention has been paid to zinc. In fact, whether you are omnivorous or vegetarian, it is not difficult to put together a diet which provides adequate protein and iron. By contrast, consuming the recommended levels of zinc seems to be more of a challenge for both omnivores *and* vegetarians. At this time, there are many unanswered questions regarding the role played by zinc in health maintenance, the adequacy of zinc in our overall food supply, the suitability of recommended allowances and the zinc status of North Americans. For these reasons, our discussion here will primarily focus on the positive aspects of achieving adequate zinc intake with vegetarian foods.

Zinc in the Body

Zinc has a central role in metabolism and ensuring an adequate intake is important throughout the life cycle. Zinc plays a part in enzyme function in all cells; it is essential for reproduction, growth, sexual maturation, wound healing and for our immune systems. Zinc has a role in our ability to taste; some seniors who have lost the sense of taste are actually zinc deficient. Infants and children who are not getting enough zinc will have slower physical growth and poor appetites.

Lab Tests

There is not a single, specific and sensitive way to assess zinc status; instead a combination of tests is used. Thus, testing is expensive and is not done on a routine basis, with the result that we have limited feedback about the zinc status of North Americans. In her book *Principles of Nutritional Assessment*, a taste test has been described by Gibson, which can be used along with laboratory tests.

Recommended Zinc Intakes

The recommended intakes for zinc in Canada and the United States are given in Table 3.12. These recommendations are based on average requirements, with an additional safety factor. In the case of zinc, the additional safety factor is particularly large, because there seems to be a wide range in people's requirements for this mineral.

Table 3.12 Recommended Intakes of Zinc

Sex	Canada	United States
Adult women	9 mg	12 mg
Adult men	12 mg	15 mg

One reason that men need more zinc is that they lose an estimated 0.6 mg zinc with each seminal emission. Ardent vegetarians might be well advised to keep a bowl of cashews on the bedside table (25 grams of these nuts provide 1.5 mg of zinc)!

Zinc in the Sample Menus in this Chapter

The zinc provided by each of the four menus presented earlier in the chapter is shown in Table 3.13.

Table 3.13 Zinc Provided in Menu Nos.1 to 4

	For 130-pound (59 kilo) person	For 170-pound (77 kilo) person
1. Omnivore Menu	12.0 mg	15.0 mg
2. Lacto-Ovo Vegetarian Menu	8.5 mg	10.7 mg
3. Lacto-Ovo Vegetarian Menu	12.3 mg	15.2 mg
4. Vegan Menu	15.5 mg	17.2 mg

Menu No. 1

In this menu, the zinc was provided primarily by the beef, chicken, dairy products and peas.

Menu No. 2

The majority of the zinc in this menu comes from the cheese and tofu in the lasagna at supper and the oatmeal, milk and toast at breakfast. The egg sandwich provides a little more zinc. The other foods – vegetables, fruits, spreads, salad dressing, cookies and pie – don't make significant contributions. Zinc falls slightly below recommended levels, but this is not likely to be a problem, since the recommended intakes include a substantial safety margin. However, zinc intakes could be increased to recommended levels very easily: by adding wheat germ to the oatmeal; by snacking on nuts; by including other foods from Table 3.14.

Menu No. 3

This lacto-ovo vegetarian menu meets the recommended intakes for zinc. Whole wheat pasta and small quantities of lentils and cheese provided the largest amount of zinc, at supper. At breakfast, oatmeal, milk, toast and almond butter all contain zinc. Hummus, pita bread and cashews are additional zinc sources.

Menu No. 4

In this vegan menu zinc comes from foods eaten throughout the day. At breakfast, cereal with wheat germ and sesame tahini (in place of butter) on toast provide zinc. The tofu salad sandwich at lunch is a good source of zinc. Tahini, used in place of salad oil, adds zinc (as well as calcium). Walnuts, given here as a snack, provide zinc and omega-3 fatty acids. Vegans also tend to use a wide assortment of grains such as brown rice, quinoa and millet; all of these make a contribution to the day's total zinc intake.

Zinc Content of Vegetarian Foods

The zinc content of a variety of foods is given in Table 3.14.

Table 3.14 Zinc in Foods

	Volume	Weight (g)	Zinc Content (mg)
Legumes and Foods Made from Legumes			
Adzuki beans	½ cup (125 mL)	115	2.0
Tofu, firm	½ cup (125 mL)	126	2.0
Tofu, regular	½ cup (125 mL)	124	1.0
Baked beans	½ cup (125 mL)	127	1.8
Tempeh	½ cup (125 mL)	83	1.5
Garbanzo beans, cooked, or hummus	½ cup (125 mL)	120	1.3
Lentils	½ cup (125 mL)	100	1.2
Miso	2 tbsp (30 mL)	34	1.2
Assorted legumes (black, kidney, lima, mung, pinto beans or split peas), cooked	½ cup (125 mL)	90	1.0
Peanut butter	2 tbsp (30 mL)	32	0.9
Nuts and seeds (dried) and butters			
Pumpkin or flax seeds	¼ cup (60 mL)	34	2.62
Tahini, unroasted	2 tbsp (30 mL)	30	1.4-2.9
Cashews or sunflower seeds	¼ cup (60 mL)	36	1.8
Cashew butter	2 tbsp (30 mL)	32	1.6
Pecans	¼ cup (60 mL)	27	1.5
Almonds	¼ cup (60 mL)	36	1.1
Almond butter	2 tbsp (30 mL)	32	1.0
Walnuts	¼ cup (60 mL)	27	0.8
Grains and Cereal Foods			
Wheat germ	2 tbsp (30 mL)	15	2.1
Quinoa, uncooked	¼ (60 mL)	42	1.4
Millet, uncooked	¼ (60 mL)	50	0.8
Brown rice, cooked	½ cup (125 mL)	98	0.6
Oatmeal, cooked	½ cup (125 mL)	130	0.6
Whole wheat bread	1 slice	25	0.4-0.6
White bread	1 slice	24	0.2
Vegetables			
Peas, raw or cooked	½ cup (125 mL)	80	1.0
Potato, with skin	1	202	0.6
Fruits			
Avocado	1	173	0.7
Milk and Milk Products			
Milk	½ cup (125 mL)	122	0.5
Cheddar cheese	½ oz	14	0.4
Other Foods			
Nutritional yeast powder	1 tbsp (15 mL)	6.7	1.0
Egg	1 large	50	0.7

For purposes of comparison:

Beef hamburger, lean, broiled	2 oz	56	3.0
Chicken, roasted light meat	2 oz	56	0.7
Cod	2 oz	56	0.2

In vegetarian diets which have been shown to support good zinc status, we see a reliance on nuts, legumes, a variety of whole grains, and processed soy products such as tofu, tempeh and soy-based meat analogues. Lacto-ovo vegetarians derive additional zinc from eggs and dairy products. The way foods are prepared or processed is an important factor in the availability of zinc from plant foods. Vegetarian diets have the potential to be low in zinc, so make the most of the zinc in your diet.

Substances that Inhibit Zinc Availability

CALCIUM SUPPLEMENTS
When people take calcium supplements together with plant foods, a zinc-calcium-phytate complex is formed in which the zinc is tightly bound and not available for absorption. Be careful not to take calcium supplements at the same time as zinc-rich foods.

OXALATES
As with iron, oxalates in spinach and rhubarb bind zinc, making it unavailable.

PHYTATES AND WHEAT BRAN SUPPLEMENTS
As we saw in the iron section of this chapter, the phytates that are associated with fiber in raw plant foods can reduce the availability of minerals. While a certain amount of dietary phytate appears to be beneficial overall, excessively high ratios of phytate to zinc can reduce zinc absorption; this can occur when unleavened bread is a mainstay or when substantial amounts of raw wheat bran are added as a supplement. The addition of raw wheat bran to a plant-based diet is neither necessary nor advisable.

Processes that Enhance Zinc Availability

Preparation methods such as the soaking of legumes, the yeasting of bread and the sprouting of seeds all increase the availability of zinc from plant foods. For example, when chickpeas are soaked (or sprouted) before being cooked and made into hummus, enzymes break down the phytates and release zinc so that it can be easily absorbed. When bread is rising at the bakery, or on your kitchen counter, zinc is being made available. Roasted nuts contain substantially less phytate than raw nuts. Science is just beginning to understand some of the food preparation methods that long-term vegetarians have been using for years to ensure good nutrition. Fortunately for the people with busy lifestyles, the places we can shop are also becoming more health oriented, so we can purchase these foods ready-made.

Single Mineral Supplements

Don't rush out and buy zinc pills. Zinc, iron, copper and calcium all interact with one another, and large intakes of one of these can interfere with your utilization of another mineral. Unless medically indicated, avoid taking a single mineral supplement. If you wish to use supplements, a multivitamin-mineral complex containing quantities at recommended levels (rather than higher) will be more supportive of good health. Check that the supplement you use contains zinc; many do not.

Guidelines for Maximizing Zinc Intake

For optimum zinc intake from your diet follow these guidelines.

1. Consume a variety of zinc-rich foods. Eat zinc sources throughout the day, including whole grains, wheat germ, tofu, tempeh, miso, legumes, nuts and seeds. Lacto-ovo vegetarians can add eggs and dairy products.

2. Make the most of the zinc in your diet. Use legumes (which have been soaked), yeasted breads, roasted nuts and sprouts.

3. Eat whole foods rather than refined foods. Products such as white flour have lost much of the zinc in the refining process. Large amounts of wheat bran, added to a diet high in whole grains and legumes, are not only unnecessary, but can interfere with mineral absorption.

It is clear that meats can be safely removed from the diet, giving all the advantages of lower intakes of saturated fat and cholesterol while at the same time meeting the needs for protein, iron and zinc. Generally, these nutrients are not as concentrated in plant foods as they are in animal foods, but we don't need such concentrated sources. In fact, as we'll see in the next chapter, eating these *less*-concentrated sources of protein may help our calcium balance.

Removing meat from the diet is a vegetarian's first step. But what about dairy products? Can we live without them – healthfully?

WITHOUT DAIRY
PRODUCTS

urrent thinking is that the lentil is one of nature's most perfect foods. I remember when milk was one of nature's most perfect foods, but that was a long time ago. Now it is the lentil, the kidney bean, the rugged cereals; these are the perfect foods.

J. Carroll, San Francisco Chronicle

It used to be so simple. But, these days, North Americans are receiving many messages about the use of dairy products.

On the one hand, our culture teaches us that milk and its products are an essential food group; government publications tell us that we *must* eat foods from each group to be healthy. Children learn that if they don't drink their milk, they won't grow strong bones. Adults get the impression that the best way to prevent, or even cure, osteoporosis is to drink more milk.

On the other hand, we hear reports of cow's milk causing allergies, congestion and diabetes. In fact, there are even recommendations *against* using milk by some physicians.

So, what is the truth? Is milk nature's most perfect food, or is it poison?

In reality, cow's milk is neither nature's perfect food (except for a baby calf), nor poison. Canadian and American food guides recommend that we consume, at different ages, in the range of two to four cups of milk daily, or comparable amounts of cheese or yogurt. Many North Americans and Europeans rely on milk and its products as major sources of calcium, vitamin D and riboflavin. With the North American style of eating, it can be a challenge to get these nutrients without milk. But this doesn't make cow's milk an essential food.

Some people do not use dairy products at all, for a variety of reasons. Many other people consume less than recommended amounts of these products. Yet, there are no provisions in our food guides for those individuals who don't consume dairy products. Thus, many people are under the impression that if dairy products are not used, calcium supplements are essential. It would be beneficial if our food guides went one step further and provided guidance about alternative sources for the nutrients milk provides. In order to see what the food alternatives are, we need to look at the eating patterns of cultures in Africa or the Orient that don't include milk in their diets, and yet have bone health as good or better than ours.

REASONS WHY PEOPLE LIMIT OR ELIMINATE DAIRY PRODUCTS

When asked why they use little or no dairy products, the reasons that people give generally fall into three categories: common cultural practices, human health and compassion for animals.

Cultural Usage

For the First Nations people, and for many immigrants who are a part of the ethnic melting pot of North America, milk is not a traditional food. There are cultures throughout the world that have not kept dairy cattle and yet developed balanced and nutritious eating patterns. They found other sources of the nutrients in milk. It is worth noting that some of these cultures show rates of osteoporosis *far* lower than the rates for Canada, the United States and Sweden, countries with high dairy consumption.

Health Reasons

Dairy products, as it turns out, are not "nature's perfect food" for a lot of people. Health reasons for not using milk include these:

LACTOSE INTOLERANCE

After about four years of age, when nature probably intended our weaning from human milk to be complete, many people stop synthesizing the digestive enzyme lactase. They develop an intolerance to lactose, the sugar in milk; in 2% milk, one third of the calories are from lactose. It is estimated that 60–90 percent of non-Caucasians and 5–15 percent of Caucasians show some degree of lactose intolerance. Sometimes a limited use of milk and cultured products such as yogurt or hard cheese is acceptable for these people.

ALLERGY AND SENSITIVITY TO MILK PROTEINS

Dairy products are a leading cause of food allergy and food sensitivity. Four proteins in milk can cause a wide variety of allergic responses in people of all ages, but primarily in infants and young children.

FAT CONTENT

Whole cow's milk is a high fat fluid, designed by nature to turn a 60–70-pound (27 to 30 kilo) calf into a 300–600-pound (135 to 275 kilo) cow in one year. Many milk products such as cheese and butter, even in some of the low-fat versions, are still higher in total fat, saturated fat and cholesterol than many consumers want. As we saw in Table 3.7, (page 48), 2% milk, which has become much more popular than whole milk, still derives a third of its total calories from fat.

JUVENILE DIABETES

There is evidence that for a small proportion of children with a particular genetic makeup, juvenile diabetes may have been initiated by the ingestion of protein from cow's milk during infancy.

Reasons of Compassion for Animals

DAIRY COWS

Our agricultural industry clearly tries very hard to feed healthy food to a growing population. However, in meeting the demand for high quality dairy products at low prices, factory farming has moved a long way from the story book picture of contented cows, grazing in green fields with a calf frolicking nearby. While in some places this picture is still true, increasing numbers of the more than ten million dairy cows in North America live in factory farm conditions. Many dairy cows are separated from their calves immediately after delivery, to prevent the development of bonding between cow and calf. The life span of a dairy cow is five years rather than the natural 12–15.

When we look at the issues of hormone use with dairy cattle, we start to get a glimpse of the changing face of agriculture in North America. The treatment of cows with a synthesized hormone, rbST (recombinant bovine somatotropin) leads to an increase of 10 percent or more in milk production. Use of the hormone has been passed by the Food and Drug Administration in the United States; at the time of publication, it was not licensed for use in Canada.

The milk produced appears to be safe for human consumption, and prior use of the hormone cannot be detected in the milk. The concern for the rbST-treated dairy cow, however, is associated with long periods of negative energy balance (weight loss), and increased vulnerability to illness (mastitis). The Council on Scientific Affairs of the American Medical Association stated in 1991 "the long-term effects of rbST on cows have not been evaluated. However, dairy cows experience an average of only three lactations before sacrifice for meat production. Therefore, those studies evaluating the influence of rbST on the health of the animal over a period of three lactations cover the agriculturally productive life of the dairy animal."

For some people, the origins of the white beverage that we grew up on seem to be changing a little too much for comfort.

VEAL CALVES

As repeated pregnancies are necessary for the continued yield of milk by the dairy cow, during her three to four years of milk production, she is "freshened" (impregnated) once a year. A female calf may join the army of milk producers. A male calf is likely to become tender white veal, after being raised for about 14 to 24 weeks, in confined conditions which prevent normal muscle development. The stomachs of calves may be used to provide the rennet needed in cheese production.

People often choose not to eat meat because of an unwillingness to consume animal flesh. As vegetarians become more knowledgeable about the origins of their food, it becomes apparent that the production of dairy products is closely connected with the meat industry. As a result, a decreased use of dairy products often follows the elimination of meat.

The Need for Alternatives to Dairy Products on Food Guides

One or more of these cultural, health or animal-related reasons can be sufficiently compelling to convince some people not to use dairy products, or to use only small amounts. At the XXIII International Dairy Congress, it was reported that a 29-country survey showed a decline in consumption of fluid milk. In developed countries, this was attributed to increased numbers of immigrants from countries where milk is not a staple food, and the pursuit of healthier diets, lower in fat and cholesterol.

When people don't use meat, fish and poultry, they will generally replace these foods with legumes, tofu and nuts. This replacement is supported by the presence of the "Meat Alternates" on food guides, which gives an official stamp of approval to the plant foods that provide iron, protein and zinc. On the other hand, government endorsed food guides give no hint that the nutrients in milk can also be found in alternative foods. Thus, people who use little or no dairy products have a limited awareness of the replacement foods which need to be included in their diets.

The Canadian and American food guides, as they are presently constructed, adequately address the needs of many North Americans. However, they are of limited value to others who, for a variety of reasons, use little or no milk. To increase the usefulness and appeal of our food guides, foods that are calcium-rich dairy alternatives should be listed side by side with dairy products, and be called "Milk Alternates."

The Vegetarian Food Guide, given in Chapter 8 of this book, includes a "Milk and Milk Alternates" food group. Here we lay the foundation for this food group and for meeting one's needs for calcium, vitamin D and riboflavin on a plant-based diet. We begin with the mineral that is most abundant in our bodies.

CALCIUM

Calcium is the mineral of the decade. It is featured on billboards, radio and TV advertisements; it fills the supplement shelves of pharmacies and health food stores. It is found in milk – and in plants. In this chapter, we address one myth that is prevalent in our society:

> *Myth:* It is virtually impossible for your diet to meet your calcium needs without milk and milk products.

It is a commonly held belief that without milk, we must either take supplements or face certain osteoporosis. This myth is based on three misconceptions. First, that our calcium status is dependent on very high intakes of calcium, rather than on calcium balance (more about this later). Second, that there are not calcium-rich alternatives to milk products. Third, that the calcium from plants is less available. In this next section, we will look at the truth behind these misconceptions. Before we tackle the myth, it's important to have some understanding of the role of calcium in the body.

Calcium in the Body

Over 99 percent of the calcium in the body is found in bones and teeth. The calcium in bones is in a state of constant turnover and bone is being remodeled throughout our lives. Even though only 1 percent of the calcium in our bodies is found in blood and in other tissues, its function here is vital. Calcium is a part of all cell membranes and is involved with muscle contraction and relaxation, blood clotting, the transmission of nerve impulses, and the absorption of vitamin B_{12}.

Calcium Balance

The body maintains its levels of calcium in blood and bones with a complex system of checks and balances. Even as you read this, your body is adjusting the amount of calcium in your blood, keeping it at an exact level. To maintain this level, you have a limited ability to change the proportion absorbed from foods and to alter the quantity of calcium lost in urine. You can also draw on the calcium stored in bone, if necessary. The difference between calcium intake and calcium losses from the body is known as calcium balance.

THE NEED FOR POSITIVE CALCIUM BALANCE EARLY IN LIFE

Throughout the growing years, we need to maintain a positive calcium balance by taking in more calcium than we lose. It is of prime importance that a good foundation of calcium be laid in bones during the first quarter century of life, and that we attain "peak bone mass" during this time (for specific guidelines, see Chapter 9). Generally, people who are most in need of calcium absorb the highest percentage from the diet, so that absorption is greatest during pregnancy, lactation and the growing years. Thus, children may absorb up to 75 percent of dietary calcium, as compared with rates of 20–40 percent observed in young adults.

CALICIUM LOSSES AND BONE MAINTENANCE LATER IN LIFE

Beyond the mid 30s, natural bone loss begins in men and women. For this period of our lives, we can expect to have a slight negative calcium balance. Calcium loss accelerates around the time of menopause in women, then slows down again. Your diet and lifestyle choices throughout these years can help keep your bones strong by maximizing calcium absorption and minimizing calcium loss. Thus, although you don't need excessive calcium supplements, adequate calcium intake is certainly important.

FACTORS CONTRIBUTING TO POSITIVE CALCIUM BALANCE

Your calcium status, and the amount of calcium in your bones, depends on more than just the amount of calcium in your diet. Calcium intake is just one part of the rather complex equation of calcium balance. A great many nutrients interact with calcium, and can affect its absorption from foods and our losses in urine. Vitamin D has a key role in helping calcium absorption. Boron, a mineral found in vegetables, fruits, nuts and legumes, may have a role in preventing calcium loss.

And apart from diet, exercise is of the utmost importance. Weight-bearing exercise such as walking, running or cycling, done at least three times a week, is a significant factor in helping us retain the calcium we have.

FACTORS CONTRIBUTING TO NEGATIVE CALCIUM BALANCE

"Calcium thieves" such as excess protein or salt can cause substantial calcium losses. Other factors such as alcohol intake, smoking, heavy intakes of caffeinated beverages (coffee, tea and some soft drinks) and prolonged periods of inactivity can also tip the balance in a negative direction.

Of particular interest to vegetarians and near-vegetarians are studies which have shown that the amount of calcium lost in urine is increased with high intakes of protein. When we take in more protein than we need, the breakdown and excretion of the excess sulphur-containing amino acids causes the urine to become more acidic. As the urine becomes more acidic, it carries out calcium with it. Meat, poultry, fish, eggs and dairy products are concentrated sources of protein, and of sulfur amino acids. Plant foods also contain these sulfur amino acids, which are essential for building body protein. However, plant foods are less concentrated sources of total protein and of these amino acids, so excesses are less likely. While calcium losses are counteracted, at least in part, by the high phosphorus levels in foods such as meats, increasingly our high protein intake is being targeted as a significant factor contributing to our high incidence of osteoporosis. As we saw in the last chapter, North Americans tend to consume, *on average*, about 100 grams of protein daily, far in excess of the recommended 50 to 70 grams. Two thirds of this protein is of animal origin.

Vegetarians tend to have total protein intakes closer to recommended levels; this appears to be advantageous to calcium balance.

ASSESSMENT OF CALCIUM STATUS

The calcium status of an individual cannot be assessed by routine blood tests. This is because we generally keep our blood calcium level constant, drawing from the calcium in bone when necessary. More complex bone density tests (called "dual photon densitometry") can be used to estimate calcium stored in bone, but bone tests reflect more than just calcium status, since many nutrients are involved in the building of bone. Furthermore, lifestyle factors such as exercise and smoking affect calcium balance.

This has complicated the establishment of recommended levels. According to Health and Welfare Canada's Scientific Review Committee, in their 1990 Nutrition Recommendations report, "Defining the adult requirement for calcium has proved to be one of the most difficult problems in the history of human nutrition."

Recommended Calcium Intakes

The Canadian recommended intakes for adults are in the range of 700–800 mg per day. American recommendations are 800 mg for adults above 24 years of age, and 1200 mg daily for younger adults. Markedly different recommendations for adults have been set by the World Health Organization (400–500 mg/day) and Japan (600 mg).

Health and Welfare Canada's Scientific Review Committee makes the following points:

> Beyond weaning age, children and adults of various countries and food cultures subsist on diets differing markedly in calcium content. These differences in calcium intake, which are due mainly to the relative strengths of the dairy industry, have not been demonstrated to have any consequences for nutritional health. . . . It cannot be assumed, however, that the low calcium intake of women living in countries with a cereal-based food economy (400–500 mg/day) is necessarily adequate for women consuming a Western diet.

Certainly we do need adequate calcium intake, especially during the growing, bone-building years. However, exactly *what level of calcium intake can be considered adequate* is a matter of considerable debate among experts, because:

1. There is no easy, routine way to assess calcium status.
2. The body has the capacity to adapt to a wide range of calcium intakes.
3. Eating patterns and other habits differ from country to country in many ways that affect calcium balance.

For those whose lifestyle choices support calcium retention, smaller quantities of dietary calcium *may* be adequate. These lifestyle choices include physical fitness, adequate vitamin D, non-smoking, and avoidance of excess protein, alcohol, caffeine and salt. But there are many questions yet to be answered; little research has been done on the effects of lifelong vegan diets on bone health.

For this reason, it seems advisable for vegetarians to use the same recommended calcium intakes given for other North Americans. But, wait a minute. Can we really get that much calcium *without milk?*

We have come to think of dairy products as the sole source of calcium in our diets. People are often unaware that other dietary sources exist. As we will see, there are plenty of excellent plant sources, with abundant available calcium. First let's look at the four menus from the last chapter and see how much calcium they provide, and which foods provided it.

Table 4.1 Calcium Provided in Menu Nos. 1 to 4 (pages 41 to 46)

	For 130 Pound (59 kilo) Person	*For 170 Pound (77 kilo) Person*
1. Omnivore Menu	900 mg	1010 mg
2. Lacto-Ovo Vegetarian Menu (Dairy and egg emphasis)	1220 mg	1590 mg
3. Lacto-Ovo Vegetarian Menu (Less dairy and egg)	950 mg	1120 mg
4. Vegan Menu	1105 mg	1235 mg

The calcium in all of these menus exceeds the adult Canadian and American recommendations of 700–800 mg per day. To help meet the American recommendations for young adults (1200 mg), calcium-fortified products could be used as well.

An important point: in all three vegetarian menus, calcium is supplied, in small amounts, by plant foods in meals and snacks throughout the day. Research has shown that calcium is absorbed far more efficiently when it is consumed in many small doses. When the same amount of calcium is given in a few concentrated portions it is less well absorbed.

OMNIVORE MENU
Typically in North American diets, three quarters of the calcium is provided by dairy products. In the omnivore's menu, 70 percent of the calcium comes from dairy products: milk at breakfast, yogurt at lunch and, to a lesser extent, cheesecake.

LACTO OVO VEGETARIAN MENUS
In Menus 2 and 3, approximately 45–50 percent of the calcium is from dairy products. About half of the calcium is supplied by plant foods.

VEGAN MENU
In the vegan menu almost every food eaten contributes to the total, over 1000 mg of calcium. About 20 percent of this comes at breakfast, from the toast with tahini and molasses and the orange. The tofu salad sandwich, using tofu made with calcium, is a big contributor. (If nigari or magnesium are used in the tofu processing, the calcium provided by the sandwich is much lower.)

Plant Foods as Calcium Sources
Plant leaves and stems (otherwise known as green vegetables) and seeds are some of the best calcium sources around. Canadians and Americans are notorious for not eating their vegetables. In fact, a survey of 11,000 people showed that 48 percent on the day surveyed ate no vegetables at all! It is no wonder that many people have low calcium intakes, especially if they aren't fond of milk.

These calcium-rich plant foods are regularly used in other parts of the world – and they're used well. You don't end up with a mushy, tasteless green pile on your plate. Greens are seasoned deliciously and presented attractively. Seeds are often ground and provide a creamy texture to some dishes. If you are going to put together meals high in calcium without dairy products you will probably be in for a few taste adventures. The recipes in Chapter 12 will help you get started. Table 4.2 gives the calcium contents of a range of foods that contain calcium, some common, others perhaps unfamiliar.

Table 4.2 Calcium in Foods

Legumes and Foods Made from Legumes	Volume	Weight (g)	Calcium Content (mg)
Tofu, firm (made with calcium)	¼ cup (60 mL)	63	430★
Tofu, firm (made with nigari)	¼ cup (60 mL)	63	129
Tofu, regular (made with calcium)	¼ cup (60 mL)	63	220★
Tofu, regular (made with nigari)	¼ cup (60 mL)	63	67
Natto miso (a soy condiment)	¼ cup (60 mL)	44	96
Hummus	½ cup (125 mL)	122	81
White beans	½ cup (125 mL)	90	81
Tempeh (a fermented soy product)	½ cup (125 mL)	83	77
Navy beans	½ cup (125 mL)	91	64
Black turtle beans	½ cup (125 mL)	93	52
Pinto beans	½ cup (125 mL)	86	41
Seeds and Nuts			
Whole sesame seeds	2 tbsp (25 mL)	56	176
Tahini (sesame butter)	2 tbsp (25 mL)	56	128
Almond butter	3 tbsp (45 mL)	48	129
Almonds, dry roasted	⅓ cup (80 mL)	42	120–176
Vegetables and Fruits			
Broccoli, cooked	1 cup (250 mL)	156	178
Okra, frozen, cooked	1 cup (250 mL)	184	176
Chinese cabbage, cooked	1 cup (250 mL)	170	158
Collard greens	1 cup (250 mL)	190	148
Mustard greens, cooked	1 cup (250 mL)	140	104
Kale, cooked	1 cup (250 mL)	130	94
Rutabaga, cooked	1 cup (250 mL)	170	72
Figs, dried	5 medium	94	135
Orange	1 medium	140	56
Seaweeds (Sea Vegetables)			
Hijiki, dry	¼ cup (60 mL)	10	162
Wakame, dry	¼ cup (60 mL)	10	104
Grain			
Amaranth, cooked	1 cup (250 mL)	132	276

Other Foods

Canned pink salmon (with bones)	3 oz	85	181
Milk, whole, 2% or skim	½ cup (125 mL)	122	144–151
Blackstrap molasses	1 tbsp (15 mL)	20	137
Calcium fortified soy beverages★★	½ cup (125 mL)	125	95–160

★ Calcium values are from U.S. Department of Agriculture; values may vary in different areas, check with local suppliers.

★★ At the time of writing, sale of these beverages is not permitted in Canada.

In the production of tofu, either a calcium or a magnesium salt is used as part of the process. Check the label to see if the tofu you are buying has added calcium; for the non-packaged variety you'll have to ask the supplier. Non-dairy milk alternates have come a long way, since some of the early unappealing soy milks. A variety of calcium-fortified foods, from tortillas to soy milks, are available on the American market. Due to more restrictive laws on fortification, these are not available in Canadian supermarkets, although they may be obtained worldwide through Seventh-day Adventist ABC stores.

Some of the foods listed in Table 4.2 are high in calories, while others are low. Sesame tahini and tofu are at the higher end of the range, and are excellent for increasing the caloric intakes of children and underweight adults. The vegetables and seaweeds are extremely low in fat and calories. All of these foods provide other minerals in addition to calcium. Native people living in coastal areas of North America traditionally used local seaweeds, including kelp and dulse, and have obtained some of their calcium from these.

Seaweeds are actually vegetables from the sea, and have a long history of use in Japan. Some Japanese dishes use seaweed as a main ingredient. When Westerners start out, they often prefer smaller amounts providing saltiness and seasoning, or in Western food variations such as the type of sushi known as California roll. In the recipe section (Chapter 12) we include the exceptionally high-calcium hijiki seaweed as an option in the delicious "Green Sea Soup" and the stir fry. Miso soup is a delicious appetizer; in Japan it is also a regular breakfast food.

Most grains are not good calcium sources. In some countries people have increased their calcium intakes by using flour which has been fortified by adding calcium carbonate; this is routinely done in Israel. Some people fortify their own flour this way, with calcium purchased from a local pharmacy. Amaranth, an ancient grain from South America, has an unusually high calcium content. It's a new product to North Americans; we're just learning how to use it. It can be cooked together with three parts of rice, but it will probably become more popular in the processed forms – breakfast cereals, flours and pastas – that are beginning to make their appearance in the marketplace.

Calcium Availability from Foods

Overall we absorb 30 to 50 percent of the calcium in the North American diet. Recent studies by Weaver have shown that the absorption of calcium from some vegetables is much higher than was formerly believed, although it is important to remember that they are also less concentrated sources of calcium than dairy products. Table 4.3 shows the calcium absorption from foods when portions containing comparable amounts of calcium were given. When we combine the information from Table 4.2 and Table 4.3, we find that some plant foods can be real calcium powerhouses in our diets. So, although greens are much less concentrated sources of calcium than milk, because the calcium in some greens is more readily available, they can make substantial contributions to daily calcium intake. In fact, this is the case in many parts of the world where dairy products are not regularly consumed.

Table 4.3 Percentage of Calcium Absorbed from Foods

	Percentage Absorbed
Vegetables, cooked	50–70%
(broccoli, brussels sprouts, chinese and green cabbage,	
cauliflower, kale, kohlrabi, mustard greens, rutabaga,	
turnip greens, watercress)	
Milk	32%
Tofu	31%
Almonds, sesame seeds	21%
Beans, cooked (pinto, small red, white)	17%
Spinach, cooked	5%

Preparation techniques, which make food appetizing, at the same time often increase the availability of calcium from plant foods: soaking (beans), sprouting (seeds and legumes), yeasting and fermentation (bread, miso) and roasting (nuts) release calcium so that we can absorb it. See Chapter 7 for a further discussion on mineral absorption.

There are a few plant foods which, although they contain plenty of calcium, are not good sources of this mineral, due to their high oxalate contents. These include spinach, beet greens, swiss chard and rhubarb. As you can see in Table 4.3, little of the calcium in spinach is available for absorption.

North American Dietary Intakes of Calcium

OVERALL POPULATION

American studies dating back to the 1950s have shown that calcium is one of the three nutrients most often consumed below recommended levels. In particular, intakes of calcium in the diets of North American women show a wide range, with many falling short of desired levels. Many women do not consume the amounts of dairy products suggested in food guides; non-dairy alternatives might be a welcome addition.

VEGETARIANS

Vegetarians were shown in the 1977/1978 National Food Consumption Survey (USDA, 1984) to have calcium intakes that were higher than those of the general population at all ages. Calcium intakes of the vegetarians ranged from 7 to 54 percent higher for comparable age groups. Particularly interesting were findings for young women from 9 to 34 years of age. In these years of bone mineralization, calcium intakes of vegetarians were 17 to 39 percent higher than the intakes of omnivores. This survey grouped lacto-ovo vegetarians and vegans together.

VEGANS

The few studies that have been done on adult vegans show intakes in the range of 500 to 1000 mg calcium, although some individuals had lower intakes. A study of 40 vegans in Israel showed their average calcium intake to be 825 mg per day. In this study, nuts and seeds provided one third of the calcium. People also ate seaweeds, as well as more common plant sources of calcium. Vegans use greens, soy products, nuts and seeds as calcium sources. Some studies of vegan children have shown low calcium intakes; this is certainly a cause for concern, because bone mineralization occurs in the growing years. Our Vegetarian Food Guide, as well as guidelines in Chapter 9, will help people of all ages achieve adequate intakes of calcium.

Incidence of Osteoporosis

A number of studies have been done comparing the long-term effects on bone density of lacto-vegetarian diets and of omnivorous diets. Marsh studied 1600 lacto-ovo vegetarians in Michigan and found that, whereas female omnivores had lost 35 percent of bone mass by 80 years of age, female vegetarians had lost only 18 percent. No differences were reported for men. She suggested that the lacto-ovo vegetarian lifestyle of the women studied, including their lower intakes of animal protein, appeared to be a protective factor in postmenopausal bone loss.

From the research that has been done, the few vegans studied do not appear to show lower bone density than omnivores.

Calcium Supplements

There is a role for calcium supplements, but as with other supplements, they should not be assumed to be adequate replacements for real food. When we depend on nutritious foods, we end up with a balance of all of the nutrients we need for building bone and for other body functions. Nature provides all of these together, in greens, beans, nuts and seeds. Supplemental calcium may not be as well absorbed as small amounts in food throughout the day.

If calcium intake from foods is inadequate, supplements can be useful, but for people in good health, there appears to be no advantage in higher-than-recommended intakes. In fact, excesses of calcium can bind the mineral zinc, making it unavailable. People who are predisposed to the formation of kidney stones should avoid intakes of calcium that are above recommended levels.

It is certainly possible to meet recommended levels of calcium intake at any age without the use of dairy products. Those vegans and near-vegans who consume a variety of the calcium-rich plant foods eaten throughout the day will obtain sufficient calcium. Others, who are not using these foods, would be well advised to begin incorporating them into their diets. Plant sources of calcium include green vegetables, tofu made with calcium, nuts, seeds and blackstrap molasses. Other plant foods can also contribute small amounts of calcium. The Vegetarian Food Guide given in Chapter 8 includes a Milk and Milk Alternates group.

Overall guidelines are given at the end of this chapter under: "Seven Simple Steps for Strong Bones (For the Non-Dairy Set)." Now let's look at a vitamin that forms a strong partnership with calcium.

VITAMIN D: THE SUN WORSHIPPER'S VITAMIN

When we expose our skin to sunlight, even for just a few minutes, vitamin D is formed. Vitamin D is also commonly added to milk. These two very different sources – sunlight and fortified foods – are the main ways we get vitamin D.

The importance of sunlight to the sturdiness of the skeleton was referred to even in ancient times. More recently, folk wisdom suggested that recovery from some diseases would be speeded by time spent in the sun. In the twentieth century, we found that certain ultraviolet rays in sunlight would help our bodies create vitamin D. It was also discovered that vitamin D could be taken orally, in foods or supplements, and that both routes were equally effective treatments for a common disease called rickets.

The Role of Vitamin D in the Body

Vitamin D is essential for the proper formation of the skeleton. If we have too little vitamin D, the skeleton will be inadequately mineralized, leading to a condition called rickets in children, and osteomalacia in adults. One of the best known roles of vitamin D is to maintain blood calcium at exactly the right level. It does this by regulating the movements of calcium in three places: absorption in the intestine, losses through the urine, and storage in the bones.

Origins of Food Fortification with Vitamin D

From the 17th to the 19th century, rickets plagued children who played in the narrow, dark streets of industrial cities (or worked indoors). In 1900, over 85 percent of the children in some smoggy urban areas of North America and Europe had this crippling disease. Subsequently, the roles of vitamin D and sunlight in curing rickets were identified. In the United States and Canada, cow's milk was chosen as a vehicle for vitamin D to reach the population as a whole, and to reach children in particular. As a result, rickets has become rare here.

Natural Food Sources of Vitamin D

There is little doubt that before the era of vitamin supplementation and food fortification, sunlight was the major provider of vitamin D for most of the world's population. Vitamin D is naturally present in few foods. Fish oils are a notable exception; these oils have provided vitamin D to Inuit and other northern people in areas where sunlight is limited. Eggs can also provide vitamin D in varying amounts if the chickens have been fed supplements. The exposure of certain plant foods to ultraviolet light has also been demonstrated to produce a form of vitamin D (vitamin D_2). For example, certain seaweeds, dried in the sun, have shown vitamin D_2 activity.

Our Current Sources of Vitamin D

North Americans generally get vitamin D from fortified foods, sunlight and supplements. Vitamin D_3 used in fortified foods and supplements is generally of animal origin, often from the livers of fatty fish or from the skins of animals. Vegans can use vitamin D_2 (ergocalciferol), available as a prescription drug.

FORTIFIED FOOD SOURCES

Foods that are often fortified with vitamin D include cow's milk, margarine, infant formulas and goat's milk. In the United States and Britain, fortified soy milks, cereals and vegan margarines (free of dairy products) are available. Vitamin D-fortified foods that are acceptable to vegans are not widely available in Canada. It would be helpful for Canadians who do not use dairy products if the nutrient fortification of alternative drinks such as soy beverages were permitted.

SUNLIGHT AS A VITAMIN D SOURCE

People who are regularly exposed to adequate amounts of sunlight have no requirement for vitamin D from foods. When our skin is exposed to the ultraviolet light in sunshine, we can make vitamin D out of a cholesterol compound, naturally present in the skin. To determine whether an individual is getting enough sunlight for adequate vitamin D production, a number of factors must be taken into consideration.

Age

The capacity of the skin to produce vitamin D in the elderly is approximately half that of younger people. Infants and children need more vitamin D to help absorb calcium for quickly growing bones; nature has cleverly arranged that they also have a greater capacity to produce the vitamin.

Skin color

People with dark skins require substantially more exposure to sunlight for vitamin D production. Whereas light-skinned people need 10–15 minutes of sunlight a day, people with increasingly darker skin need from 30 minutes to 3 hours daily (on face and hands). The melanin pigment in dark skin absorbs some of the ultraviolet radiation. This appears to be a protective adaptation, developed by people in sunny climates. It has been suggested that, over the evolution of mankind, as people moved to northern latitudes, skin pigmentation decreased to allow for adequate production of vitamin D. If you've ever wondered about those blond, light-skinned Scandinavians in the north, and the darker-skinned people close to the equator – these differences probably developed partly because of vitamin D!

Use of sunscreen

Sunscreen protection factors (SPF) of 8 and above will prevent vitamin D synthesis. Our need for vitamin D must be balanced with the obvious need for protection from overexposure to the sun, especially in the hot hours of the day. For vitamin D synthesis, midmorning sun is fine.

Type of clothing worn

Vitamin D production varies with the amount of clothing one is wearing, which affects the surface area of skin exposed. For example, the attire of some Middle Eastern women covers the head and face, preventing vitamin D production.

Sunlamps

Sunlamps can be used to produce vitamin D in the skin. They may also cause skin damage, so controlled ultraviolet light chambers are recommended.

Time of year and geographical location

Vitamin D production in skin differs seasonally and according to the latitude at which we live, as these factors affect the amount of ultraviolet radiation. On a cloudy summer day, even the "skyshine" will stimulate some vitamin D production. We have the ability to store vitamin D for the months with less sunshine. It's all right to get more sun in the summer and less in the winter, although our serum levels of the vitamin do drop. It has been estimated that there is at least a 16–fold difference in the amount of ultraviolet radiation received even on sunny days in winter, compared to summer. The "vitamin D winter," during which little or no vitamin D production occurs in skin, is longer at northern latitudes. It may be too long for the limited vitamin D reserves of infants and children, so they will need a supplement. Table 4.4 shows months without vitamin D production at specific latitudes and locations.

Table 4.4 Months Without Vitamin D Production at Specific Locations and Latitudes

Latitudes and location	Months without vitamin D production
61° N (Bergen, Norway)	October to March
52° N (Edmonton)	November to February
42° N (Boston)	December to January
34° N (Los Angeles)	none

You can roughly estimate your vitamin D winter by using the closest latitude. Shorter periods of time in the sun would be appropriate in the southern parts of the United States; as one moves north, longer exposures are needed for an equivalent amount of vitamin D production. Overexposure to the sun does *not* result in the production of harmful excesses of vitamin D, although it can, of course, lead to skin problems. Moderate sun exposure seems the wisest course.

As you might have guessed, making a recommendation for the minimum sunlight exposure necessary for vitamin D production can be complicated by all of the above factors. However, the following guidelines will help you meet your vitamin D needs. You can choose sunlight, fortified foods, supplements or a combination.

GUIDELINE FOR GETTING ENOUGH VITAMIN D FROM SUN EXPOSURE

A general guideline for North Americans, at the more populated latitudes, is an average of 10 to 15 minutes of sun daily, midmorning to late afternoon, on the face and hands, for light-skinned people. Darker-skinned people need more (30 minutes to three hours daily, depending on skin color).

GUIDELINES FOR GETTING ENOUGH
VITAMIN D FROM FOODS AND SUPPLEMENTS

Use vitamin D-fortified foods or supplements to provide the total recommended adult intakes shown in Table 4.5. (The American recommendations include a larger safety margin.) Recommended intakes for vitamin D are sometimes given in micrograms (µg) and sometimes expressed in International Units (2.5 µg = 100 International Units).

Table 4.5 Recommended Intakes of Vitamin D

	Canadian	*American*
Adults 19 to 24	2.5 µg	10 µg
Adults 25 to 50	2.5 µg	5 µg
Adults 50 and over	5 µg	5 µg

Following the guidelines above, individuals can get their vitamin D from sunlight, fortified foods, supplements or a combination of sources. Recommended intakes for pregnancy, lactation, infants and children are outlined in Chapter 9 and in Appendix 2.

EXCESS VITAMIN D

People must be particularly careful not to consume more than recommended amounts of vitamin D. Too much vitamin D (five times the recommended intake) over an extended period of time can cause "hypercalcemia" – too much calcium in the blood – which is a serious condition. This can occur with high dosage supplements or a combination of milk, other fortified foods and supplements.

RIBOFLAVIN

We'll turn our attention to one other vitamin, commonly found in dairy products but also available from many plant foods. You've probably seen its name as you sat at breakfast, reading the side of your cereal box. Riboflavin is involved with energy metabolism and is active in every cell in the body. It also helps to maintain body tissues, including skin, and mucous membranes such as those in the mouth and eyes. Riboflavin deficiencies, although rare, show up as cracks at the corner of the mouth and changes in the tongue and mucous membranes of the mouth.

Recommended Intakes of Riboflavin

Since our need for riboflavin is tied to our use of energy, the recommended intake is stated in terms of the calories we burn. The Canadian recommendation is 0.5 mg/1000 calories; the American recommendation is 0.6 mg/1000 calories, with a minimum recommendation of 1.2 mg.

Each of the four menus in Chapter 3 provides more than one and a half times the recommended intake of riboflavin. The vegan menu contains the greatest amount of riboflavin – 225 percent of the recommended intake.

Riboflavin in Diets With and Without Dairy Products

A third of North Americans' dietary riboflavin comes from dairy products and another third comes from meat, poultry, fish and eggs. Thus, there is sometimes concern that vegetarian diets and diets without dairy products will be low in riboflavin. It is true that in a few studies, vegetarians have shown riboflavin deficiencies. This is both surprising and unnecessary because riboflavin is available in many plant foods.

In a vegan diet, one third of the riboflavin may come from vegetables and fruits, a quarter from legumes, nuts and seeds and the rest from grains. Vegans often include foods not commonly used by omnivores. Foods such as nutritional yeast, yeast extracts, wheat germ and sprouts are good sources of riboflavin and other nutrients.

In fact, it is not difficult to obtain sufficient riboflavin in a diet without dairy products. Whole grains (rice, rye, millet, wheat) and enriched flours provide riboflavin in amounts very similar to the 0.5 or 0.6 mg per 1000 calories suggested in our recommended intakes. Including riboflavin-rich foods can also inspire you to try out some new vegetables. You're likely to get small amounts – about 10 percent of your recommended riboflavin intake – from each serving of a great many foods throughout the day: grains, vegetables, legumes, soy milk, dried fruit, nuts and seeds. Table 4.6 lists a few of the food sources of riboflavin in vegetarian diets; there are many others not on this list.

Table 4.6 Riboflavin in Foods

	Volume	Weight (grams)	Riboflavin (milligrams)
Yeast			
Nutritional yeast, Red Star T6635+ flakes	1 tbsp (15 mL)	4	2.4
Legumes and Legume Products			
Beans (assorted varieties), cooked	1 cup (250 mL)	190–200	.08–.16
Tofu, tempeh	½ cup (125 mL)	125	.09–.13
Nuts and Seeds			
Almonds	3 tbsp (45 mL)	48	.30
Sesame tahini	2 tbsp (30 mL)	30	.14

Grains

Wheat germ	2 tbsp (30 mL)	14	.12
Whole wheat bread	1 slice	24	.08
Enriched white bread	1 slice	24	.07
Enriched cereals (see labels)			.40

Vegetables

Broccoli, cooked	1 cup (250 mL)	156	.32
Mushrooms, raw	1 cup (250 mL)	70	.32
Peas, boiled	1 cup (250 mL)	160	.24
Avocado, California	1 medium	173	.21
Lotus root	10 slices	81	.18
Sweet potato	1	114	.15
Sprouts (alfalfa, mung, soy)	1 cup (250 mL)	105	.13–.21
Asparagus	6 spears	90	.11

Fruits

Raspberries, strawberries	1 cup (250 mL)	123	.11
Figs, dried	5	94	.09

Dairy Products and Eggs

Milk, whole, 2%, skim	½ cup (125 mL)	122	.17–.21
Yogurt	½ cup (125 mL)	114	.16
Egg	1	50	.14

When people use little or no dairy products it is important that they choose other sources for the riboflavin found in milk and milk products. Include some of the wide variety of foods listed in Table 4.6. Riboflavin is found in many of the same plant sources as calcium, and it also turns up in some unexpected foods like peas, avocado and raspberries. You'll easily meet recommended riboflavin intakes by following the Vegetarian Food Guide given in Chapter 8.

We find over and over in vegetarian diets that an adequate intake of vitamins and minerals is achieved by eating nutritious foods throughout the day, so that all (or almost all) of the meals and snacks count. A French study (Millet, 1989) noted that although vegetarians had lower caloric intakes than omnivores, the intake of vitamins and minerals was generally higher, because nutritious foods were selected.

Let's return to the two bone-building nutrients discussed earlier in this chapter. The following guidelines will help you to obtain sufficient calcium and vitamin D in a diet with little or no dairy products. Your plant-based diet can give you lifelong support.

Seven Simple Steps for Strong Bones (For the Non-Dairy Set)

1. Follow the recommendations in the Milk and Milk Alternates section of the Vegetarian Food Guide.

• Eat dark green vegetables *daily*. Include broccoli, kale, bok choy and sui choy on your regular shopping list. Find an Oriental grocery store; grow greens in your garden, or on your balcony (kale grows even in cold weather). Learn some delicious ways to prepare greens (see Chapter 12 for ideas). Minerals are lost in the cooking water, so steam vegetables or use the mineral-rich cooking water in soups or in grain preparation.

• Make sesame seeds and nuts a part of your meals and snacks. Find delicious ways to use sesame tahini. On toast or bread, perhaps with black-strap molasses, it provides calcium, iron and zinc all at once! Tahini is also an excellent base for salad dressings.

• Try Oriental favorites, such as sushi, made with the seaweed nori. Use other sea vegetables such as hijiki in stir-fries and soups.

• Use tofu made with calcium. For those people who aren't sure they like tofu, realize that, like flour, it is an ingredient. You wouldn't want to eat a bowl of flour, though you may love many baked goods. Tofu is unusually versatile; it can be made into everything from soup to dessert, so it can be used often without your menus becoming repetitious (see Chapter 12).

2. Emphasize these important foods, along with an overall good diet, during the growing years. Infants need breast milk or fortified soy formula; as children get older they can add fortified soy milks (where available).

3. Take advantage of some of the calcium-fortified foods where they are available. Use these if necessary to bring your total calcium intake up to recommended levels.

4. Don't keep company with the calcium thieves; avoid high intakes of salt, alcohol, caffeine and concentrated protein foods. A good overall diet along with some weight-bearing exercise will help you keep the calcium you have throughout life.

5. When you go out for dinner, frequent Japanese, Chinese, Middle Eastern and vegetarian restaurants. These will cater to your "non-dairy calcium" needs.

6. Sitting indoors and watching people on TV run around in the sun will not help you make vitamin D. You have to actually go outside yourself! Ten minutes a day of summer sun will be sufficient for Caucasians. Dark-skinned people may need substantially more. People living in northern latitudes will require foods fortified with vitamin D or a supplement.

7. Exercise is a prime bone strengthener; walking, jogging and other weight-bearing exercise can be key to your lifelong bone health.

VEGANISM: MORE FOOD FOR THOUGHT

 "pure vegetarian" diet could be the eventual destination of some people who have begun to move away from animal foods. Wherever you are on the continuum between omnivorous and vegan diets, you will probably find it reassuring to know that a diet totally free of animal products can keep you in excellent health.

At one time, vegan diets were considered to be risky by scientific experts, but by 1975, Dr. W. Crosby and a committee representing the American National Academy of Sciences had concluded that a vegan diet is a safe dietary option: "individual pure vegetarians from many populations of the world have maintained seemingly excellent health." They advocated that vegans take particular care in certain areas: first, to supplement their diets with vitamin B_{12}; second, to eat a wide variety of foods. The need for care in planning the diets of children was emphasized. It is now clear that vegan diets can be adequate throughout the growing years, as long as there is a focus on foods high in calories and other nutrients (for specific recommendations, see Chapter 9).

In Chapter 3 we looked at plant sources of protein, iron and zinc for people who don't include meat, poultry or fish in their diet. Chapter 4 covered sources of calcium, vitamin D and riboflavin for those who don't use dairy products. In this chapter, we address the two additional points for vegans made by the National Academy of Sciences: ensuring reliable sources of vitamin B_{12}, and obtaining a varied diet. The material in this chapter is also important for the many near-vegans who include *few* dairy products, eggs, or other foods of animal origin in their diets.

VITAMIN B12

Vitamin B_{12} was the last vitamin to be discovered; it was finally isolated as recently as 1947. Vitamin B_{12} is a complex molecule, similar in many respects to hemoglobin. Whereas hemoglobin has an atom of iron in a central position, the mineral cobalt is at the center in vitamin B_{12}.

Vitamin B_{12} in the Body

ROLE AND DEFICIENCY SYMPTOMS

Vitamin B_{12} is involved in the metabolism of certain amino acids and fatty acids. It plays a role in cell division and the maturation of red blood cells, and it helps to maintain the protective sheaths surrounding nerve fibers.

Most cases of vitamin B_{12} deficiency occur not among vegetarians but in the general population. One deficiency symptom is a type of anemia (megaloblastic anemia), in which red blood cells do not mature properly. Deficiency of vitamin B_{12} can also lead to damage to the nerves and spinal cord. Symptoms of deficiency are weakness and fatigue, difficulty with balance when walking and numbness and tingling in fingers and toes, like a "pins and needles" sensation. Other symptoms are confusion, inability to concentrate and changes in the color and surface of the tongue. Nerve damage from prolonged vitamin B_{12} deficiency can be severe and irreversible, but it rarely occurs because deficiencies are generally diagnosed before that stage.

An adequate intake of vitamin B_{12} is important at all stages of life, but particularly for pregnant and lactating women, infants and children. Babies are especially vulnerable, because they do not have stores of the vitamin to draw on. Reports of deficiency are so rare that single cases are reported in the scientific literature. But the consequences of vitamin B_{12} deficiency are serious, and they can easily be prevented by supplementation.

ABSORPTION

Over 95 percent of all B_{12} deficiencies reported in the United States occur not because of inadequate B_{12} in the diet but because of a diminished ability to absorb the vitamin as people age. Vitamin B_{12} is absorbed in the small intestine. Its absorption depends on the presence of three different substances: gastric acid (the acid in our stomachs), digestive enzymes and a substance called intrinsic factor. These three prepare B_{12} to be absorbed. As people age, gastric acidity decreases, so that by 60 years of age, 1 percent of people have lost the ability to absorb the vitamin. It is estimated that by the time we're 127, we would all have lost this ability. (This is difficult to prove, though!) Some of the senior citizens who are admitted to nursing homes with a diagnosis of confusion in fact are suffering from a loss of ability to absorb vitamin B_{12}. Where this is true, in many cases it can be reversed quickly by injections of the vitamin.

For vegans, the important issue is generally not absorption, but just making sure that intake is adequate. This is because the dietary sources of this vitamin are almost exclusively animal foods.

STORAGE

Excess vitamin B_{12} can be stored in the liver and other tissues. In fact, we can store a supply that will last three years or more. Because we can efficiently recycle the vitamin in our systems, the stores of some people last as long as 20 years.

Laboratory Testing for Vitamin B_{12}

Fortunately, vitamin B_{12} deficiency can be detected in the early stages by laboratory tests. If there is any doubt about B_{12} status, it is very important to have serum B_{12} levels checked. If necessary, further testing of MMA (methyl malonic acid) in the urine can be done; this determines the quantities of a substance that will build up if B_{12} levels are low. Long-term vegans (and near-vegans) are well advised to have lab tests done at regular medical checkups. Anyone with low lab values needs to include a reliable source of vitamin B_{12}.

Dr. Michael Klaper, a specialist in vegan health issues, says "because the liver's store is approximately 1,000 days, anyone who has been a vegan for more than three years should get his or her vitamin B_{12} level checked, and if it is below 130 picograms per mL, should add B_{12}-containing plant foods or supplements to the diet."

Recommended Intakes for Vitamin B_{12}

We need only very minute amounts of vitamin B_{12}. This is because the vitamin is so effectively conserved by the body; amounts that are released into the intestine (in bile) are almost totally reabsorbed. The recommended intakes have large margins of safety. The Canadian recommended daily intake for adults is 1 µg and the American recommendation is 2 µg.

Our Sources of Vitamin B_{12}

The *actual* sources of vitamin B_{12} are some very helpful bacteria capable of building the intricate vitamin B_{12} molecule. Higher forms of life, such as animals and humans, do not have this capability. We rely on these bacteria for our supply of B_{12}. The bacteria thrive in the lower intestines of animals and humans and can make all of the vitamin B_{12} we need. Unfortunately, although the bacteria are present, we can't absorb the vitamin because we absorb vitamin B_{12} at the upper end of the intestine, not lower down, where the bacteria are manufacturing it (and the bacteria don't travel upstream). This is not such an ideal arrangement! (It appears that some people have small amounts of bacterial synthesis of vitamin B_{12} in the mouth and small intestine that provide sources of this vitamin they can absorb. But this source cannot be relied upon.) Therefore, food sources or supplements of B_{12} are essential.

VITAMIN B_{12} IN ANIMAL FOODS

Animals derive vitamin B_{12} from bacterial synthesis; humans get it sometimes from B_{12} injections or supplements. Vitamin B_{12} is widely distributed in animal tissues. It is stored in the liver of animals, and is also present in meat, fish, poultry, eggs, milk and milk products.

VITAMIN B_{12} IN PLANT FOODS

Vitamin B_{12} is not present *in* plant foods in significant amounts. It can be present *on* plant foods, in minute amounts of dirt or bacterial contamination on the outside of the plants. Of course, when plant foods are scrupulously cleaned, the bacteria are no longer present.

Different agricultural production methods can result in wide variations in B_{12} levels. For example, when crops are grown in cobalt-rich soils, fertilized with manure (which contains B_{12} from intestinal production) and crop rotation is practiced, there can be substantial amounts of vitamin B_{12} in the bacterial contamination on plants.

In traditional methods of making fermented foods such as tempeh and miso there were more bacteria present – and more vitamin B_{12}. These production methods did not have the sanitary controls of modern techniques. For this reason, some foods thought of as vegan sources of B_{12} no longer contain the vitamin. Similarly, the amount of B_{12} on seaweeds depends both on the type of seaweed and on the bacteria present in the water in which it grew. These foods may have some B_{12}, but it is not advisable to risk one's health by relying on that chance.

The progress that humanity has made in matters of hygiene is laudable, and has certainly cut down on infectious disease, but in the case of B_{12}, changed methods of agricultural and food production have had the effect of decreasing availability. Studies have shown increased risk of vitamin B_{12} deficiency when vegans moved from countries with less hygienic supplies of food and water to developed countries.

Determining the exact amount of B_{12} in foods has proven to be a tricky process; there is much controversy about which foods are good sources for humans. The amounts available from a specific food may be uncertain, for three reasons:

1. changes have occurred with methods of agriculture;
2. more hygienic food-processing methods have been developed;
3. the presence of compounds very similar to B_{12}, called analogues, have led to inaccurate estimates of the amount of the usable vitamin in foods.

VITAMIN B_{12} ANALOGUES IN FOODS

Vitamin B_{12} analogues are substances that look like B_{12} but have structural differences so that they don't function the same way in the body. In the past, the standard way of determining the vitamin B_{12} content of a food has been to grow a particular bacteria (*L. leichmannii*) on an extract of the food and see how much growth occurs. These bacteria need a certain portion of the vitamin B_{12} molecule in order to multiply. The difficulty with this method is that bacteria can grow well on vitamin B_{12} *or* its analogues, whereas humans can use only the vitamin itself. The standard methods of estimating the amount of vitamin B_{12} in foods such as tempeh, miso, seaweed and spirulina have been based on bacterial growth, and thus have reported the quantities of analogue present, as well as the B_{12} usable by humans.

Another method, differential radioassay, can be used to distinguish true vitamin B_{12}. By this method, it has become apparent that much of what was formerly believed to be vitamin B_{12} in certain foods is, in fact, analogues.

Although vitamin B_{12} has been around for a long time, it is only recently that we've identified, named and studied it. Thus, there are a number of points that invite further research.

EFFECT OF VITAMIN C MEGADOSES ON VITAMIN B_{12}

Megadoses of vitamin C from supplements have become increasingly popular. A disadvantage of taking large amounts of vitamin C (more than 500 mg at once) is that these large doses appear to be able to destroy vitamin B_{12} by converting it to analogues. The megadoses of vitamin C found in many supplements are not advised for this reason, and could actually be detrimental. Vegans generally take in at least two to three times the recommended intakes of vitamin C just from food, but this intake of vitamin C spread over the day presents no problems.

ACTUAL VITAMIN B_{12} CONTENTS OF FOODS

One reliable food source of vitamin B_{12}, acceptable to vegans, is a particular brand of nutritional yeast, Red Star T-6635+. This yeast is grown on a vitamin B_{12}-enriched medium. It can sometimes be found in the bulk food section of health food stores and is available in powder or flakes. Often, to be certain of getting the correct brand, it is necessary to ask the store manager. It can be sprinkled on salads, grains or casseroles, adding a cheeselike flavour. In the recipe section of this book it is used in a tofu recipe and a gravy. Other brands of nutritional yeast are *not* reliable B_{12} sources. The amounts of usable vitamin B_{12} in this yeast, and in some foods used by lacto-ovo vegetarians, are shown in Table 5.1.

Table 5.1 Vitamin B_{12} in Foods Used by Vegetarians

	Volume	Weight (g)	Vitamin B_{12} Content (µg)
Nutritional Yeast (Red Star T-6635+):			
powder	1 tsp (5 mL)	2	1.0
flakes	2 tsp (10 mL)	2	1.0
Egg, large	1	50	0.7
Milk, whole, 2% or skim	1 cup (250 mL)	244	0.9
Yogurt	6 oz (175 mL)	170	0.6
Cheese	1 oz	28	0.2

VITAMIN B_{12} FORTIFICATION OF FOODS

In the United States, vitamin B_{12} (of bacterial origin) is added to a variety of foods: certain breakfast cereals, breads, soymilks and meat analogues (for quanitities, read labels). In Canada, although vitamin B_{12} fortification is permitted in meat analogues, such as tofuburgers, often these foods are *not* fortified. Soymilks, breakfast cereals and other products are not fortified with vitamin B_{12} in Canada.

THE VEGAN NEED FOR
VITAMIN B_{12}-FORTIFIED FOODS OR SUPPLEMENTS

Although some vegan adults have gone for years in apparent good health without identifiable B_{12} sources, others have shown deficiency symptoms. Infants, when breast fed by vegan mothers whose B_{12} intake was inadequate, have ended up in hospital with serious and irreversible nerve damage. For these reasons, it is essential to ensure a reliable source. Since the vitamin can be stored, larger amounts can be taken at intervals, if this is preferred to daily intake.

VITAMIN B_{12} SUPPLEMENTS

For safety, the best course for vegans is to meet recommended intakes with yeast grown on a B_{12}-enriched medium, with fortified foods or with a vitamin B_{12} supplement. During pregnancy, lactation and for vegan infants and children, this precaution is particularly important (for recommendations, see Chapter 9). *There is no point in taking chances with a shortage of this nutrient.* For infants and children, soy formulas fortified with vitamin B_{12} are a good choice.

IMPORTANCE OF A VARIED DIET

The second key to successful vegan eating is variety; don't *just* cut out animal foods. There is a whole world of plant foods to explore; this can be the beginning of a food tour around the globe. People sometimes have the impression that mealtimes without animal products are going to be pretty monotonous events. Instead, new vegans generally find that their food horizons expand tremendously and that they begin to use many new plant foods with which they were previously unfamiliar. This is definitely the way to do it. Ingenious alternatives to many dishes have been developed: delicious gravies without meat fat, creamy pies without dairy products and baked goods without eggs or milk. Learning how to cook the grains and legumes from other parts of the world will also serve to introduce you to many new seasonings and cooking methods. Those who don't cook can explore ethnic delis and restaurants as well as the vegan options at health food restaurants.

Such variety offers *more* than flavor and interest. Each legume, grain or nut has certain nutritional advantages: quinoa has abundant protein; amaranth provides calcium; and so on. A varied diet helps us to balance our nutritional needs for more than 50 nutrients daily.

In the most successful dietary transitions, highly nutritious ingredients often replace items much lower in nutritional value. For example, tahini replaces a fat or oil, and blackstrap molasses may be used instead of sugar. Whole wheat flour and dried fruits can take the place of highly refined flours and sweeteners in muffins and other baking. Some foods not commonly thought of as nutrient contributors provide trace minerals. For example, many herbal teas can provide small amounts of zinc and iron. The amounts in a cup may seem small, but over the course of a day, they certainly prove more nutritious than soda pop!

Due to the increasing popularity of vegetarian menus, new convenience foods are also available. Thus, after an initial orientation period, the new way of eating becomes just as easy as the old. An emphasis on a varied diet is an important part of healthful vegan eating.

Cautions with Macrobiotic and Restricted Vegan Diets

Studies of people on macrobiotic diets have demonstrated the need for care with vitamin B_{12} intake, and the problems that can arise when children are given vegan diets that are too restricted. Frequently, people following macrobiotic patterns do not use supplements or fortified foods, and center their diets on carbohydrate foods, with a secondary emphasis on vegetables. Beans, tofu and fruit are eaten, but in limited quantities. Many macrobiotics are vegan, although some use occasional dairy products or fish.

One New England study with a macrobiotic community found the following:

1. As many as half of the adults had low levels of serum vitamin B_{12}.

2. Those who had been on the macrobiotic diet for the longest period of time tended to have lower serum levels (however, some individuals had low but adequate serum B_{12} even after 12–25 years).

3. Although people consumed seaweeds, miso and tempeh, intake of these foods generally did not result in improved vitamin B_{12} status.

4. Children were found to be to be significantly smaller in height and weight than were children raised on less restrictive diets.

This and similar studies on macrobiotic communities in Holland have pointed out the serious consequences of overly restrictive diets, particularly when used with children. Diets were found to be inadequate in calories, fat and protein, and in a number of nutrients required for optimal growth.

On the other hand, many children on less restrictive vegan diets have shown excellent growth patterns.

POSITIVE ASPECTS OF MACROBIOTIC DIETS

Taking into account the above reservations, macrobiotic eating patterns do have interesting and valuable ideas to contribute. Nutritional concepts with Eastern origins, such as the macrobiotic system, emphasize balance in food choices in ways that are quite different from our Western concept of the "four food groups." A few of the valuable ideas to be gained from an understanding of macrobiotics are an emphasis on chewing foods, on digestion and on using foods which will shift the blood and urine in an alkaline direction (meat-centered diets tend to result in more acidic body fluids). Western nutrition texts generally ignore or underemphasize these topics.

People can end up with the best of both worlds when they use the Western scientific concepts as a basis for building a nutritionally adequate diet, and then add some of the Eastern ideas of health and nutrition to this foundation. This will ensure adequate nutrient intake at all ages and support optimal growth in children.

TABLE SALT, SEA SALT AND IODINE

Vegans and other vegetarians often buy sea salt rather than table salt. In fact, table salt would be a better choice, as it has been fortified with the essential mineral iodine. In several studies, the iodine intake of vegans was reported to be low – approximately one to two thirds of the recommended daily intake. (The vegans studied did not show signs of iodine deficiency, however.) In Canada, all table salt is fortified with iodine; in the United States some brands are fortified with this mineral. The recommended daily intake of iodine is provided by ⅓ teaspoon (2 mL) of fortified table salt. Sea salt delivers little iodine unless it has been fortified, because iodine becomes a gas and is lost during the drying process.

FORTIFICATION OF FOODS

North American legislation regarding the fortification of foods was developed in order to reduce the incidence of specific deficiency diseases occurring in the general population. These policies were designed for people consuming mixed diets, and have proven to be an effective means of preventing these deficiencies. Specific commonly used foods, such as milk and table salt, were chosen to be the means by which a particular nutrient reached a target population. These policies were not tailored to suit the needs of those adopting alternative diets. An awareness of fortification policies can be helpful to those who are not using these foods. For example, vitamin D, added to milk, has prevented rickets in a great many children. Vegans must *themselves* take the responsibility of ensuring that they and their children receive adequate sunlight or else use supplements.

Foods that are fortified with vitamin B_{12} can be suitable sources for this nutrient in vegan diets. At present, these are more readily available in the United States than in Canada.

For vegan preschoolers, an extended use of formula, which is fortified with vitamin B_{12}, D and calcium, will ensure adequate nutrient intake. For other vegans in the growing years, the use of fortified non-dairy beverages is recommended. Use either commercial varieties or the recipe given in Chapter 9.

HEALTH ADVANTAGES OF VEGAN DIETS

Well-designed vegan diets offer the possibility of excellent health. Studies comparing the caloric distribution of protein, carbohydrate and fat of vegans with those of omnivores show vegan patterns to be much closer to national recommendations. The long-term effects of vegan diets remain to be seen. Individuals and communities choosing strict vegetarian diets are creating a natural experiment. The scientific community will be watching with interest to see the potential benefits of lowered rates of chronic diseases, with increasing numbers of people adopting these dietary patterns. Because these diets are innovative, and are not the norm in this culture, people need to be well informed and to select alternative sources for nutrients found in animal foods.

It is clear that there are many health advantages to be gained by following a vegan or near-vegan diet in the prevention of chronic disease. In addition to these health advantages, all nutrient needs can be met.

FATS AND OILS:
A BALANCING ACT

uring the past couple of decades, fat has received some unflattering press from both the popular media and the scientific world. Consumers have been made painfully aware that an excessive consumption of fat can contribute to heart disease, and research suggests that it may play a significant role in the development of other chronic diseases such as cancer and diabetes. Many of the benefits of a vegetarian diet have been attributed to the fact that it is generally lower in fat than an omnivorous diet. Although the emphasis on reducing total fat in the diet is well justified, you must also consider the types of fats you are eating, and the relative amounts of these fats in your diet. The more research that unfolds, the more we see that the connection between dietary fat and health goes far beyond the issue of how much fat we eat. Achieving a healthful balance of fat in your diet requires more than simply taking meat off your menu; it means making some choices that are based on a clear understanding of fats and their relation to health and disease.

BACK TO BASICS: THE STRUCTURE OF FAT

Fats and oils are known as lipids in the scientific world, although we often refer to them simply as fats. The major distinguishing feature between fats and oils is that at room temperature fats are solid, while oils are liquid. Fats are generally found in animal foods such as meat, poultry and dairy products, while oils are commonly derived from plant seeds like olive, rape seed, corn and sunflower.

Fats and oils are made up of basic units called fatty acids. Fatty acids do not generally roam free in the body: most of them travel in threesomes as a part of larger molecules called triglycerides. Most of the fatty acids that we need for survival can be produced in the body, but there are two that we cannot make, and must obtain from food: the essential fatty acids.

Fatty Acid Categories

Fatty acids are classified as saturated, monounsaturated and polyunsaturated. Foods containing fat are made up of a mixture of fatty acids from each of these three categories, although we often focus on one fat which is present in the greatest quantity. For example, corn oil, which contains about 13 percent saturates, 25 percent monounsaturates and 62 percent polyunsaturates, is referred to as a polyunsaturated oil. The breakdown of these fatty acids in a variety of fats and oils is shown in Table 6.1.

Table 6.1 Comparison of Dietary Fats

Dietary Fat	Fatty Acid Content			
			Polyunsaturated Fat	
	Saturated Fat	*Monounsaturated Fat*	*Linoleic Acid (omega-6)*	*Alpha-Linolenic Acid (omega-3)*
Flax oil	9%	20%	17%	54%
Pumpkin oil	9%	34%	42%	15%
Canola oil	6%	58%	26%	10%
Safflower oil	9%	13%	78%	trace
Sunflower oil	11%	20%	69%	0%
Sesame oil	15%	46%	41%	0%
Corn oil	13%	25%	61%	1%
Olive oil	14%	77%	8%	1%
Soybean oil	15%	24%	54%	7%
Walnut oil	16%	28%	51%	5%
Peanut oil	18%	48%	34%	0%
Lard	41%	47%	11%	1%
Palm oil	51%	39%	10%	0%
Beef fat	52%	44%	3%	1%
Butterfat	66%	30%	2%	2%
Coconut oil	92%	6%	2%	0%
Chicken fat	31%	47%	21%	1%
Pacific salmon fat	32%	37%	1%	30%

SATURATED FATTY ACIDS

Fatty acid molecules are made up of chains of carbon atoms with hydrogen and oxygen atoms attached. When a fatty acid molecule is completely packed or "saturated" with hydrogen atoms along its carbon chains, it is called a saturated fat. Foods rich in saturated fats are generally solid at room temperature. The main sources of saturated fats are:

- animal fat (such as lard – the fat in red meat – and, to a lesser extent, poultry);
- dairy fat (milk, butter, cheese, cream and other dairy products);
- tropical "oils" (thick oils such as coconut, palm and palm kernel);
- cocoa butter;
- hydrogenated fats (such as shortening and hard margarines).

Although these foods are high in saturated fat, they also contain monounsaturated and polyunsaturated fats. Saturated fats are often considered "bad" because they are the biggest dietary contributor to high blood cholesterol levels.

Not all saturated fatty acids are created equal. Some have far more potential for raising cholesterol than others. For example, stearic acid, which predominates in cocoa butter, does not seem to affect blood cholesterol levels as much as palmitic acid, which predominates in palm oil.

MONOUNSATURATED FATTY ACIDS

When a fatty acid molecule has a single point that is not saturated with hydrogen atoms, it is called a monounsaturated fatty acid. Foods rich in monounsaturated fats are generally liquid at room temperature and semi-solid when refrigerated, as with olive oil. The principle dietary sources of monounsaturated fatty acids are:

- olive oil, canola oil and peanut oil;
- avocados and olives;
- hazelnuts, pistachios, almonds, macadamia nuts and pecans.

Up until the mid 1980s it was believed that monounsaturated fats had a neutral effect on blood cholesterol levels. We now know that monounsaturated fatty acids are as effective, and perhaps even more effective, than polyunsaturates in lowering blood cholesterol levels. Monosaturates lower LDL cholesterol ("bad" cholesterol), but do not lower HDL cholesterol ("good" cholesterol). They may even help to raise it.

POLYUNSATURATED FATTY ACIDS

When a fatty acid has two or more points that are not saturated with hydrogen atoms it is called a polyunsaturated fatty acid. If the first point of unsaturation occurs on the third carbon, the fatty acid is a member of the *omega-3 fatty acid* family. If the first first point of unsaturation appears on the sixth carbon, the fatty acid is a member of the *omega-6 fatty acid* family. Each of these two fatty acid families includes a parent *essential fatty acid* (the kind we must have but our bodies cannot manufacture). In the omega-3 family, alpha-linolenic acid is the essential fatty acid, and in the omega-6 family, linoleic acid is the essential fatty acid. We must receive food sources of these two essential fatty acids for survival.

Polyunsaturated fats tend to be liquid at room temperature. The principal dietary sources of omega-3 and omega-6 polyunsaturated fats are as follows:

Sources of Omega-3 Fatty Acids:
- nuts and seeds (flaxseed or linseed, walnuts and pumpkin seeds);
- vegetable oils (flax, perilla, canola and soybean oils);
- dark green vegetables;
- fish and seafood;
- wheat germ.

Sources of Omega-6 Fatty Acids:
- vegetable oils (safflower oil, sunflower oil, soybean oil and corn oil);
- nuts and seeds (walnuts, sunflower seeds, sesame seeds, poppy seeds and pumpkin seeds);
- wheat germ.

Polyunsaturated fats have received both praise and criticism regarding their effects on health and disease. On the one hand omega-6 fatty acids lower blood cholesterol levels (although they may reduce both the "good" HDL cholesterol and the "bad" LDL cholesterol). Omega-3 fatty acids lower triglyceride levels and blood pressure. On the other hand polyunsaturated fatty acids can go rancid very quickly. This can result in the formation of harmful chemicals and contribute to disease processes.

Cholesterol and other Sterols

Sterols are another group of lipids that are very important to human health. There are over 30 sterols found in nature, the most widely recognized being cholesterol. This important sterol is an essential part of our cells. Since our bodies produce about 800 mg per day, we do not need dietary sources of cholesterol. Too much dietary cholesterol can cause an increase in our blood cholesterol levels, thus increasing our risk for heart disease.

Health experts often recommend an intake of not more than 300 mg per day of total dietary cholesterol for the general population (over 2 years of age) and an even lower level for cholesterol-reducing therapeutic diets. Cholesterol is found only in animal foods. The most concentrated sources of cholesterol are organ meats and eggs: one egg contains over 200 mg of cholesterol.

Contrary to what many people have been led to believe, there is little difference between the cholesterol content of meat, poultry or fish. An animal food does not have to be high in saturated fat to be high in cholesterol, as cholesterol is stored primarily in lean tissue.

Plants also contain sterols, but these sterols are not known to have negative consequences for health. Indeed, it has been suggested that plant sterols may reduce the absorption of cholesterol from animal foods, thereby possibly offering some degree of protection against heart disease.

THE FUNCTIONS OF FATS AND OILS

In our concerns about the undesirable health consequences of an *excessive* consumption of fats and oils, we have almost lost sight of the fact that fats perform vital functions in our bodies. Both essential and non-essential fats play important roles in promoting health.

THE ROLE OF NON-ESSENTIAL FATS

Gram for gram, fats are the most concentrated source of energy, providing nine calories per gram, as compared to four calories per gram for either protein or carbohydrate. They serve as our main energy stores, supply insulation for the body, protect our vital organs and provide physical "padding." When our body fat drops below a healthy level, we become intolerant to cold, and in more extreme cases we develop a fine covering of body hair (as is often seen in cases of anorexia nervosa). Fats also aid in the absorption and transportation of fat-soluble vitamins, including vitamins A, D, E and K.

THE ROLE OF ESSENTIAL FATTY ACIDS

Essential fatty acids are necessary for the formation of healthy cell membranes and the proper development of eye and brain tissue. They are also involved in energy production and in the metabolism of cholesterol and triglycerides. Essential fatty acids from both the omega-3 and omega-6 families are metabolized to produce hormone-like substances called eicosanoids. These substances help to regulate numerous vital body functions such as blood clotting, blood pressure, immune response and reactions to injury. Eicosanoids formed from omega-3 fatty acids tend to lower blood clotting, blood pressure and inflammatory responses in our bodies. Eicosanoids formed from omega-6 fatty acids play a role in response to shock or injury. For optimal functioning of all body systems, we need a balance of eicosanoids formed from fatty acids of both families.

Essential Fatty Acid Balance

Historical sources suggest that humans evolved on a diet containing a much higher proportion of omega-3 to omega-6 fatty acids than the average diet of today. There are a number of reasons for this change in our diet. In the past, we obtained abundant omega-3 fatty acids from wild plants and from the fish and game which consumed these plants. Today many of the foods we eat have been processed and packaged so that they can be safely transported and stored for extended periods of time. Foods rich in omega-3 fatty acids are highly perishable and therefore have been rejected for use in most commercial foods. Also, we now consume far greater quantities of foods rich in omega-6 fatty acids: fried foods, high-fat snack foods, commercial baked goods, convenience foods, margarines, shortenings and vegetable oils.

The reduction of omega-3 fatty acids in the diet is now recognized as something that can have a negative impact on health. Indeed, excessive eicosanoids formed from the omega-6 family can result in increased incidence of heart disease, immune-inflammatory disorders, arthritis, asthma and headaches.

Scientists and nutritionists use the ratio of omega-6s to omega-3s to determine the balance or relative amounts of essential fatty acids in the diet. The typical North American diet provides a ratio of approximately 10:1 or greater. Experts from around the world recommend a ratio that is closer to 4:1 to 6:1. (It is interesting to note that the ratio in human milk is 4:1.)

A vegetarian diet is not necessarily better than an omnivorous diet in its omega-6 to omega-3 ratio. Recall the sample menus provided in Chapter 3. The omega-6 to omega-3 ratios for the different eating styles are shown in Table 6.5 on page 116. The omnivorous diet (menu no. 1) has a ratio of 9:1. The lacto-ovo vegetarian diet (menu no. 2), which is high in eggs and dairy products, has a slightly higher ratio of 11:1. By comparison, the lacto-ovo diet, with less dairy and egg (menu no. 3) has a ratio of 6:1, and the vegan diet (menu no. 4), which excludes all dairy and eggs and includes omega-3 fatty-acid-rich foods, has a ratio of only 4:1. Although this may all seem quite confusing, promoting a healthy balance of omega-3 and omega-6 fatty acids in the vegetarian diet is really not so difficult. Simply select foods that are rich in omega-3 fatty acids such as walnuts, pumpkin seeds, flax seeds, leafy plants and soybeans on a regular basis. Use foods that are rich in omega-6 fatty acids in moderation (see sources of polyunsaturated fats on page 105).

Unsaturated Fats and Free Radical Reactions

Free radicals are unstable molecules which are highly reactive. When they react with other molecules, often new free radicals are formed, producing chain reactions. Lipid peroxidation is one such chain reaction. A single free radical triggers a reaction altering literally hundreds of fatty acid molecules.

When this happens in the body, it can cause irreparable damage to cell membranes and genetic material. Fatty acid molecules can also decompose to yield a range of products which are highly toxic to body tissues. This kind of reaction can also occur in foods, particularly those foods that are rich in polyunsaturated fats. Air, ultra-violet light or heat can initiate lipid peroxidation in such foods causing deterioration and rancidity.

There has been tremendous interest in the impact of free radicals on health and disease during recent years. Free radicals have been implicated in over 50 disease states. In some cases free radicals play a role in the cause of disease, while in others they are simply products of the disease.

In cardiovascular disease, lipid peroxidation can damage blood vessels and contribute to the accumulation of plaque along their walls. Lipid peroxidation products have also been implicated in both the initiation and promotion of some cancerous tumors. In rheumatoid arthritis, the end products of lipid peroxidation increase as the disease gets worse. Although there are still many questions regarding the role of free radicals in disease states, we can expect some important answers from research that is presently underway.

PROTECTION FROM FREE RADICALS

If lipid peroxidation were to go on with nothing to stop it, it would eventually completely destroy our body cells. Fortunately, many foods contain substances called antioxidants that can protect us from the ravages of lipid peroxidation. Some antioxidants can stabilize free radicals. Other antioxidants serve to prevent the chain reaction by tying up chemicals that increase the rate of oxidation. Plant foods contain antioxidants such as beta-carotene, vitamins C and E and selenium, along with their polyunsaturated fats. When oils are extracted from these foods, as in the case of commercial oil refining, these natural antioxidants are reduced. Food manufacturers sometimes add synthetic antioxidants to help prevent rancidity and increase the shelf life of these foods.

There has been considerable discussion on the role of antioxidants in reducing free radical reactions in our bodies. Some experts advise supplemental antioxidants, particularly for individuals who are at high risk for disease, such as smokers, people living in polluted areas, and those with a high family incidence of cancer or heart disease. Others feel that we need to learn more about the usefulness of such supplements before making any recommendations.

The one thing they all seem to agree on is that it is important to eat foods that are naturally rich sources of antioxidants such as fruits, vegetables and whole grains, every day.

Some scientists suggest that we limit our intake of polyunsaturated fats to not more than 10 percent of total calories in order to reduce our exposure to the products of lipid peroxidation. Although there is currently little solid evidence to either support or contradict this recommendation, there are few benefits to consuming a greater percentage. By the same token, we need some polyunsaturated fats in our diets to insure that we get enough essential fatty acids.

THE PROCESSING OF FATS AND OILS

Virtually all of the concentrated fats and oils that we consume are processed in some way. The first step is the extraction of oils from the whole food, such as corn, olives or sunflower seeds. Further refining helps to rid the oil of offensive odors, toxins and organisms, and to ensure a safe and acceptable product. As well, fats and oils are processed to alter their taste, texture and shelf life. Some of the techniques employed in the processing result in changes that could have undesirable consequences for health.

Commercial Oil Production

Prior to World War I, the extraction of fresh oil from various foods was a cottage industry. Fresh pressed oils were delivered to the door each week and used shortly after delivery. Seeds were pressed without the use of heat, chemicals or deodorization. This way of processing oil did little damage to valuable omega-3 fatty acids and to protective natural antioxidants such as vitamin E.

New methods of processing oils developed after World War I greatly increased their shelf life, and many of these techniques are still in use today. The modern processing of oils includes oil extraction, degumming, refining, bleaching and deodorization.

EXTRACTION
Oils are extracted from seeds by mechanically pressing them or by mixing heated, dehulled and chopped or ground seeds with a solvent such as hexane. When solvent extraction is used, the solvent is later evaporated off the oil at temperatures of about 150°C. The primary objective in this first step is to produce a clean, crude oil product. In some cases the oil is filtered after mechanical pressing and sold as unrefined oil. More often, the oil undergoes further refining processes.

DEGUMMING
This process removes a variety of substances including phospholipids that would otherwise separate out during storage.

REFINING

An alkaline refining treatment removes free fatty acids that can cause rancidity and reduce the quality of the oil. Refining also helps to remove toxic substances that are naturally present in many plants. Phospholipids and minerals are also reduced during this procedure.

BLEACHING

Often, oils have a strong yellow or reddish hue that is considered undesirable, so it's bleached out. In the bleaching process, oils are heated to temperatures of about 80 to 110° C, and mixed with a substance that will absorb unwanted pigments. During this phase, some of the polyunsaturated fatty acids may undergo lipid peroxidation.

DEODORIZATION

This final stage removes undesirable odors and tastes from the oil. Deodorization also reduces the content of many other substances including pesticide residues, toxins and products of lipid peroxidation formed during the bleaching phase. It also reduces fat-soluble vitamins such as vitamin E and beta carotene (vitamin A). In the deodorization, oils are heated to 220 to 270° C for an hour or more. These high temperatures can result in some structural changes in the fatty acid molecules, and small amounts of trans fatty acids are produced. (See explanation of trans fatty acids on page 111.)

These processing methods produce tasteless, odorless, clear and stable oils that can sit on supermarket shelves for long periods of time without going rancid. On the down side, some of the substances that make oils valuable to us, including essential fatty acids and vitamin E, are damaged or diminished in the process.

WHAT ABOUT "COLD PRESSED" OILS?

A number of companies produce oils that are labeled "cold pressed." These are rarely similar to oils processed at the turn of the century. The term "cold pressed" means that the oil was not subjected to external heat *during the pressing process*. It does not necessarily mean that high temperatures were not reached from the friction of the seeds during the pressing or that the oil was not subjected to further refining and deodorization processes. Some "cold pressed" oils have undergone only mechanical pressing, but there are no guarantees. There is currently no legislation that controls the use of this term. There are some *mechanically pressed, unrefined oils* on the market today, but they are available only on a limited basis. These oils are very susceptible to rancidity and are therefore kept under refrigeration and generally sold in health food stores.

The one exception is olive oil. Because olive oil is made up mainly of the more stable monounsaturated fatty acids, it can be safely kept at room temperature for several months and is suitable for commercial use. The oil extracted from the first pressing of olives is called extra virgin. This oil has a full flavor and aroma, and contains most of the beneficial substances that are naturally present in the olives. Virgin olive oil can come from the first or second pressing and is of somewhat lower quality. Pure olive oil comes from the second pressing and is higher in solid particles so it must undergo some refining to make it acceptable to the consumer.

For many oils, the refining process is just the first stage of their transformation. A sizable proportion of these oils will go on to become hydrogenated or partially hydrogenated.

Hydrogenation

Hydrogenation is a commercial process that converts liquid oils into hard fats by the addition of hydrogen. Oils can be hydrogenated to varying degrees depending on the hardness desired. The most common examples of hydrogenated fats include shortenings, margarines and partially hydrogenated vegetable fats used for frying and in processed foods.

Hydrogenation is looked upon favorably by food producers as it improves the spreadability, shelf life and "mouth feel" of fat. It also increases its melting point, allowing for high-temperature cooking and frying. However, hydrogenation is regarded less favorably by health experts because it results in the conversion of a portion of the unsaturated fat molecules to trans fatty acids and a lesser portion of unsaturated fats to saturated fatty acids.

TRANS FATTY ACIDS

A trans fatty acid molecule has the same chemical formula as a "normal" fatty acid molecule, but its hydrogen atoms are in a different spacial arrangement. One of the results of the hydrogenation of mono- and polyunsaturated fats is the creation of trans fatty acids. The high temperatures used in the deodorization phase of the refining of unhydrogenated oils also converts a limited amount of fatty acids (about 2 percent) to the trans form. When an unsaturated fat molecule is changed to a trans form, its melting point increases and it becomes solid at room temperature. Thus, it offers the same benefits for food production as saturated fats, but is cheaper and quicker than converting unsaturated fats to saturates.

A fatty acid molecule with a trans configuration is still technically an "unsaturated fat." However, it behaves quite differently both in foods and in our bodies. Essential fatty acids with a trans configuration can no longer perform the critical functions of these nutrients in our bodies. In addition, these essential fatty acid "impostors" can interfere with the formation of long chain omega-6 and omega-3 fatty acids and increase the body's need for "genuine" essential fatty acids. In addition, trans fatty acids may alter the ratio of HDL:LDL cholesterol in a way that can increase the risk of heart disease.

The chemical structure of trans fatty acids makes them a bit of a nightmare when it comes to food labeling. There seems to be no real consensus between countries on how to deal with trans fatty acids on labels. In Canada, food manufacturers are permitted to list only polyunsaturates and monounsaturates with a "normal" (not "trans") configuration. In addition, total fat and saturated fat are declared. Thus, the trans can be calculated simply by subtracting the sum of the individual fatty acids (saturates, monounsaturates and polyunsaturates) from the total fat content. Canadian consumers often mistakenly assume that when a small amount of saturated fats are declared on a label, that the food contains low levels of undesirable fats.

In the United States, trans fatty acids are declared as monounsaturated fats. Although many of the trans fatty acids are indeed monounsaturated, the fact that they are of the trans variety is completely hidden. The consumer is deceived into thinking that these are the good monounsaturated fats that help to protect us from heart disease.

FATS AND OILS IN A HEALTHY VEGETARIAN DIET

Turning toward the practical aspects of the fats in our diets, there are two principle considerations:

1. How much fat should a vegetarian diet contain?
2. What types of fat should a healthy vegetarian diet include?

The Question of Quantity

We have been told that we need to cut back on fat, but even the experts have difficulty agreeing just how much. The World Health Organization (WHO) suggests that adults receive between 15 and 30 percent of their calories as fat. They add, however, that the 30 percent is an interim recommendation for nations with high-fat intakes, and that further benefits can be expected with a reduction toward 15 percent. Many national governments, including both the Canadian and the United States governments, recommend a total fat intake of not more than 30 percent of calories. They add that saturated fat should not exceed 10 percent of energy intake. An upper limit for cholesterol, of not more than 300 mg/day, is also suggested.

When attempting to determine a healthy level of fat intake, there are several things you need to consider. First, what is your state of health? If you are in good health, and your blood lipid levels are normal, the amounts of fat recommended for the general population by your national government and/or the WHO are reasonable. If you have high blood cholesterol levels, then you may want to go a step further and aim for the lower end of the WHO recommendations – approximately 15 percent of calories from fat. It may turn out that the quantity of fat that best supports health is somewhat dependent on the overall quality of fat in the diet. For example, a person who consumes little saturated fat and cholesterol and a good balance of essential fatty acids, may be able to maintain excellent health on a diet that is higher in total fat than a person who is eating a diet that is higher in saturated fat and cholesterol and has a poor balance of essential fatty acids.

There are also specific times during the life cycle when our needs for total fat and specific essential fatty acids increase. During infancy, a greater proportion of calories should come from fat (as is found in breast milk). It is also important for the pregnant and lactating mother to insure that her diet contains sufficient essential fatty acids. Many experts suggest that children receive a slightly greater proportion of fat than adults, and a range of 30–35 percent of calories is generally considered appropriate.

FAT IN THE NORTH AMERICAN FOOD SUPPLY

It is most revealing to take a look at sources of fat in our food supply. We don't get much fat from vegetables, fruits, grains and legumes. In fact, all of these foods combined provide less than 5 percent of the total fat in the North American food supply. About 50 percent of the fat in our foods comes from meat, fish, poultry, dairy products and eggs, and over 40 percent comes from other fats and oils.

The greatest concentration of fat is found in pure fat foods including vegetable oils, butter, margarine, shortening and lard. These foods are "*visible fats,*" or fats that we can see. One hundred percent of their calories come from fat, and they provide about four to five grams of fat per teaspoon. Many foods contain "*hidden fats,*" or fats that we don't see. Over 90 percent of the calories in salad dressings, cream cheese and heavy cream come from fat. Foods providing over 75 percent of calories from fat include high-fat meats (such as bologna, liverwurst, bacon, wieners, salami and sausage); nuts, seeds and their butters; avocados; olives; regular cheeses. Other foods high in hidden fats include regular meat, full-fat dairy products, deep-fried foods, snack foods (such as chips and buttered or microwave popcorn), crackers, chocolate bars and rich baked goods. These all get about 50-60 percent of their calories from fat.

Don't be deceived by a declaration of percent fat in a food. A frozen tofu dessert label might read "92 percent fat free." This tells you only the percentage fat by weight. The fat as a percentage of calories tells you much more. Indeed, the frozen tofu dessert derives not 8 but 46 percent of its calories from fat. Water (which contains no calories) adds weight to a food. The more water the food contains, the smaller the "percent fat by weight." For example, whole milk is only 3.5 percent fat by weight but 51 percent of calories comes from fat. Low-fat rye crackers are 7 percent fat by weight but only 15 percent of calories comes from fat. The point here is that the percentage of fat declared on a food label is of little value to you when you are trying to control the fat in your diet.

One way of limiting your fat intake is to estimate the maximum amount of fat you should get per day, and select foods that provide no more than that amount. The first step is to estimate your energy (calorie) requirements. Table 6.2 lists estimated energy needs according to sex, age and activity level. Simply multiply your ideal weight in kilograms (1 kg = 2.2 pounds) by the calories per kilogram (cal/kg) given in the chart for your age, sex and activity level. For example, if you are a 28-year-old, moderately active female, with an ideal weight of 58 kg, your energy needs would be roughly 2200 calories (58 x 38 = 2204).

Table 6.2 Estimating your caloric requirements per kilogram

Activity Level	Female 19–24	Male 19–24	Female 25–49	Male 25–49	Female 50–74	Male 50–74	Female 75+	Male 75+
Light	36	39	36	38	34	35	33	34
Moderate	38	45	38	44	36	40	37.5	35
Heavy	42	53	42	52	40	48	39	44

The second step is to estimate the amount of fat, in grams, to include in your diet. Table 6.3 provides this information based on your energy needs and the percent of fat you desire in your diet.

Table 6.3 Maximum Fat Per Day (in Grams)

	Desired Percentage of Fat				
Caloric Intake	10%	15%	20%	25%	30%
1400–1600	16–18	23–27	31–36	37–45	47–54
1600–1800	18–20	27–30	36–40	45–50	54–60
1800–2000	20–22	30–33	40–44	50–55	60–66
2000–2200	22–25	33–37	44–50	55–62	66–75
2200–2400	25–27	37–40	50–54	62–67	75–81
2400–2600	27–29	40–43	54–58	67–72	81–87
2600–2800	29–31	43–47	58–62	72–78	87–93

Finally, you'll need to keep tabs on how much fat you are getting each day. Table 6.4 provides a short list of foods and the amount of fat that they typically contain in grams per serving. More precise information is provided on the labels of many food products. Be sure to check the serving size as portions may be either smaller or larger than you typically use. The column listing the percent of calories from fat will help you to see just how much of the energy in various foods comes from fat.

Table 6.4 Fat in Food

Food/(Serving Size)	Fat grams/ serving	Fat as percent Calories
Fruits and Vegetables		
All, except those below (½ cup /125 ml or 1 med.)	trace	0–12
Avocado (⅙) or olives (10)	5	75–90
Legumes		
All, except those below (½ cup / 125 ml)	trace	1–6
Peanuts, dry roasted (1 oz / 30 g)	14	76
Soybeans, cooked (½ cup / 125 ml)	6	45
Tofu, medium (½ cup / 125 ml)	6	56
Garbanzos, cooked (½ cup / 125 ml)	2	14
Grains		
Wheat, rice, millet, barley, cooked (½ cup / 125 ml)	trace	3–7
Quinoa, oatmeal (¾ cup / 175 ml)	2	15–16
Bread, whole grain (1 slice or ½ bagel)	1	12
Pasta (1 cup / 250 ml)	1–2	3–10
Crackers, snack type (e.g., Ritz) (4 crackers)	4	51
Crackers, rye crisp type (e.g., Zwieback) (2 pieces)	1	15
Nuts and Seeds		
All, except those below (1 oz / 30 g)	13–19	73–88
Chestnuts, roasted (¼ cup / 50 ml)	½	7
Nut or seed butter (1 tbsp / 15 ml)	8–10	78–85
Dairy Products		
Milk, whole, 3.5% M.F. (1 cup / 250 ml)	8	48
Milk, 2% (1 cup / 250 ml)	5	35
Milk, skim (1 cup / 250 ml)	trace	4
Cheese, 33% M. F. (1 oz / 30 g)	9	74
Cheese, 15% M. F. (1 oz / 30 g)	4.5	54
Ice cream, 10% M. F. (½ cup / 125 ml)	14	48
Meat, Chicken, Fish and Eggs		
Lean beef and pork (3½ oz / 100 g)	7–12	30–45
Regular beef and pork (3½ oz / 100 g)	16–30	50–73
Poultry, white meat, no skin (3½ oz / 100 g)	4.5	23
Poultry, light and dark with skin (3½ oz / 100 g)	14	51
Fish, low-fat varieties (3½ oz / 100 g)	½	6–9

Fish, high-fat varieties (3½ oz / 100 g)	8–10	40–62
Egg (1 large)	5½	64
Sweet and Salty Snack Foods		
Potato chips (1 oz / 30 g)	10	61
Microwave popcorn (3 cups)	11½	54
Fruit pie (⅙th of pie)	11	39
Cake, chocolate, iced (¹⁄₁₂th of cake)	10	42
Chocolate bar, plain (1 oz / 30 g bar)	8	56
Granola bar, plain commercial type (1 bar)	4	35
Cookies, oatmeal, commercial type (2 cookies)	5	32

FAT IN THE VEGETARIAN DIET

Vegetarians tend to consume less fat, on average, than do omnivores. However, being vegetarian does not necessarily mean you will have a low-fat diet. Recall the menus in Chapter 3. The fat content of the omnivore and the first lacto-ovo vegetarian menus are similar. Vegetarian diets that are lower in eggs, high-fat dairy products and high-fat processed foods more easily meet the current recommendations for total fat and essential fatty acids. Well-planned vegan diets generally provide a healthy balance of fats.

Table 6.5 Fat Content in Various Menus

Diet Pattern	omega-6:omega-3 ratio	percent calories from fat	Cholesterol (mg)
Levels recommended by Canadian government	4:1–10:1	30 or less (15–30% WHO)	300 mg/day or less
Omnivore Menu No. 1	9:1	33%	374
Lacto-ovo Vegetarian Menu No. 2	11:1	34%	481
Lacto-ovo Vegetarian Menu No. 3	6:1	28%	55
Vegan Menu No. 4	4:1	27%	0

TRIMMING THE HIGH-FAT VEGETARIAN DIET

If your diet is too high in fat, you may need to make an effort to bring it down to a healthier level. Take a good look at where the fat in your diet is coming from, then develop a plan to reduce this fat. Remember that our food supply includes both visible fats and hidden fats. First, focus on cutting back on the visible fats, then go to work on the foods containing hidden fats.

To Cut Back on Visible Fats
- Use less margarine or butter on your foods.
- Pass up the fried foods and opt for baked, steamed or broiled.

- Cut down the amount of fat used in your recipes.
- Replace concentrated fats with low-fat alternatives (for example, use low-fat yogurt in place of mayonnaise).
- Flavor foods with salsa, fresh lemon juice, wine, broth, flavored vinegars and a variety of herbs and spices instead of fat.

To Attack Hidden Fats

- Switch from high-fat dairy products to low-fat alternatives or low-fat plant-based options (for example, instead of ice cream try fruit sherbet, rice-based frozen dessert or low-fat frozen yogurt).
- If you use eggs, do so in moderation.
- Reduce your consumption of high-fat commercial foods or replace them with low-fat options (for example, replace high-fat snack crackers with rye crisps). Many snack foods, cookies, crackers, granolas, granola bars and baked goods derive well over 40 percent of their calories from fat.
- Be conscious of how many nuts and seeds you are using. Although these are a valuable part of your diet, they are high in fat and should not be used in excess.

When you reduce the amount of fat in your diet, it doesn't mean that you have to reduce the amount of food that you are eating. Indeed, if your weight is not a problem you may need to increase the volume of food you are taking in to help compensate for the loss of the concentrated calories found in fat.

CAN A VEGETARIAN DIET BE TOO LOW IN FAT?

From the menus provided in Chapter 3, it seems as though vegans and the vegetarians who limit high-fat dairy foods and eggs do very well in terms of the quantity of both total fats and specific fatty acids in their diet. What about the vegetarian or vegan who decides to minimize fat as much as is possible? It is difficult for an adult to get too little fat, even when concentrated fats and oils are totally eliminated. However, if you also remove fat-rich whole foods such as nuts, seeds and their butters, tofu and other soy products, wheat germ, olives and avocados, your intake of essential fatty acids, particularly from the omega-3 family, may be too low. If you have decided to remove visible fats and oils from your diet, you can be sure to get sufficient essential fatty acids by following the vegetarian food guide in Chapter 8. Low-fat vegetarian or vegan diets containing approximately 10 percent fat have proven effective in treating atherosclerosis. However, limiting fat to this extent is not necessary for healthy adults and is not suitable for children.

ACHIEVING ADEQUATE OMEGA-3 FATTY ACIDS

In light of the concern regarding the proportion of omega-3 fatty acids to omega-6 fatty acids, it is important to insure that sufficient omega-3 fatty acids are included daily in the vegetarian diet. A healthy adult consuming 2000 calories could achieve the recommended essential fatty acids with 60 calories (6½ gms) of pure linoleic acid (omega-6) and a minimum of 12 calories (1⅓ gms) of pure alpha-linolenic acid (omega-3). Obtaining this amount of omega-6s is easy on almost any diet. The task is not so simple with the omega-3s. Many experts recommend that an omnivore consume fish at least two to three times per week while vegetarians must rely on plant sources of omega-3s.

Each of the following plant foods supply the recommended 1⅓ grams of omega-3s in the serving sizes suggested:
- ½ tsp (2 mL) flax oil (linseed)
- 2 tsp (10 mL) ground flax seed
- 1 tbsp (15 mL) canola or soybean oil
- 3 tbsp (50 mL) walnuts or pumpkin seeds

These plant foods provide comparable amounts of omega-3 fatty acids to 3 oz (90 g) oily fish such as salmon, trout, sardines, herring or mackerel. Other foods such as wheat germ and dark green vegetables (such as broccoli, kale and collard greens) can add smaller amounts of valuable alpha-linolenic acid. You can incorporate omega-3-rich foods in your diet by sprinkling walnuts or wheat germ on your cereal, snacking on a handful of pumpkin seeds or including a dark green salad with a flax oil dressing with dinner.

In some situations, greater proportions of omega-3 fatty acids may be of value – particularly disorders involving inflammation or compromised immune function (for example, atopic dermatitis, arthritis and lupus). Although some small studies have confirmed beneficial results using omega-3 fatty acids for such conditions, considerable research must be completed in this area before any specific recommendations can be made. At present, it would seem prudent for those suffering from these types of disorders to ensure that a good source of omega-3 fatty acids is included in the diet on a daily basis.

THE QUESTION OF QUALITY

When it comes to the quality of fat, there is a stark contrast between the high-quality fats found in plant foods such as soybeans, flax seeds, dark greens, olives, avocados, nuts and seeds, and the chemically altered fats found in margarine, shortening and partially hydrogenated vegetables oils that are so prevalent in North American diets. Even the vegetable oils on our grocery store shelves have been subjected to intense refining that removes much of the healthful contents of the original plants, including their protective antioxidants.

Adopting a vegetarian diet with a limited amount of high-fat dairy products and eggs can mean a reduction in the intake of fat, including saturated fat. But a vegetarian diet doesn't guarantee that our choices of concentrated fats will improve. There is no law against a vegetarian using plenty of margarine or butter on bread, eating French fries that have been cooked in partially hydrogenated vegetable oils, snacking on pies, cakes, cookies and other baked goods containing shortening, tropical oils or partially hydrogenated vegetable oils. There is nothing to stop us from indulging in sizable quantities of refined oils that are extremely high in omega-6 fatty acids, but almost void of omega-3 fatty acids. Indeed, to insure that a vegetarian diet provides appropriate amounts of high-quality fats, we must select food with care.

When selecting whole foods, it is relatively easy to make good fat choices. Simply emphasize plant foods (including those that provide omega-3 fatty acids) and limit high-fat dairy products and eggs. Nuts, seeds and their butters, avocados, olives, soybeans, garbanzos and tofu are all excellent sources of good-quality fats. If your diet contained no concentrated fats and oils, or prepared foods containing fats, you could be confident that these wholesome plant foods would provide all the essential fats that your body requires. Just as you can get all the carbohydrates that your body needs from whole foods, without any concentrated sugars or sweets, so you can get all of the fat that your body needs without using *any* concentrated fats and oils.

Most whole foods contain some fats. The fats in plant foods are generally unsaturated. The more unsaturated a fat, the more quickly it undergoes lipid peroxidation which can result in the production of toxic chemicals. When this occurs in a food, it develops a most objectionable flavor and odor and becomes rancid. Perhaps this is nature's way of telling us that a food has lost its freshness and is no longer wholesome. When we obtain good-quality oils or food that is rich in essential fatty acids, especially those of the omega-3 family, we must handle these foods with care.

Nuts and seeds that are naturally preserved by a hard shell or coat will keep for about a year in a cool, dry place. Once this coat has been removed, they will keep up to four months in the refrigerator. Walnuts and pumpkin seeds may not keep as long due to their high omega-3 fatty acid content. Ground flax seed and wheat germ should always be kept in the freezer as they go rancid very quickly. Unrefined oils, with the exception of olive oil which is primarily monounsaturated fat, should always be refrigerated. Buy these oils in small quantities to use within a month. Oils can be frozen for later use if desired.

Step by Step: Improving the Quality of Fats in Your Diet

STEP 1. MINIMIZE HYDROGENATED FATS

Minimize your use of hydrogenated and partially hydrogenated fats (including shortening, hydrogenated margarines) and processed foods containing these fats. Be aware that hydrogenated fats are used extensively in all types of commercially prepared foods including crackers, cookies, cakes, pastries, frozen convenience foods and snack foods. Don't be fooled by a declaration of "all vegetable oil" on the label. This vegetable oil is often at least partially hydrogenated. Be sure to read the list of ingredients! Remember that ingredients are listed by weight, from the highest to the lowest. Hydrogenated vegetable oils are also frequently used in restaurants for deep frying. When eating out, pass on the fries and opt for a baked potato or rice. When preparing baked goods at home, experiment with vegetable oils and nut butters instead of using hard fats.

STEP 2. LIMIT FOODS RICH IN SATURATED FATS

Limit your use of foods rich in saturated fats: eggs, butter, cheese and other high-fat dairy foods, coconut and coconut oil, palm oil and palm kernel oil. Reduce your consumption of non-hydrogenated soft margarines that are made with saturated vegetable fats such as palm oil rather than partially hydrogenated vegetable oils. Replace high-fat dairy products with low-fat or non-fat products. In baking, substitute ground flax seeds for eggs (see recipe section). Go lightly on butter and non-hydrogenated margarines; try mixing butter, soy lecithin spread or soft (preferably non-hydrogenated) margarine with a good quality oil (ideally one which is rich in omega-3 fatty acids such as flax or canola oil). Better yet, try one of the "butters" in the recipe section.

STEP 3. CUT BACK ON REFINED OILS

Reduce your consumption of foods that use large amounts of refined cooking oils in their preparation. Avoid deep frying. In most recipes cooking oil can be reduced by about ⅓ to ½ without affecting the quality of the product. In some cases cooking oil can be replaced with applesauce, lecithin and/or ground flax seed. When using refined oils, select those that contain some omega-3 fatty acids such as canola or soybean oils. Safflower and sunflower oil are also acceptable choices, although they contain a high percentage of omega-6 fatty acids and only traces of omega-3 fatty acids.

STEP 4. SELECT UNREFINED, MECHANICALLY PRESSED OILS

Whenever possible, select unrefined oils that have been mechanically pressed. Olive oil, preferably extra-virgin, is a good choice. Other oils pressed from organic seeds without the use of harsh chemicals are available on a limited basis. Although these oils are not generally available in large supermarkets, they can be purchased in health food stores (stored in refrigerators). Many health food stores also carry oils that are labeled "cold pressed." These oils are not necessarily superior to the regular supermarket varieties, because they may have been processed with harsh solvents and subjected to high temperatures at later stages of the refining process.

STEP 5. RELY ON WHOLE FOODS FOR THE BULK OF YOUR FAT

The best place to get your fat is from whole foods. Try spreading almond butter or non-hydrogenated peanut butter (most supermarket varieties are hydrogenated – read the label) on your toast instead of margarine or butter. Make salad dressings with tahini and lemon juice (see recipe section). Sprinkle walnuts or pumpkin seeds on your cereal and in your salad. Slice some avocado or olives for your sandwiches. Include dark greens in your daily menu. Add a sprinkle of flaxseed and wheat germ to your porridge and baked goods.

FIBER: THE GIFT
FROM PLANTS

iber has been in the news for the past 15 years. It's been discovered to be a valuable part of the defense against colon cancer, bowel disorders, coronary heart disease and diabetes. We are finding that the steady diet of many North Americans — refined cereals, bagels with cream cheese and burgers on white buns — lacks this essential protective component. *Fiber is found only in plant foods.* Foods of animal origin contain no fiber at all, and the refined grains that many Westerners consume have lost most of their original fiber content.

For those who have switched to vegetarian diets, an increased consumption of plant foods automatically results in more dietary fiber than is found in a meat-centered diet. Because of this, the concerns of vegetarians about fiber might differ from those of omnivores. What, then, are the important fiber issues, from a vegetarian viewpoint?

At one extreme, some vegetarians may still consume diets with *insufficient* fiber, if they continue to rely on refined foods and simply replace meat, poultry and fish with dairy products and eggs. At the other extreme, it has been suggested that some vegetarian diets may provide *too much fiber*, particularly for specific age groups such as children and the elderly.

Before we can examine these extremes more carefully we must understand our need for the various types of dietary fiber. This will help us to determine optimum dietary fiber levels.

The Roots of Fiber

Fiber and whole foods have long been a part of medical wisdom and folk remedies. In North America, during the early part of the 19th century, Sylvester Graham, an evangelical preacher, advocated an increased use of whole grains and developed a version of the crackers that still bear his name. Later in that century, Dr. John Harvey Kellogg, managing a health sanitarium in Michigan, inspired a return to the use of high-fiber foods. Kellogg encouraged the use of plant-based diets for healing. At the same time, he launched the well known line of breakfast cereals.

By the late 1800s, the majority of North Americans were going in a different direction from that advocated by Graham and Kellogg. The milling of grains, introduced in 1875, resulted in a removal of the bran (outer coating of whole grains) and germ (from which the seed germinates). People began to enjoy the light baked products that could be produced using refined flours. Removal of the germ gave flours a substantially longer shelf life. (The germ contains essential oils; this makes whole grain flours more vulnerable to spoilage.) Removal of the bran meant a further decrease in nutritional value, with a loss of many vitamins (folate and vitamin B_6) and minerals (magnesium and zinc) – and 80 percent of the fiber, as shown in Figure 7.1. Midway through the 20th century, four of these nutrients (three of the B vitamins and iron) were returned to refined flours, through the process of enrichment.

Figure 7.1 Some Nutrients in Breads

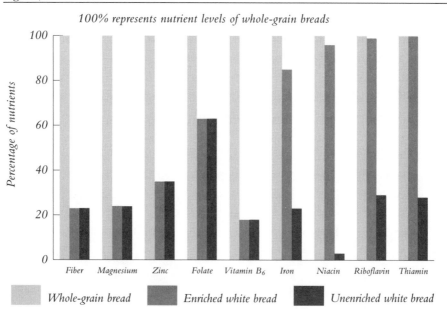

The World Health Organization Study Group estimates that the daily diet of early man as a hunter-gatherer provided approximately 40 grams of fiber; later peasant agriculturalists consumed 60 to 120 grams per day. High levels, in the range of 70 grams per day, are observed in diets of people in third world countries today. Current North American intakes of fiber are in the range of 10 to 18 grams a day, on average. As fiber intake plummeted through the early part of the 20th century, consumption of meat and other animal products rose. The resulting low-fiber, high-fat diet that has become the North American norm is now being linked with constipation, hemorrhoids, diverticulitis and irritable bowel syndrome.

Other diseases thought to be preventable, at least in part, by an increase in fiber intake are gallstones, appendicitis, varicose veins, hiatus hernia, obesity, hypoglycemia, heart disease, high blood pressure and cancer of the colon.

As our scientists begin to unravel the part played by fiber in the prevention of chronic diseases, many people are taking more interest in plant-based diets. Others, including some vegetarians, are responding to the research and headlines by consuming great quantities of fiber pills. Sales of fiber supplements and "added fiber" products are skyrocketing; "high fiber" diets are gaining in popularity.

Are fiber pills the solution to many of our chronic diseases? To find out, let's see what fiber is, and what it does.

What is Fiber?

Fiber is the foodstuff that remains undigested when food enters the large intestine. Fiber itself is made up of long chains of sugar and sugar-like molecules, joined together by bonds that our digestive enzymes cannot break down. For the most part, the sugar present is glucose; however, because we can't digest fiber, its glucose is unavailable to us as a fuel. Whenever we eat vegetables, fruits, legumes, grains (especially whole grains), nuts and seeds, we're taking in fiber. There are two categories of fiber: soluble and insoluble. Generally each food contains a mixture of types of fiber from each of these two categories. For example, oat bran has become well known for its substantial contribution of soluble fiber; in addition, oats contain various types of insoluble fiber.

SOLUBLE FIBER

Pectins, gums and mucilages are forms of soluble fiber found inside and around plant cells, helping to "glue" plant cells together. Each is composed of chains of sugars and related substances. Pectin is the substance in fruit which causes jams and jellies to gel. Oats contain a gum, giving oatmeal its sticky consistency. The gums from kidney beans are evident in the thickened water which develops when beans are cooked and canned. Rich sources of soluble fiber include fruits, vegetables, seaweeds, legumes and certain grains and seeds. Soluble forms of fiber dissolve or swell when put into water. This effect can be observed if ground psyllium seeds, a source of mucilage found in many commercial laxatives, are placed in water.

INSOLUBLE FIBER

Cellulose, the form of fiber that is found in abundance throughout the plant kingdom, consists of linear chains of glucose. Cellulose provides plants with fibrous structures of great strength. Hemicelluloses (found in the outer layer of whole grains such as whole wheat) and lignins (found, for example, in broccoli) contain other sugars and sugar-like molecules bonded together. These compounds generally will not dissolve in water, and so are called insoluble fiber. They do, however, attract and soak up water.

Dietary Fiber: Just Passing Through?

We don't digest any of these varieties of fiber in our stomachs and small intestines. Fiber is not a vitamin or a mineral, and it doesn't provide us with calories. So why do we need dietary fiber?

In part, the beneficial action of fiber results from its ability to attract and hold water as it passes through the intestine. Fiber, along with this water, supplies mass to the feces, creating a large, soft stool which stimulates the intestinal muscles. This allows the stool to move through the large intestine easily and quickly.

The fiber from foods passes through the digestive tract without being absorbed, exerting an intestinal cleansing action and keeping the digestive tract clean. Recent research indicates that in its journey it takes with it many substances which could otherwise trigger disease processes. These substances include bile acids, which can irritate the cells lining the colon, and a variety of other substances which need to be eliminated.

Fiber in Relation to Health and Disease

Because of this cleansing action, fiber plays a significant role in the prevention of a great many diseases. Here are just a few of the roles fiber plays in keeping us healthy.

FIBER, DIVERTICULITIS AND HEMORRHOIDS

Diets *low in insoluble fiber* result in small, hard feces; these require one to exert excessive pressure in the large intestine (colon) during defecation, with the possibility of damage in the lower intestine; diverticula may result. Diverticula are small pockets or bulges on the walls of the lower intestine. They occur in about half of elderly North Americans, most often without causing harm. However, in some individuals, diverticula may become inflamed, creating diverticulitis. In third world countries, where fiber intake is higher, people seldom have diverticula.

Without adequate fiber, the stool cannot absorb much water, so it remains small and unyielding. The intestine has to work hard to move such stools through its entire length, which may be as much as 29 feet; intense muscular contractions are required, generating high internal pressures. The final passage of these abrasive stools is also usually characterized by extra pressure, hence the frequent occurrence of hemorrhoids.

FIBER AND COLON CANCER

Colon cancer, a leading cause of cancer deaths in North America, has also been linked to a lack of dietary fiber. Exactly how fiber exerts its protective role is not clear at present, however it appears that fiber decreases the effects of potential carcinogens (cancer-causing agents) on the inner wall of the large intestine in the following ways:

1. The larger, more liquid stool dilutes the carcinogens.
2. Fiber binds the carcinogens.
3. As fiber speeds the passage of the stool through the large intestine, the time for contact is decreased.

Both insoluble and soluble fiber have parts to play in decreasing our intestinal contact with carcinogens, thus a wide variety of whole grains, fruits, vegetables and legumes are protective. Recent Finnish research demonstrated that when people switched to a vegan diet, within a week there was a marked reduction in four enzymes associated with the production of carcinogens in the intestine, indicating a further protective effect of plant-based diets.

FIBER AND HEART DISEASE

When researchers first suggested that oat bran could lower blood cholesterol, it seemed strange to many people in the medical field that fiber, which is not absorbed into the bloodstream, could affect the amount of a substance circulating in the blood. However, further studies proved those researchers to be correct. Oat bran really does lower blood cholesterol and thus reduces risk of heart disease. It appears that soluble fiber can prevent the absorption of excess cholesterol by carrying it out of the body. This includes cholesterol in the foods we eat as well as the cholesterol we secrete into the intestine in the form of bile acids. Soluble fiber in other foods – the pectin in fruit, the gums in legumes – has also been found effective in lowering cholesterol.

Since plant-based diets tend to be lower in total fat and cholesterol as well as being higher in fiber, there is a multiple benefit.

FIBER, DIABETES AND CONTROL OF BLOOD-SUGAR LEVELS

Soluble fiber is also a useful dietary component for controlling blood-sugar levels in diabetes. While it does not reduce the incidence of diabetes, a diet high in soluble fiber seems to allow diabetics to live longer and better. Diabetes is a disorder of the body's ability to deal with starches or sugars. Starches are actually long chains of sugars; these chains must be broken down by digestive enzymes before they can be absorbed into the bloodstream. Because it takes time for the enzymes to break down the starch, the sugar enters the bloodstream gradually. Sugar, on the other hand, is absorbed into the blood immediately. It has been known for some time that diabetics (and most other people) can more easily handle carbohydrate when it is eaten as starch rather than as sugar. It has recently become evident that diabetics tolerate carbohydrate even better when the starchy foods also contain soluble fiber. Most starchy foods happen to contain some soluble fiber, but some foods, such as legumes, are particularly rich sources.

AND THAT'S NOT ALL

The litany of benefits grows, as we learn more about the health-promoting roles played by the various types of fiber. Although the information presented here may have already converted you to a fiber fan, several questions still need to be addressed before you put your high-fiber theories into practice. One question that might have occurred to you already is:

Why Not Just Use Fiber Supplements?

The term "fiber supplements" can refer to either fiber tablets or a concentrated form of natural fiber such as wheat bran. There are a number of disadvantages to such supplements: they can be ineffective, and they can have undesirable side effects.

For insoluble fiber to work in producing a softer stool, the fiber particles have to be quite large. The finely ground insoluble fiber of wheat bran supplements appears to have lost the protective function provided by the longer strands of fiber naturally present in whole grains.

Also, problems can occur if concentrated sources of fiber are consumed with insufficient water. Recall that one of the ways insoluble fiber works is to absorb water. For the fiber to be effective, water has to be consumed at the same time as the bran. When the whole grain kernel is eaten, this happens automatically, as the grain is cooked with and absorbs water. That safeguard is removed when the bran alone is added to a meal or dish that contains little water. Eating bran without adequate water could result in a bowel obstruction – a painful and potentially dangerous condition producing the opposite effect from what most bran eaters want to accomplish.

In addition, wheat bran supplements are high in phytates. The absorption of minerals is affected by the amount of phytate present in the intestinal contents. If the diet contains marginal levels of minerals – such as iron, calcium, magnesium and zinc – the extra phytate introduced with the bran might bind enough of the minerals to cause mineral deficiency. Vegetarians relying on highly refined products such as white bread may have a marginal zinc intake to begin with; if bran is added to increase fiber intake, the bran may bind what little zinc there is in the diet. A better option is to get fiber from a variety of plant foods, including whole grains.

Finally, individuals relying on a single fiber supplement such as wheat bran will miss the health benefits of other types of fiber found, for example, in citrus fruit, strawberries, chickpeas or almonds. Similarly, the addition of a commercial laxative to a highly refined diet can't replace a variety of whole foods.

Fiber supplements, either as single purified sources of fiber or commercial laxatives, are no substitute for the rich blend of fibers provided by nature. We don't yet understand what every individual type of fiber does. Nature has put together a complex blend in each food. Every element in the blend, each molecular pattern, seems to have its own unique role to play in some aspect of health maintenance.

Returning to our earlier question: Can we simply continue with highly refined diets, and add fiber pills? Certainly we can include *some* refined foods without ill effect, and fiber supplements can help with constipation. But our best bet is a return to an increased intake of whole foods, with their full complement of the various types of dietary fiber.

The Extremes: Too Much or Too Little Fiber

TOO LITTLE FIBER

A lacto-ovo vegetarian diet based on white rice, baked goods made with refined flour and moderate amounts of fruits and vegetables is likely to be in the same range as the typical North American diet: 10 to 18 grams of fiber per day. A shift to whole grain products, and the inclusion of legumes and nut or seed butters, quickly doubles the fiber intake, bringing the total fiber up into the health-promoting range, as well as providing a wide variety of types of fiber.

Vegetarians who enthusiatically begin juicing most of their fruits and vegetables are losing the majority of the valuable fiber from these foods.

TOO MUCH FIBER

For the average bulge-battling North American adult, there is not likely to be a problem with consuming too much fiber when the dietary sources are whole plant foods.

Growing children need a different dietary emphasis. Children have small stomachs and appetites, and they need to consume enough calories for growth. When children are fed diets high in roughage, growth may be compromised because such a large volume of food is required to get enough calories. For example, to obtain the 50 calories found in ¼ cup (50 mL) of tofu, a child would have to consume 1 cup (250 mL) of cauliflower or 5 cups (750 mL) of alfalfa sprouts! In order to ensure that adequate calories are consumed by children, special attention should be paid to providing children with enough fat. Much of their food should be cooked and some refined foods can be offered. It is recommended that infants under two years old obtain as much as 35 percent of their calories from fat (Chapter 9 explains how this can be achieved). Cooking does not change the amount of fiber in a food, but it does change the effect of the fiber. The fibers become smaller, softer and more compact, leaving space in the stomach for additional food. Limiting fiber intake also helps children to maximize vitamin and mineral absorption, as discussed in the next section.

For those elderly vegetarians whose total food intake is small, cooked vegetables and fruits may be more suitable.

FIBER, PHYTATES AND MINERALS

Studies have been done to determine whether high intakes of dietary fiber result in inadequate mineral absorption. Some of this research has been done by adding raw wheat bran or other single fiber sources to the laboratory food of animals such as rats; the findings from these studies have limited relevance when applied to humans on varied vegetarian diets. Other studies have used a single food, most often wheat bran, to increase total dietary fiber of humans. Again, these studies are not directly applicable when we are looking at the effects of balanced vegetarian diets on mineral absorption. Well designed vegetarian diets provide a wide variety of types of fiber from a diverse selection of plant sources.

It is also significant that the methods used by vegetarians to *prepare* foods substantially increase mineral availability; these methods differ from the food preparation done in many animal and human research studies. During the pre-soaking of beans, the yeast raising of bread doughs, the sprouting of seeds or legumes and the roasting of nuts, minerals are released from bound forms. Other traditional methods of food preparation, such as fermentation, make minerals in foods far more available than they are in the raw form. As an example, fermentation of soybeans is used to make some Japanese foods such as tempeh, miso and natto.

Thus, while early research on fiber, phytate and mineral absorption led to concerns about mineral losses, our perspective is changing. Fiber and phytate *can* carry some of the minerals in our food supply through the intestine and out of the body. In some cases, this turns out to be an advantage, as when these processes protect us from iron overload. Fiber and phytates also provide health benefits in regulating the absorption of glucose from starch.

With any type of diet, we absorb only a fraction of the minerals in foods we consume. This fraction can vary considerably, depending on a great many factors. For example, when people take in small amounts of calcium from many food sources throughout the day, a substantially higher percentage of the calcium is likely to be absorbed than from the same amount of calcium given in a single dose. The individual who needs more calcium or iron will have a higher rate of absorption than the individual with abundant mineral stores. Traditional food preparation methods developed by cultures around the world, and modern versions of these, have resulted in increased mineral availability. On the other hand, the refining of products results in considerable loss of many minerals.

For these reasons, there is little cause for the concern expressed by early researchers regarding mineral absorption by people on vegetarian diets. Naturally, these diets must include mineral-rich plant foods, and special care must be taken not to overload certain age groups, such as children, with bulky, high-fiber foods.

In summarizing the effects of fiber and phytate on the availability of minerals from plant foods, we can quote the World Health Organization:

> Studies from the eastern Mediterranean region suggest that very high intakes of unleavened bread, where the cereal phytate has not been destroyed by the endogenous phytase in the grain, do lead to problems of mineral malabsorption. However, this seems to be a problem of food preparation rather than of the diet as such. In human physiological studies, exchanging full grain cereals for refined starches low in fiber does not lead to calcium, zinc or iron malabsorption, because the whole grain

provides an additional intake of the minerals that compensates for any reduced mineral availability. Oxalate-rich foods such as spinach do, however, limit mineral absorption. The intake of fiber from a mixed diet providing the maximum proposed adult limit of 54 grams of total dietary fiber has been shown to allow the maintenance of mineral balance, but this conclusion may not apply to fiber-rich foods made by the addition of bran, which contains extra phytates as well as fiber.

This panel of experts goes on to state that there appears to be no advantage to intakes of dietary fiber in excess of 40 grams per day, and propose 37–40 grams as an upper limit. A diet composed of whole grains, products made from whole grains, vegetables and a variety of other plant foods will supply all types of fiber, without the limitations of single high-fiber supplements.

Guidelines for Increasing Your Fiber Intake

1. Choose whole grain products instead of refined breads and cereals.
The bread you use for your morning toast, sandwiches at noon and evening snack can be your best fiber booster. If you select breads made with wheat, rye, or many other grains, and perhaps added nuts or seeds, you'll include many types of fiber in a single food. Crackers, pastas or pancake mixes can also be good sources of fiber if they are made with whole grains; in addition they will retain their original balance of nutrients. Since there are so many cereals on the market and since fiber content is often given on the label, the following selection guide may be helpful.

4 grams of fiber per serving or more = excellent source
2–4 grams of fiber per serving = good source
less than 2 grams per serving = poor source

Grains eaten on their own, such as rice, are best eaten in their whole grain form. For variety in baking, any uncooked grain, such as millet, triticale or oats, can be turned into flour in a blender. Try using combinations of flours in pancakes, muffins, cookies or breads.

2. Eat plenty of fruits and vegetables.
You may have become accustomed to eating your standard fruits and vegetables in certain quantities or with certain meals; dare to break those patterns! You can include potatoes (pre-cooked) in a stir-fry instead of serving them beside meat, and you can build a meal around broccoli. How about trying a new fruit or vegetable every month? You can learn about preparing unfamiliar

foods from cookbooks, neighbors or from your grocer. Children can get acquainted with new vegetables by helping to prepare them for a salad or a pizza.

3. Make your diet rich in legumes and nuts.

There is great variety in the legume family, as it comprises not only beans but also lentils, dried and fresh peas and peanuts. There are many quick alternatives in this group; other dishes are easy and take little of your time, but are slow cooking. Occasionally when you spend a day or an evening at home, put a big pot of beans, peas or lentils on to cook. Then freeze single or family-size portions. You can freeze garbanzo beans for later use in hummus; pinto or kidney beans for chili. Your freezer can also be stocked with homemade, ready to heat-and-eat soups. Red lentils are the fastest to prepare; they can be cooked from their dried state in 25–30 minutes. Most supermarkets have expanded their bean horizons tremendously and now offer canned soups, canned beans and deli products such as hummus, bean salads, lentil soups and bean tortillas.

Nuts are an excellent convenience food, either eaten as a snack or used in dishes such as casseroles, salads or stir-fries. They can be used raw, roasted or ground. Whether intact or slightly ground in a blender, nuts and seeds can be used in baking. When they are ground for a longer period of time, they become butters for use on bread or in sauces. Tahini, almond and other nut butters are favorites, whether purchased or homemade.

Gradual Introduction of Fiber

Boost your fiber intake in gradual steps. We all have helpful intestinal bacteria that assist in digesting our food. The population of bacteria present depends on the kinds of food we eat; it takes time for the right bacteria to become dominant when you change your diet. Here are some suggestions to ease the transition:

a) Start with the legumes that are easiest to digest. These tend to be the smaller ones, such as split peas, lentils, adzuki beans and mung beans. Gradually introduce the bigger beans to your diet.

b) Increase your use of legumes gradually over a period of a month or two. Start with small servings once or twice a week, and gradually increase both serving size and frequency.

c) Soak the larger beans such as garbanzo, kidney or other beans of similar size. The gas-producing potential of legumes is reduced when they are soaked before cooking. Discard the soaking water and cook using fresh water.

d) Chew legumes well. Digestion is better when foods are chewed thoroughly; enzymes naturally present in the saliva begin the process.

The Gas Crisis: International Solutions

Often people are somewhat cautious about getting too full of beans, owing to their reputation in the aroma department. Note that gaseous emissions are *not* an essential part of bean eating. Legumes and a great variety of vegetables are used without ill effect by populations around the world. As we realize the substantial health benefits of these foods, we start to wonder what these people know that we don't!

It helps to understand the origins of intestinal gas, so that you can eliminate potential digestive difficulties. Starches and sugars from plant foods are absorbed in the small intestine, leaving the indigestible fiber to pass along to the large intestine. In the large intestine, bacteria digest short, fiber-like molecules, which are present along with the fiber; a product of this bacterial action can be gas. To minimize those moments when you don't know whether to look at each other or blame the dog, use these tips from people around the world.

• In North America a product called Beano is available in stores. Beano is an enzyme preparation which, when consumed at the same time as a bean dish, breaks down much of the indigestible carbohydrate that can cause these uncomfortable side effects. Add a few drops to prepared bean dishes just before eating; the enzymes in the Beano break down the fiber-like molecules, so that we can absorb them as sugars in the intestine. Presto! No gas. Beano does not change the flavor of the food, and has no side effects. (Just one precaution: do not use Beano if you are allergic to penicillin.)

• The Japanese use a seaweed called kombu, with a similar improvement in digestibility. Kombu is added during the cooking of legume dishes, and is removed before the dish is served.

• In India, an herbal extract called asafoetida, grown in Afghanistan, is sometimes added to cooked foods for adults. Fennel, which is often added to curries, bean dishes and teas is also found to be helpful for digestion.

• Latin Americans prevent their gas problems with a herb similar to parsley, called epazoate. Epazoate, which grows wild on the west coast of North America, is used as a seasoning for bean dishes and is a component of many chili powders.

Ingredients in traditional dishes from around the world frequently have benefits beyond adding flavor!

Recommended Intakes of Fiber

These recommendations are based on the use of whole foods rather than a diet made high in fiber through the addition of wheat bran (which, as explained earlier, can impair mineral absorption). Current North American fiber intakes range from a low of 8–10 grams per day in many typical diets to a high of 30–50 grams per day in some vegan diets. Table 7.1 shows fiber intakes of four sample diets. There do not appear to be advantages to fiber intake in excess of 40 grams per day. Caution about excessive fiber intake should be exercised in the diets of children.

The newest recommendations from expert committees around the world suggest that we aim for at least 30 grams per day. So for your short- and long-term health, accept the gift that only plants can give.

Table 7.1 Approximate Fiber Content of Various Meals

Standard American Diet	Refined Vegetarian	Health-Conscious Vegetarian	High-Fiber Vegan
Breakfasts			
bacon and eggs (0)	buttermilk pancakes or French toast (1.2)	1 cup/250 mL bran flakes (5.0)	1 cup/250 mL multigrain hot cereal with raisins (5.3)
2 slices white toast with honey (1.2)	syrup (0)	1 slice whole wheat toast with low-fat cheese (1.6)	1 slice multigrain bread with peanut butter (3.0)
1 cup/250 mL orange juice from frozen concentrate (0.2)	½ cup/125 mL strawberries (2.0)	1 medium banana (1.8)	½ grapefruit (2.5)
milk (0)	milk (0)	milk (0)	soy milk (0)
Total = 1.4 g	Total = 3.2 g	Total = 8.4 g	Total = 10.8 g
Lunches			
beef burger patty and bun (1.5)	cheese sandwich on white bread with lettuce (1.4)	peanut butter and honey sandwich on whole wheat (4.0)	tofu "cheese" sandwich on whole wheat with sprouts and tomato (3.5)
French fries with ketchup (2.5)	lettuce with green pepper and onion (1.5)	⅓ cup/75 mL carrot sticks (2.0)	1½ cups/375 mL lentil soup (4.0)
milkshake (0)	½ cup/125 mL grapes (0.5)	1 medium apple (3.0)	1 medium fresh pear (4.3)
Total = 4.0 g	Total = 3.4 g	Total = 9.0 g	Total = 11.8 g
Suppers			
½ 10 in./25 cm pepperoni pizza (1.5)	broccoli quiche (1.8)	vegetarian lasagna with spinach (4.0)	1 cup/250 mL vegetarian chili (5.0)
tossed salad, mainly lettuce (1.0)	1 cup/250 mL white rice (0.6)	½ cup/125 mL baked winter squash (3.0)	1½ cups/375 mL brown rice (4.9)
	½ cup/125 mL mixed vegetables (3.6)	¾ cup/175 mL coleslaw (2.5)	kale and carrot salad with tahini dressing (3.0)
1 piece chocolate cake (0.5)	½ cup/125 mL apple crisp (2.0)	1 cup/250 mL mixed fresh fruit salad (2.0)	1 fresh orange (2.5)
Total = 3.0 g	Total = 8.0 g	Total = 11.5 g	Total = 15.4 g
Approximate total fiber for the day			
8.4 g	14.6 g	28.9 g	38.0 g

Suggested health promoting range: 27–40 g

THE VEGETARIAN FOOD GUIDE: PUTTING IT ALL TOGETHER

ow that you know what's free of cholesterol and high in calcium and iron, you might be wondering, what's for lunch?

The next step towards great vegetarian eating is to combine all of our information about protein, zinc, fiber and omega-3 fatty acids into a guide that helps us make our daily food choices.

Food guides are products of the 20th century. The first American food guide was published in 1916, at the beginning of an exciting era when essential vitamins and minerals were identified and found to influence health. Subsequent Canadian and American food guides have changed over the years, to accompany the new, evolving science of nutrition.

Our Vegetarian Food Guide has been modeled on the current American (Pyramid) and Canadian (Rainbow) food guides, with similar numbers of servings and serving sizes. An exception is the Milk and Milk Alternates group. In the standard food guides, 1 cup (250 mL) milk equals one serving. In the Vegetarian Food Guide, ½ cup (125 mL) milk equals one serving. This approach leads to more appropriate serving sizes for the calcium-rich plant foods that can be used as milk alternates. At the same time, the number of servings from this group is doubled.

The food guide that follows can be very flexible, allowing for food preferences, economic constraints and differing caloric needs. When you follow the plan, making a variety of choices from day to day, you can be confident that your nutrient needs will be met.

THE VEGETARIAN FOOD GUIDE*

Select a *variety* from the following food groups each day.

Grain Products: 5–12 servings

Whole grains are recommended.

Examples of 1 serving:

Breads:	Bread, **1 slice** (28 g)
	Roll, pita bread, tortilla, chapati, roti, bannock, scone, hamburger or hot dog bun, **1** (30–40 g)
	Bagel, **½** (28 g)
Hot & cold cereals:	Cereal, cooked, **½ cup** (125 mL)
	Cereal, ready-to-eat, **¾ cup** (175 mL)
Pasta & grains:	Pasta, rice, quinoa or other grain, cooked, **½ cup** (125 mL)
Other:	Pancake, waffle or muffin, **1 small or ½ large**(40 g)
	Wheat germ, **2 tbsp** (25 mL)
	Crackers, **2 to 6** (28 g)

Vegetables and Fruits: 5–10 servings

Examples of 1 serving:

Vegetable or fruit (such as potato, carrot, tomato, apple, banana, orange, peach or citrus fruit), **1 medium**

Vegetable or fruit, fresh, frozen or cooked, **½ cup** (125 mL)

Vegetable or fruit juice, **½ cup** (125 mL)

Small fruit (such as apricot or plum), **2**

Salad, **1 cup** (250 mL)

Many vegetables and fruits are excellent sources of vitamin C. Some that will provide more than 30 mg of vitamin C in a ½ cup (125 mL) serving are broccoli, brussels sprouts, cauliflower, collards, peppers, snow peas, cantaloupe, citrus fruits and juices, guava, kiwi fruit, papaya, strawberries and vitamin C-fortified juices.

* See pages 160 and 169 for specific servings suitable for children.

Beans & Bean Alternates: 2–4 servings

Pregnant and Lactating Women: 3–4 servings

For increased iron absorption, eat a vitamin C source (vegetable or fruit) at the same time.

Examples of 1 serving:

Legumes (beans or lentils), cooked, ½ cup (125 mL)
Tofu or tempeh, ½ cup (125 g)
Meat analogues (such as tofuburgers), 1 patty (70–80 g)
Nuts or seeds, 3–4 tbsp (50 mL)
Nut or seed butter, 2–3 tbsp (25–50 mL)
Soy milk, 1 cup (250 mL)
Egg, 1 large

Milk & Milk Alternates: 4–6 servings

Youths (10–17 years) and Pregnant and Lactating Women: 6–8 servings

The serving size for milk is ½ cup (125 mL). Tofu made with calcium is a high calcium source; greens are lower, so choose a variety. **This list does not include unfortified non-dairy beverages because they tend to be very low in calcium (see labels for details).**

Bonus: With some of these foods you get 2 for the price of 1, in that they count as vegetable servings or as beans and bean alternates servings as well.

Examples of 1 serving:

Seeds & nuts:	Sesame tahini, 2 tbsp (25 mL)
	Almond butter, 3 tbsp (50 mL)
	Almonds, ⅓ cup (75 mL)
Vegetables:	Greens (kale, collards, sui choy, bok choy, okra, broccoli), cooked, 1 cup (250 mL)
	Greens (kale, sui choy, broccoli), raw, 2 cups (500 mL)
	Seaweed (hijiki), dried, ¼ cup (50 mL, 10 g)
Legume foods:	Tofu made with calcium, ½ cup (125 mL)
	Legumes (soybeans, baked white beans, navy, great northern, black turtle beans), cooked, 1 cup, (250 mL)
	Legumes (chickpeas, pinto, butter, kidney), 1½ cups (375 mL)
Other foods:	Blackstrap molasses, 1 tbsp (15 mL)
	Figs, dried, 5 (100 g)
	Calcium-fortified foods and beverages providing 150 mg calcium per serving
Dairy products:	Milk or yogurt, ½ cup (125 mL)
	Cheese, 1 oz (28 g)

FOR THOSE WHO CONSUME
LITTLE OR NO ANIMAL PRODUCTS

Vitamin B$_{12}$

Fortified food or supplement supplying 1–3 μg vitamin B$_{12}$ (depending on stage of life).

Vitamin D

Fortified food or supplement supplying 2.5–10 μg (depending on age)

or

Summer sunlight on hands and face: For light skinned people, 10–15 minutes. For dark skinned people, ½ hour or more.

Omega-3 Fatty Acid Sources: 1 serving

Pregnant and Lactating Women: 2 servings

Samples of 1 serving:

Walnuts, pumpkin seeds, **3 tbsp** (50 mL)
Oil, flax seed, ½ **tsp** (2 mL)
Oil (canola, soybean), **1 tbsp** (15 mL)

More About the Vegetarian Food Guide

Note that one of the keys to successful use of a food guide is the selection of a *variety* of foods. For example, riboflavin is found in some foods that you probably wouldn't use every day, such as mushrooms, sweet potatoes, avocados and figs. Riboflavin is also provided by foods that may show up fairly regularly on your diet, because they are such concentrated sources of nutrients: wheat germ, broccoli, almonds, beans and nutritional yeast. When you focus on the most nutritious foods, but also choose variety, you'll maximize your nutrient intake.

GRAIN PRODUCTS

This group forms the basis of the vegetarian style of eating, contributing calories as well as the B vitamins and minerals which support our energy production. Yeasted breads have increased mineral availability, and whole grain products provide fiber as well as protein. Fortified dry cereals and wheat germ are also good choices.

Does 5–12 servings sound like a lot? It's really not. For example, a cup of cooked cereal at breakfast, a sandwich with two slices of bread at lunch, and a cup of rice or pasta at supper adds up to six servings. The basic serving size is equivalent to a slice of bread or ½ cup (125 mL) of cooked grain. Teens, young adults and physically active people may need 12 servings from this group (or even more).

VEGETABLES AND FRUITS

Make leafy greens a regular part of your diet; leaves transform the energy from the sun into food, and are particularly nutritious parts of plants. The energy they absorb ends up in other parts of the plant, such as stems (celery and asparagus), roots (carrots, turnips and beets), tubers (potatoes and yams), flowers (broccoli and cauliflower) and seeds (peas and corn). Some vegetables are actually the fruits of plants: cucumber, squash, eggplant, okra and tomatoes. Other foods that we commonly think of as fruits appeal to us because of their sweet tastes: apples, grapes, melons. Vegetables and fruits are a low-calorie way of packing in the nutrients such as vitamins A and C, folic acid and minerals.

BEANS AND BEAN ALTERNATES

Beans and peas (legumes) are the concentrated protein foods of the plant kingdom. As well, they contain iron, zinc, calcium, vitamin B_6 and fiber. Along with products such as tofu or tempeh, legumes are an important part of vegetarian meals. Meat analogues, made from legumes, sometimes in combination with nuts and grains, can be an easy and delicious way to increase your protein intake. Remember that iron absorption will be increased substantially when you eat a rich vitamin C source at the same time.

Nuts and seeds are less-concentrated sources of the same nutrients; they are also rich in essential oils. For example, walnuts and pumpkin seeds provide omega-3 fatty acids. Nut and seed butters are valuable in vegetarian diets as nutritious spreads and are sometimes used in recipes to replace oils.

To increase your intake of beans and bean alternates:
- Load up on legumes by using them in soups, stews, pasta sauces, loaves and patties, and in sandwich fillings such as hummus.
- Use tofu more often; scramble some for breakfast, add it to sandwiches for lunch and toss it into your stir-fry at dinner.
- Spread nut or seed butter on your toast instead of butter.
- Snack on nuts and seeds during the day, use them in baking and add them to salads.

Foods from this group can also be counted as "milk alternates" choices.

MILK AND MILK ALTERNATES

Certain foods you may have selected from other food groups will provide calcium as well. For example:

• If you use ½ cup (125 mL) of tofu made with calcium, or have a serving of almonds or tahini, you can *also* count these foods as a serving from the beans group.

• 1 to 1½ cups (250–375 mL) of legumes, as specified in the food guide, can be used as a milk alternate, and also as two servings from the beans group.

• A cup of green vegetables (kale, collards, bok choy, sui choy, okra or broccoli) is a milk alternate; at the same time it provides two servings from the vegetable group. In the recipe section you'll find delightful ways from around the world to cook greens such as kale and collards. There is also a delicious oriental salad based on sui choy. (Another name for sui choy is Chinese cabbage.)

Calcium-fortified products, providing approximately 150 mg calcium per serving, are equivalent to one serving from this group (check labels). *Unfortified non-dairy beverages, such as soy- or rice-based beverages, are not options from this group.* Even though they may be used in the same ways as cow's milk as a drink or in cooking, they are not nutritionally equivalent.

For those who use dairy products, ½ cup (125 mL) of milk or yogurt is a serving. If you use milk to meet your calcium needs, you do not need the separate sources of vitamin D or B_{12} listed below. Yogurt and cheese contain vitamin B_{12} but not vitamin D.

The recommended intake from this group is 4–6 servings. Youths, whose bone density is still increasing, need 6–8 servings. In Canada's Food Guide this higher intake of milk products is recommended for those 10 to 17; the American guide recommends the equivalent of 6 servings to age 24. Pregnant and lactating women need 6–8 servings.

The most practical way to meet one's calcium needs through plant foods is to *choose tahini, almond butter, dark green leafy vegetables and tofu made with calcium on a regular basis.*

FOR THOSE WHO CONSUME LITTLE OR NO ANIMAL PRODUCTS

Vitamin B_{12}

A vitamin B_{12} fortified food or supplement supplying the recommended intake is absolutely essential for those who use little or no animal products. This will be 1 µg to 3 µg depending on stage of the life cycle. See the recommended intakes for people of every age in Appendix 2. A supplement may be taken at weekly or monthly intervals as vitamin B_{12} can be stored in the body for future use.

Vitamin D

Sunlight can be a vitamin D source. Light skinned people require just a few minutes a day or a total of about 1½–2 hours a week of what is called "summer sun" on the hands and face. The months of "vitamin D winter" for some latitudes are given on page 87. For this part of the year, children will need vitamin D-fortified food or supplement; adults can store enough vitamin D for the winter. Dark skinned people may need substantially more sunlight, ½ hour or more daily. Those who don't spend appropriate amounts of time outdoors need a supplement or vitamin D- fortified food. For recommended intake levels see Appendix 2.

Omega-3 Fatty Acids

For vegans and non-vegans alike, an emphasis on foods that contain omega-3 fatty acids will help to provide an optimal balance between the essential fatty acids. In the omega-3 fatty acids section of the food guide, the foods and serving sizes listed provide approximately the Canadian recommended daily intake. Walnuts and pumpkin seeds can be added to your trail mix, salads and cereals. The oils – flax, canola and soybean – are best used in salad dressings and added to prepared foods. The brands to buy are those processed without heat. (Some oils, although labeled "cold pressed," are still subject to high heat when they are deodorized.) Store all of these omega-3 foods in the refrigerator or freezer.

Smaller amounts of omega-3 fatty acids will be obtained from certain other plant foods, such as leafy greens and wheat germ.

ADDITIONAL RECOMMENDATIONS FOR EVERYONE

Drink 6–8 glasses of water daily (this includes herb tea, water, juice and non-caffeinated beverages). About ⅓ tsp (1 mL) of regular (iodized) table salt will meet your daily iodine requirement.

Calories

For the extra calories you need above the minimum recommended intake, choose other foods from these food groups. The minimum number is suitable for those with lower caloric requirements: children, the elderly, people limiting their caloric intake, and those with low activity levels. Teens and people who are bigger or more active will need more servings. Athletes may exceed the number of servings shown here.

Assessing Your Diet

How do you figure out whether you're meeting your needs from each group?

A handy way of checking off your day's food intake is the Score Sheet below, and on pages 144 and 145. The darkened squares indicate your recommended minimum from each group.

VEGETARIAN FOOD GUIDE SCORE SHEET

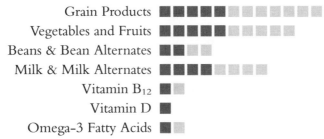

Copy the Score Sheet and use it to assess your diet for a few days. This will give you an idea of the strengths and weaknesses of your current way of eating. If you find that you're short in a certain group, choose foods from that group and put them on your shopping list. If there are some foods that you don't know how to use, check the recipes in Chapter 12; these recipes have a special emphasis on highly nutritious ingredients. After scoring your diet for a while and making a few adjustments, you can relax and realize you're on the right track.

As we learn more about nutrition, we find more reasons to eat *whole* foods. Nature has packaged foods so that they provide a great many more health supportive components than we may have realized. Although the era of vitamin discovery is complete, new substances are being found in whole foods that appear to play powerful roles in the prevention of disease. These are the phytochemicals found in such foods as garlic, onion, licorice, tofu and cooking herbs. Scientists are also investigating the parts played by trace minerals towards our overall well being. These substances are present in whole foods, but can be lost or changed with processing.

Today's discoveries are making it increasingly obvious that vitamin pills can never replace real food. (Supplements and fortified foods can sometimes help – for example, providing vitamin B_{12} to vegans.) Organic foods are good choices; in buying these products we support our health, environmentally friendly industries *and* the planet. These foods are becoming more available and less expensive, with increasing consumer demand.

Overall, the fresh and tasty plant foods are superbly designed to nourish us – at every stage of the life cycle.

USING THE VEGETARIAN FOOD GUIDE SCORE SHEET

To show you how to use the score sheet, here we rate the lacto-ovo vegetarian menu (No. 3) from page 44.

(number of servings)

Grain Products ▨▨▨▨▨✓✓▨▨▨▨

cereal, 1 cup (250 mL)	(2)
toast, 1	(1)
pita bread, 1	(1)
spaghetti, 1½ cups (375 mL)	(3)
(TOTAL: 7)	

Vegetables and Fruits ▨▨▨▨▨✓✓✓▨▨

orange juice, ½ cup (125 mL)	(1)
cherry tomatoes, 4	(1)
carrot, 1	(1)
apple, 1	(1)
tomato-vegetable sauce, 1 cup (250 mL)	(2)
green salad, 1 cup (250 mL)	(1)
banana, 1	(1)
(TOTAL: 8)	

Beans & Bean Alternates ▨▨½▨

almond butter, 1 tbsp (15 mL)	(⅓)
hummus, ½ cup (125 mL)	(1)
cashews, ¼ cup (50 mL)	(1)
lentils, ¼ cup (50 mL)	(½)
(TOTAL: 2½+)	

Milk & Milk Alternates ▨▨▨▨▨▨▨▨

2% milk, 1 cup (250 mL)	(2)
almond butter plus tahini and garbanzo beans	(1)
parmesan cheese, 2 tbsp (25 mL)	(1)
(TOTAL: 4)	

Vitamin B_{12} ▨▨

milk and cheese provides 1 μg vitamin B_{12}	(1)

Vitamin D ▨

vitamin D fortified milk and sunlight, combination	(1)

Omega-3 Fatty Acids ▨✓

flax seed oil, 1 tsp (5 mL) in dressing	(2)

VEGETARIAN FOOD GUIDE SCORE SHEET

And here's a sample analysis of the vegan pattern from page 46.

(number of servings)

Grain Products ■■■■✓✓✓✓▨▨

cereal, 1 cup (250 mL)	(2)
toast, 1	(1)
sandwich, 2 bread	(2)
rice, 1 cup (250 mL)	(2)
muffin, 1 large	(2)
(TOTAL: 9)	

Vegetables and Fruits ■■■■✓⅓▨▨▨

orange, 1	(1)
carrot, 1	(1)
apple, 1	(1)
salad, 2 cups (500 mL)	(2)
onions, ¼ cup (50 mL)	(½)
figs, 3	(1)
(TOTAL: 6½)	

Beans & Bean Alternates ■■✓▨

soy milk, 1 cup (250 mL)	(1)
tofu made with calcium, ¼ cup (50 mL)	(½)
lentils, 1 cup (250 mL)	(2)
(TOTAL: 3)	

Milk & Milk Alternates ■■■■▨▨▨▨

tahini, 2 tbsp (25 mL)	(1)
blackstrap molasses on toast and in baking, 1 tbsp (15 mL)	(1)
tofu made with calcium, ¼ cup (50 mL)	(1)
kale in salad, 1 cup (250 mL)	(½)
figs, 3	(½)
(Note: calcium fortified soy milk would add more servings)	
(TOTAL: 4)	

Vitamin B$_{12}$ ■▨

nutritional yeast, Red Star T-6635+ brand (in sandwich), 1 tsp (5 mL)	(1)

Vitamin D ■

a short walk in the sunlight at lunch break	(1)

Omega-3 Fatty Acids ■▨

walnuts, 3 tbsp (50 mL)	(1)

VEGETARIAN NUTRITION IN THE GROWING YEARS

The growing years are characterized by physical changes that result in unique nutritional requirements. During pregnancy and lactation, infancy, childhood and adolescence, our needs for a number of nutrients rise. As we consider the implications of these changes for the nutritional health of vegetarians, it becomes apparent that a basic shift in our goals must take place. We naturally move away from the adult model, which is centered on the prevention of degenerative diseases, towards a model that promotes optimal growth and development. To do this we need to put a greater emphasis on foods that are rich sources of both energy and nutrients. In so doing, the positive health consequences of a vegetarian diet can be realized for both the short and the long term.

Regardless of whether you are just beginning to cut back on animal foods, or are a vegetarian or a vegan, you can be assured that good health can be achieved during the growing years. The guidelines offered in this chapter will help to ensure that the special needs of growing bodies are met in a simple and enjoyable manner. Our approach is a cautious one, particularly in the area of vegan nutrition for children.

PREGNANCY AND LACTATION

You're pregnant, and there are few things that matter more to you right now than having a healthy baby. You may be wondering if your plant-centered diet is adequate to support this little person who shares your food. Relax. With a little good sense, you can obtain all the nutrients you need to produce a wonderfully healthy baby.

It's best to begin your pregnancy well nourished, but if your diet is less than ideal, there's no better time to improve it. Consider it an investment in the future.

Vegetarians enjoy some advantages when it comes to pregnancy and lactation, including a lower risk for obesity and hypertension. In addition, the vegetarian diet is usually loaded with nutrient-dense whole grains, fruits and vegetables, and contains few processed, high-fat extras.

Lacto-ovo vegetarians are at no greater risk for nutritional shortages during pregnancy than are omnivores. In planning a prenatal diet for the lacto-ovo vegetarian, the nutrients that need special consideration are iron, zinc and possibly protein. In comparison to the pregnant omnivore, lacto-ovo vegetarians seem to have less trouble meeting their needs for folic acid and calcium. Those who consume only small amounts of dairy products would be well advised either to follow the guidelines for vegans given in this chapter or to increase their use of dairy foods during this time.

Based on our current knowledge, it is apparent that vegan women can also have very healthy pregnancies. Vegans need to give attention to those nutrients commonly provided by dairy foods, including calcium, vitamin D and vitamin B_{12}, in addition to the nutrients that may be of concern for lacto-ovo vegetarians. Restrictive vegan diets have been linked to low birth weight in infants, thus some care is needed in planning a vegan diet during this time. On the other hand, vegans have been reported to have healthy pregnancies with no significant differences in birth weight, congenital abnormalities or other complications as compared to omnivorous women.

The recommended nutrient intakes during pregnancy and lactation for both the United States and Canada are provided in Appendix 2.

Nutrition Guidelines for Pregnant Vegetarians and Vegans

1. Aim for a weight gain of 25–35 lb (11.5–16 kg) during pregnancy.
A weight gain of 25–35 lb (11.5–16 kg) is associated with the healthiest outcome for both the mother and baby. Adolescents and women with large body frames should aim for the upper end of this range, while short women with smaller frames should aim for the lower end. For those who are underweight, a gain of 28–40 lb (12.5–18 kg) is suggested. Women who are overweight do not need to gain "fat stores" for lactation, thus a gain of 15–25 lb (7–11.5 kg) is generally sufficient. It is important to note that many people assume that they

are overweight, when in fact they are within their healthy weight range. Check with your doctor or health care provider before you decide to limit your weight gain. You may be limiting your nutrient intake unnecessarily. *Do not try to lose weight during pregnancy – it's not worth the risk!*

In order to produce the desired weight gain, about 100 extra calories per day are needed during the first trimester, and about 300 extra calories per day in the last two trimesters, in addition to normal food intake. A hundred calories amounts to little more than an apple or a banana each day, while 300 calories can be easily obtained from a ½ cup (125 mL) serving of trail mix or a peanut butter and banana sandwich. Those who are underweight or who are not gaining weight adequately will need additional calories.

If you are experiencing "morning sickness" and have a poor appetite during the first trimester, do your best to include complex carbohydrate and protein foods when you do eat. Limit sweets and fatty foods, eat several small meals a day, and drink plenty of water.

2. Eat a wide variety of nutritious foods, as outlined in the vegetarian food guide.
During pregnancy your needs for nutrients go up substantially (see Appendix 2), although your needs for calories increase by only a small amount. What this means in terms of real food is that you can't afford to eat a lot of "junk," or foods that provide little nutritional benefit. Focus on wholesome foods, as outlined in the vegetarian food guide.

To make the food guide work for you, be sure that you achieve the recommended number of servings every day. Select a wide variety of foods from within each of the groups; the more variety you include, the better balance of nutrients that you will receive. Try not to skip meals, as you need a good supply of vitamins and minerals throughout the day.

A suggested meal plan, based on the food guide, with the additions recommended during pregnancy, is provided at the end of this section.

3. Include one extra serving from the beans and bean alternates group every day.
During pregnancy, an extra serving from the beans and bean alternates group is recommended, bringing the total to three to four servings per day. This will help to increase your intake of protein, iron and zinc, which are necessary to a normal healthy pregnancy. These nutrients are important for the growth of your uterus, and your expanding blood volume, as well as the growth and development of the fetus (review Chapter 3 for more information on these nutrients). Although it is relatively easy to increase protein in your diet, it is a greater challenge to get enough iron and zinc, regardless of whether you are a

vegetarian or an omnivore. Prenatal supplements are routinely advised to help ensure that you receive enough of these essential minerals.

The following food combinations are examples of three to four servings of beans and bean alternates:

- ½ cup (125 mL) tofu and 1 cup (250 mL) kidney beans
- 3 tbsp (50 mL) almond butter and 2 soyburgers
- ¼ cup (50 mL) cashews, 1 cup (250 mL) pea soup and ½ cup (125 mL) tempeh
- 1 egg, ½ cup (125 mL) pinto beans and 1 cup (250 mL) soy milk

4. Include two to four additional servings of milk and milk alternates each day.
An additional two to four servings from the milk and milk alternates group are recommended, bringing the total to six to eight servings per day. These foods help to provide the extra calcium that you need during pregnancy. Fluid cow's milk and some fortified non-dairy beverages (read labels) – commercial or home-made (see recipe, page 164) – also contribute to your vitamin D requirements.

An increase in calcium intake is necessary during pregnancy to help ensure proper formation of your baby's bones and teeth, as well as for nerve, muscle and blood functioning. Extra vitamin D is also needed to help promote the absorption of calcium.

The necessary calcium can be obtained by consuming a minimum of six servings from the milk and milk alternates group, in addition to the smaller amounts that you receive from other foods throughout the day. The following examples each provide the equivalent of at least six servings from the milk and milk alternates group:

- 2 tbsp (25 mL) tahini, 1 tbsp (15 mL) blackstrap molasses and 1 cup (250 mL) tofu (made with calcium)
- 3 cups (375 mL) of calcium-fortified non-dairy milk (read label) or cow's milk
- 1 cup (250 mL) steamed kale, 1 cup (250 mL) baked beans, ⅓ cup (75 mL) almonds and 5 figs
- 1 cup (250 mL) broccoli, 1 cup (250 mL) black turtle beans, ¼ cup (50 mL) seaweed and 1 cup (250 mL) yogurt

Those who have difficulty eating six to eight servings of calcium rich foods may need to take a calcium supplement .

Vitamin D is easily obtained by drinking fortified cow's milk. You can also get some vitamin D from fortified margarines and non-dairy milks, although the amounts in these products are not generally enough to meet requirements. Vitamin D can also be obtained from exposure to sunlight. For those living at northern latitudes or having limited sun exposure, a vitamin D supplement is recommended.

5. Include an extra serving of foods rich in omega-3 fatty acids every day.
During pregnancy and lactation, you need more essential fatty acids to help ensure that the brain and eyes of the fetus and young infant develop normally. This can be achieved by including an extra serving of foods rich in omega-3 fatty acids in your diet every day. This brings your total intake to two servings per day. Examples of two servings of omega-3-rich foods are:
- 3 tbsp (50 mL) walnuts and and ½ tsp (2 mL) flax oil
- 3 tbsp (50 mL) pumpkin seeds and 1 tbsp (15 mL) canola oil

6. Include a reliable source of vitamin B_{12} in the diet every day.
Vitamin B_{12} needs are increased during pregnancy and lactation to allow for the expanding blood volume, and the growth and development of the baby. For lacto-ovo vegetarians, 3 cups (750 mL) of cow's milk or one egg and 2 cups (500 mL) of milk provide all the vitamin B_{12} required.

Vegans can obtain enough vitamin B_{12} using one tablepoon (15 mL) of Red Star T-6635+ yeast (large flakes), or vitamin B_{12}-fortified meat analogues and non-dairy beverages. Aim for a total of approximately 3 µg per day. Do not rely on other plant foods which have traditionally been considered vitamin B_{12} sources, as many of them contain vitamin B_{12} analogues (see Chapter 5). *If adequate vitamin B_{12}-fortified foods are not used, a supplement is necessary.*

7. A prenatal vitamin/mineral supplement is recommended for vegetarians and vegans who are at risk for under-nutrition, who have a nutrient deficiency, or who for any reason are unable to follow carefully the vegetarian food guide.
Vitamin and mineral supplements can provide some protection against nutrient shortages during pregnancy, and thus are often recommended during pregnancy for vegetarians and omnivores alike. However, they are not absolutely necessary when the diet is well planned.

There are a number of situations in which it would be wise to use a prenatal vitamin supplement. Some of the more common reasons are:
- You have entered pregnancy undernourished, underweight or otherwise nutritionally compromised.
- You do not consume the necessary amounts of animal foods or vitamin B_{12}-fortified products to get the vitamin B_{12} you require during pregnancy.
- You do not use adequate quantities of vitamin D-fortified foods, and have limited exposure to sunlight.

- You have a history of poor iron status, or iron levels that are below normal values.
- You are unable to consume the amounts of foods recommended in the food guide because of nausea, lack of appetite or any other reason.
- You smoke (remember if you do, so does your baby).

Many experts routinely advise a daily iron supplement of 30 mg per day during the last two trimesters of pregnancy. If your doctor does suggest taking a supplement or you decide that you would like to take one, it is a good idea to opt for a prenatal preparation. Refer to the recommended nutrient intakes during pregnancy in Appendix 2, and try to find a supplement that contains iron, zinc, vitamin D, vitamin B_{12} and folic acid in quantities similar to the recommended levels. Remember that a supplement does not compensate for a poor diet. Even if you do use one, your emphasis should continue to be on a healthy, balanced intake of foods.

Single nutrient supplements can be toxic to the developing baby, and are therefore best avoided unless medically indicated. Calcium and vitamin B_{12} are the two exceptions to this rule. Calcium in most prenatal supplements ranges from about 100 to 250 mg; this is insufficient to meet the needs of those who are consuming few calcium-rich foods. If you need a calcium supplement, select one that provides 500 to 1000 mg elemental calcium, depending on your dietary intake. Higher dose supplements are not advised as they provide no added benefit, and can interfere with the absorption of other nutrients.

8. Avoid alcohol during pregnancy.

Pregnant women who drink alcohol on a regular basis increase the chances of their babies being born with fetal alcohol syndrome (FAS). This devastating condition can result in disorders of the central nervous system, mental retardation, growth deficiencies and abnormal facial features. Although the risk to the infant increases with the amount of alcohol consumed, safe lower limits are not known. For this reason, alcohol should be completely avoided during pregnancy.

9. Keep caffeine consumption under 300–400 mg per day.

Caffeine passes easily across the placental barrier and is poorly metabolized by the unborn baby. During the last trimester of pregnancy, caffeine is poorly metabolized by the mother as well. The effects of caffeine on the baby are not clearly understood, although research indicates that caution is warranted. Caffeine is found primarily in coffee, tea (both black and Oriental green teas), cola beverages, chocolate and some medications. Three hundred milligrams of caffeine is the amount found in approximately three cups of regular coffee or seven colas.

Caffeine-free, grain-based beverages made from ingredients such as roasted malt, barley, chicory and carob may be useful substitutes. Although decaffeinated coffee contains minimal caffeine, it is often processed with harsh chemicals and thus there are some concerns regarding its effects during pregnancy. Herbal teas such as rosehip, mint, lemon and fruit teas are tasty alternatives. Some herbal teas – for example goldenseal, Scotch broom, sassafras, devil's claw and pennyroyal – are unsafe for use during pregnancy. If you do use herbal teas, make sure that those you select are safe.

10. Minimize your intake of environmental pollutants.
There are a number of things that you can do to minimize your intake of environmental pollutants during pregnancy. These steps are also important to reduce the possible residues in your breast milk:
- Choose organically grown fruits, vegetables and grains whenever possible. Otherwise, be sure to wash your produce well.
- Choose low-fat dairy products.
- If you use fish, avoid those from polluted lakes. Small fish have less residues. Also avoid fish oil supplements.

Additional Considerations for Breast Feeding

When you breast feed your baby, your nutrient needs continue to be higher than normal, and are very similar to what they were during pregnancy. An additional 400–500 calories per day (above non-pregnancy levels) are needed for those who are normal weight. This amount could be provided by a tofu salad sandwich and a glass of orange juice. If you are underweight, an extra 800–1000 calories per day may be necessary. This would be most easily achieved by increasing by about 200 calories per meal (for example, a glass of milk – soy or cow's, preferably calcium fortified – or juice and a slice of bread with tahini), and adding an extra snack (perhaps a bowl of cereal). If you don't get enough to eat, your milk supply could suffer.

You'll also need extra fluids while you are breast feeding. Try to remember to drink a big glass of water whenever you are nursing.

You should continue to limit your intake of caffeine while you are breast feeding. Alcohol does not need to be as strictly avoided, although it is quickly transferred to breast milk, so your intake should be minimal. Some babies are sensitive to strong flavors such as garlic, onion or hot spices, so you may have to limit these as well. If your baby has colic, eczema or chronic congestion, it could be caused by something you are eating, particularly if there is a history of allergy in your family. The food most commonly associated with these kinds of reactions is cow's milk. Try eliminating it from your diet for three days, and see if there are any improvements. Other foods to consider are those that other family members have reacted to. It may take a little perseverance to track the culprit down.

Supplements may be necessary, for the same reasons as described in guideline no. 7. Prenatal supplements can be finished off, then an adult multivitamin and mineral supplement will be sufficient. Make sure that it contains vitamins B_{12} and D, as well as zinc. Vegan breast feeding mothers must be especially careful to get a reliable source of vitamin B_{12}.

Planning an adequate prenatal diet

sample pattern	sample food choices
Breakfast	
3 grain products	1 cup (250 mL) oatmeal
1 fruit	1 tsp (2 mL) flax oil (mixed in oatmeal)
2 milk and milk alternates	½ cup (125 mL) milk
1 essential fatty acid source	(fortified non-dairy or cow's)
	1 orange
	1 slice toast
	1 tbsp (15 mL) blackstrap molasses
	1 tbsp (15 mL) tahini
Lunch	
3 grain products	2 slices whole grain bread
2 vegetables and fruit	½ cup (125 mL) tofu
2 milk and milk alternates	(tofu salad sandwich)
1 beans and bean alternates	1 cup (250 mL) sui choy salad
	1 slice banana loaf
Dinner	
2 grain products	1 cup (250 mL) millet
3 vegetables and fruits	1 cup (250 mL) curried garbanzos
1 milk and milk alternates	1 cup (250 mL) broccoli
2 beans and bean alternates	sliced melon
Snacks	
1 grain product	1 whole grain muffin
2 vegetables and fruits	1 banana
1 milk and milk alternates	5 figs
1 essential fatty acid source	1½ oz (45 g) pumpkin seeds

The totals provided by this sample plan are
> *9 grain products*
> *8 vegetables and fruits*
> *6 milk and milk alternates*
> *3 beans and bean alternates*
> *2 essential fatty acid sources*

Be sure to drink at least 6 glasses of water a day.

This pattern provides the necessary nutrients for a pregnant or lactating vegetarian, although depending on the foods selected, the iron and zinc could be low. If all animal products are avoided, a reliable source of vitamins B_{12} and D must be included. Sufficient vitamin B_{12} could be obtained by using fortified products.

INFANCY: UP TO TWO YEARS OF AGE

The first two years of life are filled with discovery. So many new colors, textures and flavors are welcomed by the adventurous infant. As parents, we must seize the opportunity to build a foundation for health that includes a wide variety of wonderful foods.

Our babies will grow at an incredible rate during these first years. We have the responsibility for ensuring that they receive all that is needed for normal growth. We must begin with a basic understanding of the unique needs of human infants, and a little common sense.

There is no doubt that a well-planned lacto-ovo vegetarian diet can provide adequate nutrition for an infant. By contrast, there is considerable debate regarding the adequacy of a vegan diet for infants, and many experts do not recommend this type of eating pattern for the first two years of life. Their concern stems from a number of reports of varying degrees of malnutrition and poor rates of growth in infants on vegan diets. It is clear that a poorly planned or overly restrictive vegan diet can have serious consequences for the growth, development and the overall health of infants. An all-plant diet is generally high in fiber, and can both compromise the digestibility of protein and other nutrients and lead to a reduced energy intake.

It is not impossible to adequately nourish a baby on a vegan diet, but the potential for inadequate nutrition should be recognized, and the diet planned accordingly. A closer look at the reports of malnourished vegan infants indicates that they are often the result of restrictive regimens that are low in protein, fat and energy, and as such are most unsuitable for infants. Many of these babies have been fed homemade or unfortified commercial milk substitutes that contain insufficient nutrients.

Studies have also shown that vegan infants can achieve normal growth and development when the diet is carefully planned to ensure enough protein, fat, calories and other nutrients.

Nutrition Guidelines for Vegetarian and Vegan Infants (birth to two years of age)

1. Infants should be breast fed for a minimum of six months, and preferably for a full two years.

Breast milk is specifically designed to meet the needs of the human infant, just as the milks of other mammals are specifically designed to meet the needs of their young. The more scientists learn about the unique composition of human milk, the more they realize that an equivalent can never be formulated in a lab.

Breast milk provides much more than simply an ideal balance of nutrients for your infant. It provides special substances that will protect your baby from infection, and helps to create a bond between you and your infant. The benefits of breast feeding can continue to provide these advantages well into the second year of life and beyond.

2. If breast feeding is not chosen, not possible or if it stops before a year of age for the lacto-ovo vegetarian infant, and two years for the vegan infant, commercial infant formula is recommended.

Commercial infant formula is the most acceptable alternative to breast milk. Experts now advise using the iron-fortified variety from birth until the introduction of high-iron solid foods, as iron deficiency is the most common nutritional problem in infants. If you stop breast feeding, or breast feed your baby fewer than three times a day, a commercial iron-fortified infant formula should be used as the replacement.

Between nine and 12 months of age, lacto-ovo vegetarian babies can switch to whole cow's milk, if they are eating at least ¾ cup (175 mL) of solid foods a day. Low-fat milks are not suitable for babies under 12 months of age, and skim milk should not be used as the main source of milk for babies under 24 months of age. Vegan babies should continue to be given infant formula for a full two years and beyond. *Fortified or unfortified soy milk, tofu milk, rice milk, nut milk and skim cow's milk should not be used as the primary milk source during the first two years of your baby's life.* These milks will not provide the nutrients necessary for optimal growth and development of your infant, and could lead to malnutrition.

3. Vegetarian infants between 12 and 24 months of age should consume at least 20 oz (625 mL) of breast milk, cow's milk or formula per day.

Milk continues to provide important nutrients for your baby in the second year of life. It helps to ensure that they receive sufficient calcium and high-quality protein to support normal growth and development.

If your baby is a lacto-ovo vegetarian, both dairy products such as milk, yogurt and cottage cheese and eggs can be used regularly to provide highly digestible protein. Plant proteins, as described for the vegan baby, can also contribute significantly to the protein needs of the lacto-ovo vegetarian baby.

If your baby is a vegan, continue to breast feed or provide formula during the second year of life, to ensure an adequate balance of nutrients. This is a very vulnerable period for infants, and the continuation of breast feeding or formula during this time greatly reduces the risk of malnutrition.

If for any reason lesser amounts of breast milk or formula are consumed during the first two years of life, it is recommended that food combinations be provided at each meal that supply high-quality protein. Soy products (such as tofu and tempeh), quinoa and amaranth have amino acid profiles similar to cow's milk, and are therefore important protein sources for the vegan infant. Other plant foods can be combined to offer similar protein quality. Plant proteins tend to be slightly lower in their digestibility, thus vegan babies require slightly more protein than lacto-ovo vegetarian babies. Examples of "all plant" combinations that work well for the older baby include pea soup with bread, tofu with rice, and bean stew with millet (refer to Chapter 3 for more information on protein complementation).

4. Breast fed infants should be given a vitamin D supplement of 10 μg per day, beginning during the first week of life.
Whether or not routine vitamin D supplementation is needed for breast fed infants is a matter of controversy. It appears that, if you receive enough vitamin D in your diet, and your baby is regularly exposed to sunlight, there is little risk for deficiency. On the other hand, if you do not consume vitamin D-fortified milk or have limited sun exposure, the vitamin D in your breast milk will be low.

Considering the uncertainty regarding the adequacy of Vitamin D in breast milk, it is generally recommended that breast fed infants be given 10 μg of vitamin D per day from birth.

Breast fed infants can receive enough vitamin D from sunlight alone, although this method is less reliable than using a supplement. Infants must be exposed to warm sunlight for at least two hours every week (to hands and face), and more for infants with dark skin.

Formula fed infants don't need a vitamin D supplement as infant formula is fortified with this nutrient.

5. Breast fed infants require an additional source of iron by six months of age. Infants on regular infant formula need extra iron by at least four months of age.

The iron stores of breast fed babies start to decline at about six months of age, and even earlier for babies who were premature. With the small amounts of highly absorbable iron from breast milk, and the iron stores from birth, many infants can maintain normal iron levels until they are nine months old or more. However, even marginal iron deficiency can slow development and cause irritability. Thus, it is generally recommended that a good source of iron be provided by six months of age for breast fed infants, and by four months of age for infants fed a non–iron-fortified formula.

For formula fed infants, iron-fortified formula or an iron supplement (at a dose of about 1 mg/kg body weight) can be used until the baby begins solid foods. Iron-fortified infant cereal is a good way to provide extra iron at this age, as most babies are ready for solid foods. Begin with a single grain cereal such as rice, barley or oat pablum so that food allergies can be easily identified if they occur. Mixed cereals can be used after the infant has been given each grain separately. These cereals can continue to provide high-quality iron up to two years of age and beyond. Sprinkle them on other cold cereals, and add them to muffins, pancakes and other baked goods.

If you do not wish to use commercial infant cereals, realize that whole grains are much lower in iron. Tofu, prune juice, fortified cream of wheat and quinoa all provide significant amounts of iron. To receive the recommended amounts of iron, your baby will need a combination of iron-rich foods such as 2 tbsp (25 mL) of tofu, 2 tbsp (25 mL) of quinoa, ¼ cup (50 mL) of prune juice and ¼ cup (50 mL) of wax beans. Other high-iron vegetarian foods are listed in table 3.11 (page 61).

6. Breast fed vegan infants should receive a vitamin B_{12} supplement of at least 0.5 µg per day from the second week of life until at least two years of age.

As a vegan mother, your breast milk can be very low in vitamin B_{12}, especially if you are not using a supplement or vitamin B_{12}-fortified foods. For this reason, your baby should receive a vitamin B_{12} supplement of at least 0.3 µg per day from birth until at least two years of age, or until such time that enough vitamin B_{12} is provided by fortified foods.

If you are a lacto-ovo vegetarian, you don't need a supplement unless your intake of milk and eggs is limited. You can get enough vitamin B_{12} from having at least 3 cups (750 mL) of milk (or equivalent dairy products), or 1 egg and 2 cups (500 mL) of milk per day.

If your baby is formula fed, a vitamin B_{12} supplement is not necessary as formula is fortified. Vitamin B_{12} supplements can be discontinued if your breast fed infant begins to consume at least 3 oz (100 mL) formula each day in addition to or in place of breast milk.

7. Fat and energy should not be restricted during the first two years of life, unless medically indicated.

Breast milk, the ideal food for infants, derives approximately 54 percent of its calories from fat; 1 cup (250 mL) of breast milk contains about 175 calories. This could well be nature's way of telling us that babies need food that is concentrated in both fat and energy. Vegetarian, and particularly vegan, diets are sometimes low in fat and energy, and are often high in fiber. Be sure to take this into account when planning your infant's diet, so baby receives enough calories, fat and protein. As you begin to introduce solid foods, follow these suggestions to help keep fat and energy at a healthy level for your infant:

- *Include plenty of low-fiber, high-protein foods in the diet.* Tofu, smooth nut and seed butters and creams, soy yogurt, soy cheese and other soy products, in addition to dairy products and eggs for the lacto-ovo vegetarian, are good choices.

- *Do not restrict fat during this time.* Low-fat or skim milk, other "low-fat" food products, and foods made with fat substitutes are not appropriate for infants. Breast milk or formula, tofu and smooth nut butters and creams are important sources of fat for the infant who does not consume animal foods. Vegetable oils can also be used in food preparation.

- *Avoid excessive fiber in the diet.* Peel thick-skinned fruits and vegetables, and don't overdo their use, as these foods are low in fat and energy. Avoid concentrated fiber products such as raw wheat bran, bran cereals and bran muffins. Use mainly whole grain breads and cereals (for example, brown rice, millet, quinoa and oatmeal bread), as they contribute important minerals to the diet; some refined breads and enriched pasta and cereals can help limit total fiber in the diet.

- *Serve regular meals with snacks in between for infants above ten months of age.* (Younger infants are still receiving enough milk between meals so that regular snacks are not as important.) Infants have very small stomach capacities, and thus should be fed frequently. Choose snacks carefully, making sure that they contribute to the infant's overall nutrient needs. A few energy-packed favorites include spreads (hummus, tofu spreads or nut butters) on crackers or rusks; bread with cheese (dairy or soy); homemade, wholesome cookies, muffins or squares; rice, cornmeal, quinoa or other whole grain puddings with fruit, and yogurt (dairy or soy).

8. Solid foods should be delayed until four to six months of age.

Not so long ago, a baby's first bite of solid food was considered a real developmental milestone. Parents spooned in solid foods by two months of age, and the babies usually ended up with more food dribbling down their faces than into their bellies. We now understand that most infants have no need for solid foods before six months of age. Some infants are ready for solids by four or five months of age, particularly if they are growing very quickly. When your baby is ready for solids, you'll know it! Here are a few of the signs:

- Your baby will be constantly hungry, even after nursing eight or ten times in a day or drinking 40 oz. (1.25 L) of formula.
- He or she will be able to sit up and give signs of satiety like turning the head away.
- Birth weight will have at least doubled.
- Your baby will be able to move solids to the back of the mouth and swallow without spitting most of it out.

There are no hard and fast rules regarding the order of introduction for solid foods after six months of age, although the sequence usually recommended is infant cereals, vegetables, fruits, then protein-rich foods. This sequence takes into consideration both the nutritional value of these first foods and the maturity of the infant's gastrointestinal system. Each infant is unique in his or her ability to chew and handle foods at various ages (don't wait till your baby has teeth; he or she can chew without them). Some infants are ready for mashed vegetables and fruits by six months, while others are not ready for these types of foods until they are eight months old.

Suggestions regarding specific quantities of foods needed between 12 and 24 months are provided in the "Getting Enough to Grow On" guidelines on page 160.

9. Avoid giving foods to infants that may cause choking or asphyxiation.
Your baby may have difficulty chewing and swallowing foods that are small, hard or seedy. Choking can occur suddenly. Always supervise your infant while they are eating. Make sure children are seated during meals and snacks. Eating on the run greatly increases the risk for infants. The following foods are commonly associated with choking in babies and should be avoided or prepared as outlined to reduce the danger of choking:

During the first 12 months avoid:
- raw, hard fruit and vegetable pieces (cook these foods for a few minutes to soften)
- grapes (later, grapes can be cut in half)
- fruits with seeds (these can be mashed and strained)

During the first three to four years avoid:
- popcorn, nuts and seeds (smooth nut butters and creams may be given)
- potato or taco chips
- small candies

> • whole tofu dogs (tofu dogs can be sliced in half or quarters, lengthwise)
> • chewing gum

10. Honey and corn syrup should not be fed to infants under one year of age.
Infant botulism is a rare but very dangerous disorder. It can happen when an infant eats a food containing *Clostridium botulinum* spores, which can produce a deadly toxin in the infant's gastrointestinal system. The foods eaten by infants that most commonly contain these spores are honey and corn syrup. In order for the *Clostridium* spores to produce the toxin, their environment must be non-acidic and anaerobic. A baby's gastrointestinal system fits this description in the early months. As the baby gets older, and is eating a variety of solid foods, his or her gastrointestinal tract becomes acidic (usually by six or eight months of age), and the toxin can no longer be produced.

Getting Enough to Grow On: A Guide for the 12–24-month-old infant

The second year of life is an important time of transition for a baby. Parents need to take special care to ensure that their baby receives a balance of foods that will make this transition a healthy one. The 12–24-month-old infant should receive the following foods each day:

Milk and Milk Alternates
3 cups (750 mL) of fomula or breast milk or a combination of the two.
It is important to continue breast feeding or formula for the vegan infant. Lacto ovo vegetarian babies can be safely switched to whole cow's milk after 12 months of age, although breast feeding is still preferable.
Other milk alternates can be given, but should not be used as a replacement for breast milk, formula or whole cow's milk (2% milk is acceptable for the baby who is getting higher fat foods such as cheese and eggs, and is growing very well).

Breads and Cereals
4–6 oz (50–75 mL) iron-fortified infant cereal plus
2–4 child-size servings of other breads and cereals per day
1 child-size serving = ½ slice of bread
                ¼ cup (50 mL) rice, quinoa, enriched pasta or
                    other cooked grain
                ½ cup (125 mL) cold cereal

Vegetables and Fruits
4–6 child-size servings per day (including 2 vegetables)
1 child-size serving = ½–1 fresh fruit
                ¼ cup (50 mL) vegetables or fruit pieces
                ¼ cup (50 mL) fruit juice

Bean and Bean Alternates
2 child-size servings per day
1 child-size serving = ¼ cup (50 mL) cooked legumes
                                      1 oz (25 g) tofu
                                      4 tsp (20 mL) nut or seed butter
                                      1 egg

CHILDREN: TWO TO TEN YEARS OF AGE

The years of childhood provide an excellent opportunity to introduce a world of interesting and enjoyable foods to impressionable little ones. By giving your children a wide variety of wholesome vegetarian foods, they'll reap the benefits twice over. First, they'll be healthier children with less likelihood of obesity than their peers. Second, they'll grow into healthier adults with a lower risk for heart disease and cancer than the population at large. So before getting too concerned about the dangers of nutritional deficiencies for children on a vegetarian diet, consider the risks that are incurred in the typical North American diet. Certainly you don't want to place your children at risk for nutritional deficiencies, but you can be assured that a balanced vegetarian diet will do no such thing.

In planning a vegetarian diet for your child, you have to consider how their needs differ from the needs of an adult. Small children have limited stomach capacities and high requirements for nutrients. A plant-centered diet, containing mainly fruits, vegetables and whole grains, can be too low in calories and other nutrients and too high in fiber to meet a child's needs, particularly during the preschool years. Vegetarian diets can be well designed to provide more concentrated sources of energy and nutrients, so that an appropriate balance of foods is achieved. A number of research studies have demonstrated that both vegetarian and vegan children can be well nourished and experience rates of growth and development similar to that of other children.

Children who are raised from birth as vegetarians generally accept a wide variety of healthful foods without any problem. If you adopt a vegetarian style of eating a number of years after your children are born, there may be a little resistance, especially if your original diet was based on highly refined foods and "meat and potato" type meals. Do not despair. There are a number of things that can be done to help ease the transition to vegetarianism for youngsters:

> • *Involve children in food selection and preparation.* Children love to help stir, knead, roll, decorate and do just about anything else in the kitchen that you think they're ready for.

- *Consider your child's preferences when planning menus.* Try to include something that they really enjoy at each meal.
- *Serve vegetarian versions of traditional favorites.* Pizza, spaghetti, lasagna, chili, burgers, hot dogs, stews and stir-fries are all popular favorites.
- *Stock the cupboards and refrigerator with a variety of foods that are both wholesome and appealing for children.*
- *Don't restrict fun foods excessively.* It can be tough to be vegetarian in the midst of friends who love cheeseburgers and chicken nuggets, so do allow some fun foods.
- *Keep offering new foods, even if they are rejected.* A child who turns up their nose at something one day could end up adopting it as their favorite meal a month later (it really does happen!).
- *Respect a child's right to dislike a few foods.* Children can't be expected to love everything; nor is it necessary for good nutrition.
- *Let your children decide when they have had enough to eat.*
- *Work on making meals a pleasant time.* Set a pretty table, light a candle and encourage positive family interaction.

As parents, we are responsible for providing our children with safe and adequate food. The whole thing can seem a little overwhelming at times, especially when the children go through periods of food refusal or strange eating behaviors. Be assured that if you provide a variety of nourishing foods in a pleasant atmosphere, your child will manage to get enough to eat.

Nutrition Guidelines for Vegetarian and Vegan Children

1. Include a variety of foods from all four food groups, as outlined in the vegetarian food guide for children.

Children learn to enjoy the foods that they grow up with. If they are served whole grains, a wide variety of vegetables and fruits, legumes, tofu and other healthful foods as described in the vegetarian food guide, they will likely accept and enjoy these kinds of foods all their lives.

Offer something from every food group at each meal whenever possible. This will help to ensure that a balance of nutrients is provided throughout the day.

Select a variety of foods from within each food group so that your children become familiar with many different tastes and textures.

Grain products

- Instead of always having the same type of sliced bread, buy a variety: rye bread, pumpernickel bread, pita bread, chapatis, bagels, multigrain rolls and oatmeal scones.

• Try different grains such as millet, quinoa, spelt, cracked wheat, barley, amaranth, Job's tears and kamut.

• Offer your children a variety of pasta including whole grain, vegetable, and pastas made from different grains.

Vegetables and fruits

• Plant some unusual vegetables, or go to an ethnic store to buy them. Involve your children, and make it a real adventure.

• Try artichokes, eggplant, zucchini, collards, kale, daikon or broccoflower (a cross between broccoli and cauliflower).

• Children often love to try unusual fruits such as mangos, Chinese pears and pomegranates.

Beans and bean alternates

• Experiment with all kinds of tofu, and use it in everything from appetizers to dessert.

• Try other soy products such as tempeh, miso and soyburgers.

• Get familiar with many different kinds of legumes. Try black beans, red lentils, pinto beans, adzuki beans, mung beans and lima beans.

Milk and milk alternates

• Introduce milk alternates such as tahini, collards, almond butter and tofu early on and make them a part of the normal fare.

• If dairy products are used, include cottage cheese and other cheeses, yogurt and puddings.

2. Preschoolers should receive 16–20 oz (500–625 mL) of cow's milk or a nutritionally comparable replacement per day. School age children should receive 16 oz of milk or milk alternates per day.

Milk continues to be a valuable source of calcium, vitamin D, riboflavin and other nutrients after the first two years of life. It is recommended that cow's milk or a suitable alternative be provided for children. One option during the early preschool years is breast milk. In many cultures, children are breast fed into the third and fourth years of life. Although this is not a common practice in our culture, it is deserving of consideration. Breast milk offers a wonderful balance of nutrients and immune protection for your child as long as it continues. Even though the amount of breast milk consumed during this time may be fairly small, it should be taken into account when determining quantities of other milks needed.

For lacto-ovo vegetarian children, whole, 2% or 1% cow's milk is suggested, depending on the needs of the individual child. If your child is overweight, a lower fat milk may be appropriate. For most children, 2% milk is suitable. Milk alternates, including dairy products other than fluid milk, can also be used, but realize that these do not provide vitamin D. The nutrient content of calcium-fortified non-dairy milk alternates is more variable, although their calcium content is similar to milk.

For vegan preschoolers two to five years of age, commercial soy-based infant formula is recommended as the most suitable alternative to breast milk or cow's milk. Many vegan parents are turned off by the fact that infant formula is a mixture of fat, sugar, protein and lots of added vitamins and minerals. You may take one look at the list of ingredients and say forget it. Remember that this formula is based on soybeans with the addition of nutrients needed to make it as similar as possible to breast milk. By using soy formula during the vulnerable preschool period, you will virtually eliminate your child's risk for nutritional deficiencies. For this reason, it is worth consideration. When formula is used, no nutritional supplements are needed. If infant formula is not used, a calcium-fortified soy milk is the next best alternative.

Calcium-fortified non-dairy milks are also the most suitable milk for the older vegan child. Some of these milks are also fortified with vitamin D, vitamin B_{12} and other nutrients, although the fortification levels may not be adequate to meet a child's daily requirements. Most fortified non-dairy milks are low in fat, thus it is important that the child receive sufficient fat to meet their needs for energy and essential fatty acids if these milks are used.

Fortified non-dairy milks are not readily available in Canada at the present time, thus it is difficult for vegan parents to find suitable milks for their children. (Let your local MP know that you would like to see these kinds of products.) If you are a vegan, and do not have access to fortified non-dairy milks, and do not wish to use formula, a homemade fortified milk can be prepared using regular soy milk (select a full-fat milk for preschool children), calcium, vitamin B_{12} and vitamin D. *This recipe is suitable only for children over two years of age, and should absolutely not be used as an infant formula.*

HOMEMADE FORTIFIED SOY MILK

Add the following supplements to 4 cups (1 litre) of soy milk:
- 2 tsp (10 mL) of calcium carbonate powder or finely crushed calcium carbonate tablets. (Note: Check the strength of the powder or tablets; aim for a total of 1200 mg of elemental calcium for the 4 cup recipe.)
- 0.6 mL of D-Visol (this provides 10 µg – 400 IU – of vitamin D).
- ½ of a 25 µg vitamin B_{12} tablet, crushed (this provides 3 µg vitamin B_{12} per cup). Stir well, or mix in a blender for 30 seconds. Store in the refrigerator. Shake the milk well before serving.

CAUTION: Measure the vitamin D very carefully. Excessive vitamin D can be toxic. Check your supplement, and do not exceed 400 IU in 4 cups (1 litre) of milk.
DO NOT USE AS AN INFANT FORMULA

Unfortified soy milks, rice milks and nut milks are not appropriate milk substitutes during the preschool period as they do not provide enough calcium or other nutrients to meet the needs of a preschooler. If these milks are used for children six years of age or older, be aware that they are not good sources of calcium or vitamin D. Be careful to ensure an adequate intake of these nutrients by selecting "milk alternates" such as tofu made with calcium, almond butter and greens, and by providing enough exposure to sunshine (see Chapter 4).

3. Provide protein-rich foods at every meal, and try to include foods from each food group whenever possible.
It is important for children to receive high-quality protein at each meal. When foods from each food group are served at mealtime, adequate protein is virtually guaranteed throughout the day.

As a lacto-ovo vegetarian, your child will receive high-quality protein from milk and eggs. When these foods are served regularly, there is seldom any difficulty meeting protein needs.

If your child is following a vegan diet, it is important that he or she receive high-quality protein throughout the day, especially during the preschool years. The following plant foods provide high-quality protein:

- soy infant formula
- soy milk
- tofu
- amaranth and quinoa
- legume and grain combinations (or other food combinations described in Chapter 3)

By using infant formula, or as a second choice, fortified full-fat soy milk (minimum of 6 g protein per cup/250 mL), from the ages of two to five years, high-quality protein will be assured. Some non-dairy milks such as rice milk, tofu beverage, potato milk and most nut milks are very low in protein, and thus should not be used until your child is at least six years old and is eating full portions of foods as described in the vegetarian food guide for children.

Quinoa, amaranth and soy products have amino acid profiles resembling that of cow's milk, thus they can be relied on as valuable protein sources. It is extremely important that foods from the beans and bean alternates group be given at least twice a day. Tofu should become a real staple. It is generally very well accepted by children, in addition to being digestible and versatile. Legumes and products such as vegetarian burgers can be eaten with grains or seeds (in butter form for children under four years of age) to provide a good balance of essential amino acids.

4. Provide foods that are concentrated in fat and energy and low in fibre as part of the regular daily fare.

The vegan diet can be very high in bulk, making it difficult for small children to meet their needs for energy. When this occurs protein is used as energy, rather than for building body tissues, and growth can be compromised. This condition is most often seen in vegan preschoolers on diets that limit fat and protein-rich foods, although it is a concern for all vegetarian children. Small children need to eat more concentrated foods throughout the day. The following suggestions will help to ensure that the vegetarian or vegan child gets enough fat and calories:

- *Provide three meals a day plus regular snacks in between.* For many children it is difficult to pack in enough food at a meal to tide them over until the next meal.
- *Don't restrict fat excessively.* Allow liberal use of tofu and other soy products, avocados and nuts, seeds and their butters. Do not feed whole nuts and seeds until four years of age because of the danger of choking. Include some fats and oils in baking and cooking. Dairy products (whole or 2% products) and eggs provide concentrated fat and energy for lacto-ovo vegetarian children.
- *Don't overdo raw foods.* Use some cooked vegetables and fruits and their juices. Make sure legumes have been well cooked.
- *Avoid the use of concentrated fiber foods in the form of wheat bran or fiber supplements.* Choose whole grain breads and cereals, but do not add extra fiber to foods. Whole grains can be cooked to increase their digestibility. Use refined grains such as pasta, crackers and couscous in lesser quantity, because of their inferior mineral content.
- *Offer plenty of low-fiber, protein-rich foods.* Great choices include tofu, nut butters and creams, soy cheese and yogurt, in addition to dairy products and eggs for the lacto-ovo vegetarian.
- *Make a special effort to provide children with appealing and wholesome snacks.* Offer nutritious squares, muffins, loaves and cookies, crackers and cheese (soy or dairy) or nut butters, yogurt (soy or dairy), and trail mixes for older children.

5. Provide your child with plant foods that are good sources of iron and zinc every day. Iron deficiency is the most widely recognized nutritional deficiency in North American children. Vegetarian and vegan children may receive insufficient iron if their diet is very high in fiber and other substances that inhibit the absorption of iron.

Lacto-ovo vegetarian children may not get enough iron if dairy products are used as the main source of protein. Dairy foods are tasty and convenient, and are often among children's favorite foods. Children who are given excessive quantities of milk to drink often have a poor appetite, as they get most of the calories that they need from the milk alone. When dairy products are the central focus, it can be difficult to make room for iron-rich legumes and greens. Limit fluid milk to not more than 20 oz (625 mL) ounces per day to help avoid this problem.

To increase the iron in your child's diet, include iron-rich foods such as tofu, dried prunes, legumes or dark greens, and a source of vitamin C with each meal. Infant cereal is an excellent source of iron. It can be added to other hot cereals, pancakes and baked goods. Remember to use cast-iron cookware when possible.

Although we seldom hear of problems relating to zinc deficiency, it is one of the nutrients that children have the most trouble getting enough of. Insufficient zinc in a child's diet can cause a lack of appetite, delays in development, and slow wound healing.

To provide your child with sufficient zinc, serve legumes, nut butters, wheat germ, miso and tofu on a regular basis. Also, be sure to use whole grains, as they contain far more zinc than their refined counterparts. Preschoolers who are drinking 20 oz (625 mL) of formula each day are getting over half the zinc that they need from the formula alone.

6. Include four or more servings of vegetables and fruits in the diet each day.
The value of vegetables is well known to one and all, but somehow most people don't manage to eat their daily quota. This situation might be remedied if we could interest our children in these fabulous foods during their formative years. Vegetables and fruits provide vitamins A and C, folic acid and a number of other important vitamins and minerals. A good rule of thumb is to include at least one serving of vegetables or fruits with every meal. Don't forget to use them as snacks as well!

• *Provide at least one vitamin C-rich fruit every day.* Oranges, grapefruits and strawberries are great choices. Juices that are naturally rich in vitamin C, such as orange or grapefruit juice, or those enriched with vitamin C such as many apple or grape juices, can also be used. Be careful not to overdo the juices; too much juice is a significant cause of chronic diarrhea in small children. Do not use fruit "drinks" or "punches" in place of juice, even if they have vitamin C added. The vitamin C is all they have: the rest is sugar, flavors and colors.

• *Get children accustomed to dark greens early on.* Broccoli is often a favorite. Use a variety of dark greens in salads, stir-fries, casseroles and spaghetti sauces.

• *Encourage an interest in vegetables and fruits by growing some in your own garden or even on your balcony.* If that isn't possible, bring children on an excursion to a farm and let them see how these foods grow.

• *Try offering dried fruits for a change.* Dried fruits are convenient, portable and nutritious. Try something different like dried peaches or pears. Unfortunately they aren't so great for the teeth, so be sure children brush after eating them.

• *Preserve the nutritional value of vegetables by cooking them in a minimum of water or steaming them.* Don't wait until they turn into a dull mush before serving them.

• *Make these healthy foods fun.* Children love kabobs, dips and fancy shapes or patterns. Fruits and vegetables are very colorful and make wonderful pictures on a plate (faces are a favorite).

7. Include a source of omega-3 fatty acids in the diet.
Omega-3 fatty acids are very important to normal growth and development and should be included in your child's diet each day.

Omega-3 Fatty Acids — Getting Enough

Food Sources	2–5-year-olds	6–10-year-olds
flax seed oil	⅓ tsp (1.5 mL)	½ tsp (2 mL)
canola and soybean oil	2 tsp (10 mL)	1 tbsp (15 mL)
walnuts and pumpkin seeds	2 tbsp (25 mL)	3 tbsp (50 mL)

• Nuts and seeds should only be used in butter form for children 4 years and under.

• Add omega-3 fatty acid-rich oil to sandwich fillings, mashed potatoes or salad dressings.

8. Include a reliable source of vitamin B_{12} in the diet every day.
Vitamin B_{12} is not supplied by plant foods to any significant degree. Thus, a special effort must be made to insure that vegetarian and particularly vegan children receive reliable sources of this nutrient.

Lacto-ovo vegetarian children can obtain enough vitamin B_{12} from one to one and a half glasses of milk or an egg and a glass of milk.

For vegan children, fortified foods or supplements must be used to ensure that enough vitamin B_{12} is available. The fortification of foods with vitamin B_{12} varies dramatically among different countries, depending on regulations (see Chapter 5). Fortified products are more widely available in the United States than in Canada. Significant dietary sources include Red Star brand T-6635+ nutritional yeast, some fortified cereals, meat analogues and non-dairy milks. Check the labels to see that at least 1 µg of vitamin B_{12} is provided each day (for Red Star yeast flakes that amounts to about 1 tsp/5 mL).

The Question of Supplements

Lacto-ovo vegetarian children can be well nourished without the use of supplements, providing that a balance of foods as described in the vegetarian food guide for two- to ten-year-olds is followed.

For vegan children, needs for all nutrients can be met if fortified foods are used. Otherwise, a supplement of vitamin B_{12} is necessary. A regular children's multi-vitamin/mineral supplement generally contains enough vitamin B_{12} – read the label. Vegan children will also need a vitamin D supplement if there is limited exposure to warm sunlight. If insufficient servings from the milk and milk alternates group are consumed, then a supplement of approximately 500 mg elemental calcium is recommended.

If a supplement is used, it is best to select one which contains a variety of vitamins and minerals including vitamin B_{12}, vitamin D, zinc and iron in amounts which approximate the RDA's or RNI's* (see Appendix 2). Many children's supplements contain no minerals except iron. Read the label. Avoid single nutrient supplements other than calcium, unless medically indicated.

Getting Enough to Grow On: A Guide for 2- to 10-year-olds

Children need smaller servings of food, more often. Appetite can fluctuate considerably in this age group, and there are going to be times when your child will eat more or less than what is suggested in the guide. Child-size servings are recommended for 2- to 5-year-olds in all groups but the milk and milk alternates group. These servings are approximately half of the portion recommended for the older child or adult. For additional examples of foods in each of the food groups, see the vegetarian food guide.

Milk and Milk Alternates: 4–6 servings per day
2–5 years: Give preschoolers 16–20 oz (500-625 mL) of cow's milk, soy formula or fortified soy milk per day. Milk and milk alternates servings should mainly come from these beverages.
6–10 years: Adult-Size Servings
one serving =
½ cup (125 mL) cow's milk, infant formula or fortified non-dairy milk
1 oz (25 g) dairy cheese or ½ cup of yogurt
¼ cup (50 mL) or 2 oz (60 g) tofu (made with calcium)
1 cup (250 mL) calcium-rich green vegetables (see food guide on page 141 for specifics)
3 tbsp (50 mL) almond butter, 1½ oz (40 g) almonds, or 2 tbsp (25 mL) tahini

---

* RDA is the American designation: Recommended Daily Allowance. RNI is the Canadian designation: Recommended Nutrient Intake

Grain Products: 5–12 servings per day

2–5 years: Child-Size Servings:

one serving =

½ slice of bread

¼ cup (50 mL) cooked grain

¼ cup (50 mL) hot cereal

⅓ cup (75 mL) cold cereal

6–10 years: Adult-Size Servings

one serving =

1 slice of bread

½ cup (125 mL) cooked grain

½ cup (125 mL) hot cereal

¾ cup (175 mL) cold cereal

Vegetables and Fruits: 5–10 servings per day (at least 2 vegetable servings)

2–5 years: Child-Size Servings

one serving =

¼ cup (50 mL) vegetables or fruits

½ whole fruit or 1 small fruit

¼ cup (50 mL) fruit or vegetable juice

6–10 years: Adult-Size Servings

one serving =

½ cup (125 mL) vegetables or fruits

1 whole fruit or 2 small fruits

½ cup (125 mL) fruit or vegetable juice

Beans and Bean Alternates: 2–3 servings per day

2–5 years: Child-Size Servings

one serving =

¼ cup (50 mL) legumes

¼ cup (50 mL) or 2 oz (60 g) tofu

1½ tbsp (25 mL) nut/seed butter

1 small egg

6–10 years: Adult-Size Servings

one serving =

½ cup (125 mL) legumes

½ cup (125 mL) or 4 oz (120 g) tofu

3 tbsp (50 mL) nut/seed butter

1 large egg

Include a source of omega-3 fatty acids in the diet.

ADOLESCENTS: AGES 11 TO 17

Many teens today are making the decision to cut meat out of their menu. Their motivation often comes from concerns about the environment or animal rights, rather than from a desire to improve the nutritional quality of their diet. This doesn't mean that food is not of prime importance. It just means that the criteria for food selection may be a little different than it is for the average health-conscious vegetarian adult. The two main criteria for food selection by teens generally are:

1) *How fast can it be ready?*

2) *Does it taste good?*

The most acceptable answers to these questions are that *it is ready* and *it tastes great.* In other words we're talking instant, delicious food. Our society is fairly well set up for instant and delicious, but not for vegetarian.

Many teens who grew up eating the standard North American fare simply stop eating meat when they become vegetarian. Instead of a hamburger and fries for lunch, they opt for a double order of fries. When chicken, potatoes and corn arrive on the dinner table, they eat only the potatoes and corn. There are a few hitches to this kind of approach. First, parents tend to be less than supportive because they see their teenager eating a very poor diet. Second, this poor diet can start to take its toll on the teen, causing him or her to feel run down.

The solution that will usually satisfy parents and teens alike is to venture into the world of nutritional alternatives to meat. The possibilities are endless. Parents generally become a little less resistant to the whole idea if they know that their teenager is getting a well balanced diet. In many cases, parents even begin to enjoy vegetarian meals, and some even end up becoming vegetarian themselves. The result could well be a healthier family.

Of course, there are also teens who have been raised on a vegetarian diet. This group generally does very well. Some studies show not only that these vegetarian teens are well nourished but also that they tend to eat less junk and fat and more fiber than meat -eating teens. A large study by John Sabate looking at Seventh-day Adventist teens showed that these vegetarians actually outgrew their omnivorous peers by an average of 1 in. (3 cm).

The nutritional needs of a vegetarian teen are no different than the needs of any other teen. Many physical changes take place, and the demands for nutrients are high. There are many things that a parent can do to help a vegetarian teen be well nourished:

• *Keep a variety of super fast and wholesome foods handy.* Stock up on fresh fruits, trail mixes, nutritious baked goods, yogurt, cottage cheese, soy cheese and whole grain breads and cereals.

• *Encourage teens to contribute to meals by helping with meal planning and preparation.* Teens can be expected to prepare whole meals or make a salad or even a nutritious dessert. This will give them a good head start for managing on their own. The recipes provided in this book are a great place to start.

• *Offer vegetarian versions of popular dinner favorites.* Many traditional items such as pizza, burgers, burritos, lasagna, chili and spaghetti can easily be made meatless.

• *Remember that your teenager is responsible for his or her own food choices.*

• *Encourage involvement in groups and activities that will increase their knowledge of vegetarianism and the vegetarian way of eating.* The vegetarian newsletter for teens, "How on Earth," is a good starting place. For subscriptions write to: How on Earth, c/o VE·Net, PO Box 3347, West Chester, PA 19381.

The guidelines that follow provide more practical tips on nutrition for teens. Don't get too concerned if everything doesn't happen precisely according to plan. Teens are very resilient and seem to be able to get through these years even under less than ideal conditions.

Nutrition Guidelines for Vegetarian and Vegan Adolescents

1. Eat a variety of foods as outlined in the vegetarian food guide.
The best way to ensure all the necessary nutrients are provided is to include many different foods from each of the food groups outlined in the vegetarian food guide. (Note that some of the amounts are different for teens than they are for adults.)

A good rule of thumb is to select something from every food group at each meal. Choose snack foods from the food guide as well, and try to vary meals from day to day, especially breakfast and lunch.

2. Include six to eight servings of milk and milk alternates every day.
The density of bones and defense against osteoporosis in later life depends, at least in part, on getting enough calcium and vitamin D during the teen years, when calcium needs are greatest.

Lacto-ovo vegetarians who use the recommended amounts of dairy products have little difficulty getting enough calcium. Studies comparing the hardness of bones in vegetarians and omnivores have shown that vegetarians generally have stronger bones. There are a number of factors that could explain these differences, but whatever the reasons, it seems as though calcium is not a problem for this group. Vitamin D needs can be easily met by fortified cow's milk, margarine and sunshine.

For vegans, getting enough calcium can be a little trickier. Calcium-fortified non-dairy milks greatly simplify matters, and are therefore highly recommended, but they are not readily available in Canada. The recipe for homemade fortified soy milk on page 164 provides a suitable alternative.

Unfortified non-dairy milks vary considerably in their calcium content, with many varieties having less than 20 mg per cup. Thus they cannot be depended upon as calcium sources. Also if an unfortified milk is used, sunlight or a supplement will have to be relied on for vitamin D (see Chapter 4).

There are a number of ways that a vegan adolescent could boost his or her calcium intake without using dairy products or fortified milks:

• *Use more tofu.* Tofu is a great food for teens: it's convenient and loaded with nutrients. Be sure to buy the type that is made with calcium. Tofu can be used for a quick breakfast scramble, an eggless "egg" salad sandwich or a tofuburger for supper. Throw pieces into soups, stews, spaghetti sauces and stir-fries.

• *Try tahini (sesame seed butter).* It's great on toast, in hummus, in soups or in baking.

• *Snack on almonds.* Almonds are also great for throwing into a stir-fry or on a salad. Use almond butter instead of peanut butter on sandwiches.

• *Use legumes more often.* Regular brown beans and pinto beans, used in Mexican cooking, are both surprisingly good sources of calcium.

• *Go for the green!* Broccoli and many dark green leafy vegetables can add lots of calcium to a meal.

• *Give blackstrap molasses a try.* Blackstrap molasses is the only sugar that is concentrated in minerals. It can be used on toast or bread as a spread (great with tahini or another nut or seed butter) or in baking for cookies, loaves and muffins.

3. Use whole grain breads and cereals most of the time.

Breads and cereals form the foundation of our diets, so they should be chosen with care. Refined grains pale by comparison to their whole grain counterparts, especially when you consider their mineral content. Teens who have been raised eating white bread, white rice and white spaghetti may find it tough making the switch. Here are a few pointers:

• *Don't give up on whole grain breads without giving them a fair try.* Buy something a little different like multigrain bagels, Russian rye or sunflower seed bread. Make a sandwich using a slice of whole grain bread and a slice of white bread.

• *Make sure bread is fresh when it's purchased.* If you buy your bread from a bakery, you just may find the whole grains a little more appealing. To keep bread fresh, freeze it right away, and take out only what you'll need for a day at a time.

• *If whole grain breads are still rejected, offer whole grain anything!* Other whole grain products like whole wheat and vegetable pastas, wild rice, cornmeal muffins or hot and cold whole grain cereals may be well accepted.

• *Be adventurous.* Cook something different like quinoa, tabbouleh salad or barley pudding. You may be pleasantly surprised by the response.

• *Use more whole grain flour in baking.* Use whole grain flour in cookies, muffins or other goodies (or you can use half white and half whole wheat) for a more nutritious treat.

• *Try healthy convenience foods.* There are all kinds of whole grain convenience foods available in health food stores and supermarkets. Many of these products are quite appealing to teens.

4. Include vegetables and/or fruits with every meal, and select them often for snacks as well.

Don't make French fries the daily vegetable. The more colorful vegetables and fruits are delicious and nutritious. One or more servings of vegetables or fruit should accompany every meal. Encouraging the consumption of fruits and vegetables is easier than you might think:

• *Keep a variety of fresh fruits on hand*. It's great to keep a big bowl out, ripe for the picking.

• *Before dinner, put out a plate of raw vegetables and dip for everyone to munch on*. It's surprising how fast these snacks can disappear when friends are over.

• *Make a couple of different vegetables at meals*. Include at least one that you know will be liked.

• *Get teens involved in growing vegetables*. It's great fun to experiment with growing foods organically. Teens can prepare all kinds of salads, stir-fries and other dishes with what they reap from the garden. Gardens also make excellent snacking grounds.

• *Keep a jug of pure fruit juice in a tightly covered container in the fridge at all times*.

• *Load up spaghetti sauces, soups and casseroles with all kinds of vegetables*.

• *Stir-fry vegetables often*. The crispy texture of a stir-fry is often more appealing than the more well cooked traditional vegetables.

• *Use fruits regularly for dessert*. Fruit salads, fruit kabobs and fresh fruit platters are all very popular options.

• *Keep plenty of dried fruits on hand as instant, portable snacks (but remember, they're not great for your teeth, so brush after eating)*.

5. Include two to three servings from the beans and bean alternates group every day. When meat goes, it needs to be replaced by alternatives that provide roughly equal nutritional value. The best replacements are legumes and foods derived from legumes. Using these foods daily is one of the bigger challenges in putting together a healthy eating plan for teens.

The main nutrients that are of concern when we eliminate meat are protein, iron and zinc. If the vegetarian food guide is followed, there is no need to worry about protein complementation. This will happen naturally over the course of the day.

Iron can be a problem for teens, especially for females who lose iron each month with menstruation. Those who are watching calories, are very active in sports or have replaced the meat in their diet mainly with cheese and eggs may also have a tough time getting enough iron. A multi-vitamin/mineral supplement with iron may be appropriate for those who have difficulty meeting their needs.

Beans and bean alternates don't have to be boring or tasteless. Here are a few tips for turning teens on to beans (and bean alternates):

• *Replace the meat with beans in favorite stew, casserole or soup recipes*. Red lentils work especially well where hamburger was used: in spaghetti sauces, sloppy Joes, cabbage rolls and tamale pies. Try a meatless version of old-fashioned beef stew with pinto, romano, navy, garbanzo or other beans.

• *Give tofu a fair chance.* Remember that tofu picks up the flavor of whatever seasonings or sauces that you use, so try it with family favorites like barbecue or sweet and sour sauce. Tofu is one of the most versatile foods imaginable. It can be a part of sandwiches, snacks, fancy main dishes and beautiful desserts.

• *Rely on old standbys.* Serve baked beans, chili, bean tortillas and vegetarian pizza more often. (Top the pizza with vegetarian sausages or pepperoni to get a meaty flavor.) These can be helpful foods for easing the transition.

• *Check out the fantastic selection of ready-made meatless options.* Vegetarian patties, sausages, loaves and luncheon slices are available in supermarkets, health food stores, ethnic stores and food co-ops. Some of these products are very meat-like. Many are delicious, and all are fast and easy to prepare.

• *Stir-fry meals more often.* Use almonds, cashews or other nuts, tofu, tempeh or firm beans such as garbanzos in place of the meat.

• *Try making loaves or patties from scratch.* These can be frozen for later use, and are much cheaper than the store-bought versions. They are also surprisingly easy to make.

• *Use eggs for a quick and tasty meal.* They can be cooked in a jiffy or used in quiches or frittatas with vegetables.

• *Use nuts, seeds and their butters.* Nuts are great for more than just snacking. Spread nut butter on morning toast, pack a tahini-carrot sandwich for lunch, and make some cashew burgers for supper.

6. Include a source of vitamin B_{12} in the diet every day.
Vitamin B_{12} is a concern for teens who are consuming only plant foods or just small quantities of dairy products and eggs. In such cases, the use of vitamin B_{12}-fortified foods (see Chapter 5 for sources) or a vitamin B_{12} supplement is necessary.

For lacto-ovo vegetarian teens, 2 cups (500 mL) of milk or an egg and a cup (250 mL) of milk each day will provide enough vitamin B_{12} to meet needs.

7. Don't skip meals.
Teenagers are famous for skipping meals. Breakfast and lunch are the meals most commonly missed. This can lead to bouts of hunger that are too often filled with nutritional wash-outs like potato chips and chocolate bars.

The answer lies in nourishing "fast" foods. There are endless quick and easy ideas for breakfast and lunch, many of which can be packed and carried along (see Chapter 12).

8. Make snacks count.

Snacks are an important part of life for most teenagers. They can make or break an otherwise marginal diet. Any food that fits into the food guide is a good snack choice. If there is a sweet tooth to contend with, try some of the treats in the recipe section. This doesn't mean extras like chocolate bars should be forever forgotten, but they should be only occasional treats.

9. Maintain a healthy weight by eating a balanced diet and exercising regularly.

Focus on overall health instead of a slim figure. If teens eat a well-balanced diet and exercise regularly, they are probably at a healthy weight.

For overweight teens who are eating a well-balanced diet, activity level is usually the key. Try for at least 30 minutes of aerobic exercise three or four times a week. Encourage walking or biking whenever possible (it's better for the environment than driving or taking a bus). Make an effort to cut back on fatty foods, especially fried foods and sweet desserts.

For those who are underweight, encourage the consumption of regular meals and snacks. Trail mixes, milkshakes, homemade muffins and other baked goods make great choices.

The Supplement Question

A teenager's need for nutritional supplements depends entirely on eating habits and individual needs. Supplements are not necessary if you are following the food guide, although there are times when they do come in handy. If supplements are needed, choose a regular (rather than high-potency or stress type) adult multi-vitamin/mineral supplement containing recommended levels of a wide range of nutrients including iron, zinc and magnesium (see Appendix 2). Calcium, at recommended levels of intake, is not generally included in such a supplement, because it would make the pills too large. If you have a difficult time getting the recommended number of servings from the milk and milk alternates group, a calcium supplement is also recommended. (Supplements should not provide more than 1200 mg of elemental calcium per day.) Otherwise, avoid single nutrient supplements unless medically indicated.

VEGETARIAN DIPLOMACY

ou did it! You finally decided to take the plunge and give up meat forever. The compassion you feel for animals, your fellow man and the environment will be felt by those for miles around you. People will look at you and say, "There goes a person who really respects life. What a hero!" Your parents will beam with pride, and your friends will call on you constantly, just so they might be seen in your presence.

A likely story? Not on planet earth. Let's face it, when you become a vegetarian, it isn't all so easy. No longer will you partake in the ritual devouring of the "bird" at Christmas. No longer will Aunt Mary treat you to your formerly favorite meal of pot roast with those golden brown potatoes cooked inside the pot. You'll feel a little awkward at the family barbecues when your dad asks you for the fourth time, "Are you sure you don't want just a little piece of this nice, juicy Porterhouse? I did it medium rare, just the way you like it." You might expect that this kind of sacrifice made in the name of compassion and global ecology would have people cheering, but instead it makes people uncomfortable.

This discomfort may not be all bad; after all, it could get people thinking about some of the issues surrounding their food choices: animal agriculture, health and the environment. But then, when it comes to family and friends, it might be a little easier if the source of their discomfort was something or someone other than you. You'd probably rather be laughing with them, supporting and encouraging them, rather than causing them discomfort.

Your vegetarianism could make your family feel as though you are turning your back on their values and culture. Food has always been central to your communication, your traditions and your celebrations. You have created a separation in the one area that your parents thought would always bind you together. Other people feel you are judging their behavior. They may be uncomfortable simply because you are different, like someone who has been indoctrinated into a cult. New acquaintances seem reluctant to get too close to you; they may think they'll offend you by their choices. If they were to become good friends with you, they may have to ask you to dinner. Entertaining a vegetarian can seem like the challenge of the decade for a person whose one and only vegetarian dinner option has been macaroni and cheese.

Of course there are those people who don't shy away when they hear the news that you are a vegetarian. They tell it like they see it. One of the favorite responses is, "It doesn't bother me a bit, but I like my meat." Then they go on to tell you how *they* care about people. They remind you of all of those poor children who are starving to death in developing countries, and try to make you feel guilty for caring about some cow. You think to yourself that perhaps a little lesson in the global food situation would be appropriate, but instead, you just say how you care about people too.

Your vegetarian diet can be a source of anxiety and frustration. You might even go so far as to say that it puts a real damper on social interaction in the world of the omnivore. Thankfully, it doesn't have to be that way.

Instead of being a source of tension for you and those around you, your vegetarian food choices can be a tool by which you share a whole new world of valuable experiences with other people. Much depends on your attitude, sense of humor and social diplomacy.

This chapter guides you through a variety of social experiences that are common to vegetarians. The first part considers the questions with which vegetarians are often faced, and offers some answers. These are meant to help boost your level of comfort and confidence in the event that such a question should come your way. The second part invites you to put yourself in a few difficult social situations. How do you think you would react? Consider the selection of responses offered in the text. The probable outcomes are also discussed. As you think about these situations and their outcomes, you will be preparing yourself to handle such situations in an effective and positive manner.

THE QUESTIONS

One of the interesting aspects of becoming a vegetarian is hearing the questions of all those people who are just a little mystified by your choice. Your answer to each question will depend, at least in part, on the situation and how the question is asked. There are many people who have a real interest in or curiosity about your experience. You might wish that you were given a couple of hours to prepare a meaningful response. Some people may be considering cutting back on, or even giving up, meat themselves, but just aren't so sure of how to go about it. This could be a real opportunity to share a few practical pointers, or some deeper insights into the real connections between our food choices and our daily lives. Still other people may just be kidding around, and in that case it would be fun to come back with an appropriately lighthearted response.

The questions most commonly posed to vegetarians are "*What do you eat?*" and "*Why are you a vegetarian?*"

Question No. 1: *What do you eat?*

"What do you eat?" is a polite way of asking the particulars about your diet. The real questions that loom in the back of the mind of the person who is asking generally relate to the taste, variety and healthfulness of the vegetarian diet, or the time needed to prepare the food. Although we've all known people who have no problem asking whatever is on their mind, many people are more subtle. When someone asks you the question "What do you eat?" you might assume that they are interested in more than what was on your dinner plate last night. The real questions could well look more like this:

QUESTIONS RELATING TO TASTE AND VARIETY

Isn't vegetarian food gross, not to mention boring?
Do you eat beans every day? Don't you get a lot of gas?
Do you really like that kind of food?
Don't you miss meat?
Do you eat fish?

For some people, the notion that a meal consists of meat, potatoes and vegetables is what limits their imagination. When the meat goes, what are you left with? A potato and a few mushy vegetables. Why would anyone voluntarily choose to eat that way? Those that have some inkling that beans or tofu could act as suitable meat replacements picture a hunk of raw tofu or pile of beans in place of that nice crispy piece of chicken.

QUESTIONS RELATING TO HEALTH AND SAFETY

Won't you get malnourished, and lose your hair?
How are you supposed to get enough protein?
Aren't you going to become anemic?
If you don't drink milk, how do you expect to get any calcium?
Do you feed your kids that way too? Do you think it's safe?

Many people wonder how one can possibly be well nourished when meat and, heaven forbid, dairy products are removed from the diet. There's also a feeling that forcing a child to partake in this sort of deprivation is akin to child abuse.

QUESTIONS RELATING TO FOOD PREPARATION

Do you spend hours slaving over a hot stove every day?
Do you grind your own wheat and bake your own bread?
Do you grow all your own vegetables, and preserve them for the winter?

Many people are under the impression that vegetarians spend their entire lives in their garden growing organic food, and in their kitchen baking bread and cooking beans.

The Answers

When someone asks *"What do you eat?"* try to get some idea of what the person really wants to know. You might even ask them if they are curious about the taste, variety or nutrition of vegetarian meals, or the time it takes to prepare them. Share your personal adventures about the transition away from meat towards that world of plants. Was it an overnight decision or a gradual change? How have you mastered the art of vegetarian cooking? What special things have helped you along the way? Has it affected your health?

Here is a sample of the kinds of responses you might make:

"I eat almost everything that you do, except instead of meat, I use tofu, beans and nuts as my main sources of protein. With these, I make vegetarian roasts with gravy, patties, casseroles and some great ethnic foods such as lasagna, chili, bean burritos and African stew. For fast and easy meals, I make tofu stir-fry, pasta dishes, tacos or burgers using commercial frozen vegetarian patties. Being vegetarian has made me a lot more adventurous with food. The variety of foods I eat now is even greater than it was when I ate meat."

Or a more in-depth version:

"You'd be surprised at the incredible variety of foods available to vegetarians. When I first started to cut back on meat, I tried tofu and different kinds of beans. I wasn't overly impressed because I really didn't know how to cook them, so I decided to take a vegetarian cooking class. I learned how to make things that I had never even heard of. We made loaves and patties from grains, tofu, beans and nuts, and great Indian and Middle Eastern food. I've never looked back. I bought some vegetarian cookbooks and tried piles of recipes. Now I feel like a pro, and I really love the food. It doesn't have to be overly time consuming either. I have at least a dozen different meals that I can put together in less than a half hour (some in less than 15 minutes). The neat thing is that my tastes have totally changed. I don't like overly sweet or fatty foods anymore. It's affected the way I feel too. I have more energy and better endurance than I've ever had."

There are the odd occasions when someone will pop the question in a light-hearted manner. You wish that you had the perfect crazy response, instead of standing there saying that you eat some good food too. How about saying something like this:

> "I eat tofu of course. Scrambled tofu for breakfast, tofu sandwiches for lunch, stir-fried tofu or tofuburgers for supper and tofu cheesecake for dessert. Thank goodness there's tofu for us vegetarians."

Question No. 2: Why are you a vegetarian?

People are often curious about what could have possibly motivated you to give up meat. Was it something "strange" like religion or animal rights, or was it just an interest in improving your health or the health of the environment? When someone asks you why you are a vegetarian, they are very likely curious about your innermost reasons for making this choice. Their real questions could look more like this:

QUESTIONS RELATING TO RELIGION

Have you changed your religion?
Have you joined some sort of weird cult?
Are you into that New Age movement?

Some people associate vegetarianism with religious extremism. They figure that if you are a vegetarian, you are probably into something fairly radical.

QUESTIONS RELATING TO ANIMAL RIGHTS

You're not one of those animal rights activists, are you?
What do you suppose would happen to the farmers if we all stopped eating meat?
You do eat chicken and fish, don't you? After all, they aren't really animals.
Why on earth would you give up dairy products? They don't actually kill the cow.

People are very curious about those that choose to stop eating meat out of concern for animals. They may feel just a little guilty themselves, or they may want to prove to themselves that it's really no big deal.

QUESTIONS RELATING TO THE ENVIRONMENT

Do you seriously think that there is a connection between meat eating and the state of the environment?

Isn't all that manure from the animals good for the soil?

Are you one of those vegetarian flower children who thinks they can save the world?

Many people have heard the odd mention of the connection with the environment, human hunger and our food choices. They may be wondering if there really is a connection or if it's just a minor point.

QUESTIONS RELATING TO HEALTH

Do you really think that vegetarians are healthier than meat eaters? The vegetarians I know don't look so hot.

Are you some sort of health food freak?

Do you think that meat is full of hormones?

Isn't vegetarianism just another fad diet?

Vegetarians have long been thought of as health food faddists. Today more and more people are hearing that this kind of diet can not only be healthful but can probably protect against disease. These people may wonder if you've gone off the deep end and are a purist, or if you really know something that they don't.

The Answers

When someone asks "Why are you a vegetarian?" they may simply be interested in your motivation, or they may want to rule out some of the stranger possibilities. As you answer, consider how you might be able to share some of the deep concerns you have about the issues that convinced you to give up meat, and possibly dairy foods as well.

"I just don't feel comfortable with the thought of eating animals."

"I feel better eating a vegetarian diet."

"I think it is one way that I can make a small contribution to the environment."

Or a more in-depth version:

"The most important reason for me is that I'm not that comfortable with the way that food animals are raised these days.

"The old Farmer Jones image of animals wandering contentedly through the fields rarely holds true today. Instead, many animals suffer from birth to death in completely unnatural surroundings. The whole scene bothers me so much that I decided to become a vegetarian.

"After taking the initial step, I started to experience some improvements in my health. My digestive problems improved a lot when I stopped eating meat and cut back on dairy products, and I felt much more energetic. I also started to read about the connections between our food choices, the environment and ecology. I was amazed to find out how much environmental devastation has occurred in order to satisfy our desire for meat. Did you know that one North American eats the same amount of meat in a year as ten average Asian families? Cows actually outweigh people on this planet. In the United States food animals consume about 70 percent of the grain that is produced.

"The more I learn, the more confident I am that my decision to become vegetarian was one of the best that I have ever made. I'd love to share a couple of books with you, if you'd like more information."

You might try a more light-hearted tone:

"I figured if it's good enough for Albert Einstein it's good enough for me!"

"I prefer not to eat anything that could bite back."

"I thought that I'd like to try to live forever."

SITUATIONS

The world may never be quite the same after you pledge your allegiance to the land of bean sprouts. People look at you a little differently. They eye your sandwich wondering what really lies between those two pieces of bread. They avoid any eye contact with you at the company barbecue for fear of having to sit beside you with their big Italian sausages. Those who have known you for years are sure that your wife has forced you into the whole thing, and that you would inhale some "real" food if only you could be certain that she wouldn't find out.

The situations you face as a vegetarian are not always easy. In some cases, you feel quite unprepared. After it's all over, you may dream up a hundred ways that you could have better handled the situation. We invite you to put yourself in the place of many different people who have gone through similar experiences.

1. WIFE AND MOTHER TURNS VEGETARIAN
WITHOUT FAMILY SUPPORT

You're the only vegetarian in the house. Your husband and two young teenagers are just not into it. You switched over to a vegetarian diet after going to a lecture with a friend who has been sharing information about vegetarianism for some time. Your husband is not thrilled. The one thing that he made absolutely clear is that he has no intention of giving up meat or eating a bunch of weird food. He likes his meat and fully intends on continuing to eat it. The kids are on Dad's side. You feel awful buying and cooking meat, but you do it anyway. Dinner for you often consists of potatoes and vegetables with a spoonful of cottage cheese. A couple of times a week, you prepare a vegetarian meal, which seems to go over all right. Lately you began to resent having to cook meat, and it has finally got to the point where you feel sick about it. You should:

> a) Be thankful that your family will eat the two vegetarian meals a week without much of a fuss, and continue to provide them with the foods they want.

> b) Tell your family that you cannot stand having meat in your house, and if they want it, they'll have to go out to a restaurant.

> c) Tell your family that you are not comfortable cooking meat anymore, and ask them to take over that task.

PROBABLE OUTCOME

a) Passive, thankful response:

This is certainly the path of least resistance as far as your family is concerned, but it doesn't seem like such a great choice for you. If this is the route you end up with, plan to progress by increasing the vegetarian meals to four or five times per week. Your family will be far less likely to notice that the meal is meatless if it is fashioned after traditional favorites such as spaghetti and lasagna. There are plenty of meals which can easily go either way. For example, when making pizza, do one with meat and one without. Burgers, hot dogs, tacos and stir-fries can all be easily made to please both the vegetarian and the meat eater.

b) No meat in my house:

This could be a disaster. Asking something like this of your family would be a little like your husband forbidding you to have tofu around because the mere look of it makes him feel sick. Try to reach some sort of a compromise.

c) Express discomfort; ask for help:

This is probably your best option. Often women are expected to make the ultimate sacrifices for their families and are taught to forget about their own needs. You are having a difficult time dealing with buying and cooking meat, so discuss your feelings with your family and solicit suggestions from them. If the solutions come directly from them everyone will be happier with the agreements reached. Indeed, you may be able to accomplish your goal without having to get angry or upset at all.

2. INVITED TO ANOTHER PERSON'S HOME FOR DINNER

You and your husband have been vegetarians for three years. When you began your new job at the dental office the staff was great. Within a couple of weeks, another dentist invited you and your husband over for dinner. Although you often eat lunch at work together, you usually bring peanut butter sandwiches and a salad, or a cheese and lettuce sandwich (sometimes even with phony baloney). As a result, your new friend has no idea that you are vegetarians.

You're not too sure how to handle the dinner invitation. You decide to:

a) Turn the invitation down, making up a good excuse.

b) Accept the invitation, not mention that you and your husband are vegetarians, and bring a vegetarian casserole with you.

c) Accept the invitation, not mention that you and your husband are vegetarians, and just show up for dinner.

d) Tell your new friend that you'd love to come to dinner, but that you'd like her to know that you are vegetarians. Offer to bring a part of the meal (a main dish would be great).

PROBABLE OUTCOMES

a) Turn invitation down:
This is an easy out, but accomplishes little. As soon as you offer the excuse, another, more convenient date will likely be suggested.

b) Accept invitation; bring casserole:
Bad move. You host will likely be offended that you have not told her of your dietary preferences. She would not have bothered to spend eighty dollars on lobster and filet had she known that you were vegetarians.

c) Accept invitation and show up:
If you are at all attached to your vegetarian diet, this answer is probably a major mistake. You may arrive to find chicken poached in a white wine sauce with baked potatoes and vegetables. You could get away with eating just the vegetables. But, then again, the potatoes could have been cooked with bacon bits and the vegetables with baby shrimps. The point is that there is no guarantee

that any of the dishes served will be free of meat, fish or poultry. If you suddenly announce that you are vegetarians, your host will likely feel very uncomfortable. Remember that the entire feast has been prepared in your honor. The main objective is to please you, the special guests. If a meat-centered meal has been prepared, the host has automatically failed at pleasing her guests.

People tend to put on their best spread for company, and in our society that usually includes meat. The hosts may even be moving towards a vegetarian diet, but because they are having special guests over, they opt for meat, because that's what's generally expected. If you do decide to go without telling your hosts that you are vegetarians, then you probably should be prepared to eat whatever is served.

d) Say that you are vegetarians:
This is the best option. Get your courage up, and say something right away. Tell her that you and your husband are vegetarians. Let her know that you'd be happy to do a shared meal, and even make the main dish. You might suggest something like a Mexican meal where both meat and bean enchiladas or tortillas could be prepared.

3. RESTAURANT WITHOUT
VEGETARIAN OPTIONS ON THE MENU

The whole office is going for lunch. As you are a fairly new addition to the team, no one is aware that you are a vegetarian. One of the guys says, "Let's not eat at that Chinese place again, let's get some real food," so you end up at the local steak house. You feel a kind of uneasiness coming on as you look at the menu – even the Caesar salad is described as being made with real bacon bits. There is some French onion soup, but of course the broth base is likely beef. You:

   a) Say that you have the stomach flu and can't eat.

   b) Order the dish with the least amount of meat, and eat around it.

   c) Ask the waiter if he could suggest any meatless options.

PROBABLE OUTCOMES
a) Can't eat; stomach flu:
All this will serve to accomplish is making you very hungry. Think about your motivation for hiding the fact that you are a vegetarian. Are you worried that these people will suddenly think less of you? Perhaps you aren't giving them enough credit. Maybe they've already decided that you're a decent person, and being vegetarian isn't likely to change their minds. They are going to find

out sooner or later, so why not save yourself a few hunger pains and make it sooner.

b) Order meat and eat around it:

At least you'll leave with something in your stomach, but did you really want to pay for that piece of steak? There are few restaurants that cannot accommodate a vegetarian, so it's really quite unnecessary for you to go to that length.

c) Ask for meatless:

You've got the idea! It's not unusual for restaurants to get this kind of request. Don't forget that many movie stars, athletes and even famous scientists are vegetarian. Some restaurants without a single vegetarian entrée on the menu make wonderful vegetarian meals. They'll cook up an awesome pasta dish filled with fresh vegetables or a colorful stir-fry with rice, and serve it with a great salad and some fresh bread. If the waiter seems less than confident about the options, arrange to speak privately with the chef, and let him know exactly what you would like. The main menu will generally give you a good idea of what could easily be prepared. If there are stir-fries on the menu, these can generally be done without the meat, as can many pasta dishes. If all else fails, ask for a baked potato with a large order of stir-fried vegetables. You may want to discuss the price as well, so you don't end up paying for a filet mignon.

Remember, when you do have a choice of where to eat, go for an ethnic restaurant. Oriental, Greek, Lebanese, African and Indian restaurants all generally provide vegetarian options (the more authentic the better). When you can, phone ahead.

4. INVITING OUT-OF-TOWN WORK ASSOCIATES TO DINNER

You have three out-of-town business associates at the office for a week. You decide to invite them all for dinner, then you go crazy for the next couple of days trying to decide what to cook. You:

a) Decide to break down and buy some fish for the occasion.

b) Make some really interesting vegetarian dishes for them to try. Tofu roast, quinoa casserole and some curried eggplant. You even whip up a nice carob pudding for dessert.

c) Opt for familiar foods, without the meat.

PROBABLE OUTCOME

a) Buy fish:

It's certainly an option, but absolutely unnecessary. You can make a lovely meal without having to buy fish.

b) Make unusual vegetarian foods:

Risky. Some people are very funny when it comes to foods that they don't recognize. You'd be better off to try this kind of meal with some friends, but not with people that you've never met.

c) Make familiar favorites:

Good choice. Chances are that no one will even notice that there is no meat on the table. Lasagna, spaghetti, chili, tortillas and crepes can all work very nicely. Be sure to have some special side dishes, fresh bread and a great dessert, like peach pie or a chocolate and fruit fondue.

5. MAKING A CELEBRATION DINNER FOR YOUR EXTENDED FAMILY

Every year you take turns with your brother and two sisters hosting the Christmas feast. This will be your first year as a vegetarian host. Jerry has let you know in no uncertain terms that he expects turkey for dinner. Ellen reminded you that it's only once a year, and that it wouldn't kill you to make this little sacrifice for the occasion. You don't want to cook a turkey, nor do you want to end up in a huge fight with your family. You decide to:

a) Give in and cook a turkey.

b) Tell your family that you just aren't comfortable cooking a turkey, but you would be happy to do everything else, if one of them brings the turkey.

c) Refuse to have a turkey in your house. Tell them that they can cook what they like when it's their turn to do the meal, but you'll do what you like when it's your turn.

d) Explain to your family that you would prefer to host a part of the celebration at your house that is separate from the Christmas turkey dinner.

e) Go to Mexico for Christmas.

PROBABLE OUTCOME

a) Make a turkey:

This option makes everyone happy except you. Sometimes in life we feel compelled to do things that go against our principles, simply because it will help to avoid difficult confrontations. In the end, there is no greater understanding of your concerns or feelings, and your family will probably conclude that you don't mind preparing meat for other people. Perhaps a compromise could be reached. It's obviously important for your family to have their traditional meal for the occasion, and it's just as important for you not to have to purchase and prepare the turkey.

b) *Have someone else bring the turkey:*

This may be a good compromise for everyone involved. You don't have to cook the turkey, but your family gets what they want for Christmas dinner. Make wonderful trimmings, and a vegetarian main dish to share. A giant stuffed squash is a great option. The vegetarian main dish often ends up as one of the more popular items of the feast.

c) *No turkey in your house:*

Sometimes it isn't what you say that creates a problem, it's how you say it. Remember that having turkey for Christmas is very important to your family, as it is for most people. Telling them that they can't do that this year is probably not a good idea. It could create a lot of tension during the season when peace, joy and love are supposed to fill our hearts and homes. This is not to say that you should give in and have a turkey in your house when you are really very uncomfortable with that, but rather that there may be a better way of reaching that end.

d) *Offer to do something else:*

This is the best solution for those who do not wish to have a turkey dinner in their home. There are so many ways to participate in the celebration other than hosting Christmas dinner. How about offering a Christmas Eve games night at your house, and serve appetizers such as spinach dip with sourdough bread, stuffed mushrooms, fresh fruit kabobs and some special Christmas baking. Another alternative which could be great fun is a brunch and skating party. This type of activity could become a new, healthy tradition for your family.

Everyone will become more comfortable with vegetarian foods and your vegetarianism as a whole, over time. Expose them to your favorite vegetarian dishes when they come for a meal, and be sure to bring plenty of food to share when you go to visit them.

e) *Go to Mexico:*

This isn't a bad idea, but you'll be faced with the turkey problem again next year!

6. TEEN GETS RAZZED ABOUT WEARING LEATHER SHOES

Your teenager is a confirmed vegetarian. In fact, he was a vegetarian two years before you were. He brings tofu sandwiches to school, and doesn't seem to care what other kids say about it. One day he comes home rather upset, and confides in you that the kids have been bugging him at school about wearing leather shoes. They tell him that if he really cared about animals then he wouldn't wear leather. They even go so far as to say there isn't a whole lot of difference between wearing leather shoes and eating a big steak. He asks you for some advice. You tell him to:

a) Just ignore people like that.

b) Remind them that at least he does something. Then go out and buy some non-leather shoes so that he doesn't have to worry about being bugged about it anymore.

c) Tell the other kids that it's not an "all or nothing" situation. He's just cut out meat, so far, and is trying to buy fewer things that have been made with animal products, but it isn't all that easy. Remind them that leather shoes will last for years, a steak doesn't last more than a few minutes.

PROBABLE OUTCOME

a) Ignore them:

This won't help your teenager to effectively handle these difficult situations.

b) You do something:

Once again, be careful about the way you say things. Rather than saying "at least I do something," which implies that *they* don't, you can say, "I'm trying, but I still have a way to go." This gives the message, without putting anyone down. Buying new shoes when they aren't really needed certainly doesn't help the environment. Wait until new shoes are needed, then consider going leather-free (which does not necessarily guarantee that it has been made without animal products).

c) Not all or nothing:

This is a great start. There is only so much any of us can do at any one time. It is interesting for people to learn the actual extent of animal products in almost everything we use in this society. In truth, it is impossible to be free of all animal products, unless you are a living on some island with nothing from civilization to assist you. The soap, shampoo and creams we use often contain animal products. The strings of musical instruments and tennis rackets (yes, even the plastic ones use animal products in their manufacturing), films and videos, paint and the steel in our cars all contain animal products. Even cotton clothing and the soles of non-leather shoes have often been made with some part of an animal. Environmentally speaking, a pair of leather shoes that is worn for a few years, then passed on to someone else, makes a lot more sense than four ounces of meat every day. In regards to animal rights, you'll be responsible for the death of a lot fewer cows if you wear leather shoes than if you eat meat every day.

7. YOUR FIRST BUSINESS CONVENTION AS A VEGAN

It's the first convention you've attended since becoming a vegan. It was never too difficult as a lacto-ovo vegetarian, as most places are happy to prepare an omelet on short notice. You aren't so sure how easy things will be now that you have eliminated milk and eggs. It's nice to know that the airlines offer vegan meals in addition to the regular vegetarian options. You make sure to have your meals ordered when you book your flight. You are pleasantly surprised with the meal; lentil loaf with tomato sauce, rice, broccoli, a whole grain dinner roll and some fresh strawberries for dessert. You arrive at the convention center, to find a little basket of fresh fruit in your room. What a bonus! Maybe it won't be so bad after all.

Next morning you go down for breakfast, and order some oatmeal, unbuttered whole wheat toast, and fresh squeezed orange juice. Lunch is to be over a meeting, so you figure it will be a buffet. You are fairly certain that you'll at least get salad, potatoes and a roll. To your dismay, lunch is a catered sit-down meal. No sooner do you sit down than a plate arrives in front of you. A ham quiche, with a tiny side salad and a white roll. Your stomach turns as the aroma of the ham fills the air. You decide to:

a) Eat the roll and salad, and check the agenda to see if another similar affair has been planned, so that you can be sure to order ahead next time.

b) Decide that you can wait until dinner to eat.

c) Tell the waiter that you are a vegetarian and ask if you could get something else to eat.

PROBABLE OUTCOME

a) Eat the roll and salad:
This is probably the easiest thing to do, but it's not necessarily your best option. The person two seats away could receive a beautiful vegetarian plate just as you are finishing your dinner roll. (You only have to experience that feeling once or twice to clue in to the fact that it pays to ask.)

b) Wait until dinner:
You'll end up so hungry that the next time you'll remember to pre-order vegan food.

c) Ask for something else:
What have you got to lose? Most good hotels are very accommodating. You'll often end up with a meal that will have those around you wishing that they had the same. The worst thing that could happen is that the waiter says he is very

sorry, they can't prepare anything else. We have never actually seen this happen, so the chances are pretty good that you'll get some reasonable alternative.

GUIDELINES FOR GETTING ALONG

1. Care about animals and the environment, but love your fellow man.
Your concern for animals demonstrates a deep reverence for life, and a gentle heart. Your concern for the environment demonstrates an understanding of the fragility of the earth, and an able mind. These are certainly admirable qualities, but they need to be carefully balanced with love for your fellow man. If you really want to make this world a better place, begin by considering the consequences of what you say and do on the lives of your neighbors. Remember that every person, regardless of his occupation or interests, has something of value to offer.

2. Take the time to listen to other people, and lift them up with your words.
It is so easy to pass judgment or belittle someone without really understanding them. By listening to other people, not only can you get to know them better but you can be a support and encouragement to them. As an added benefit, you will probably learn something. Putting people down does nothing but hurt them and push them away. Instead, try to lift people up with your words.

3. Share your experiences in a positive way.
In our society, where meat is front and center of most social interactions involving food, the vegetarian can feel a little intimidated. Think of people like George Bernard Shaw and Gandhi who made the same choice as you. Rather than retreating from social interaction, go forth proudly, as a vegetarian with something to share.

You can try to impress people with long sermons about the sins of meat eating, expecting to convert the masses into peace loving tofu munchers, but you'll likely be in for a real disappointment. Instead, inspire them with your example of healthy living. You might want to invite friends for a vegetarian meal, or bring a delicious vegetarian dish to the staff party. Share recipes and books with them. You might even ask them to join you for a vegetarian cooking class.

4. Learn to laugh at yourself and some of the predicaments you get yourself into.
You can go through life with a sour and serious view of just about everything,

or you can take a step back and realize that there *is* a little humor in most awkward situations. Loosen up, and laugh a little. It will likely add as many years to your life as your vegetarian diet.

Although it may not be easy for you, try to forgive and forget. People often speak before thinking, and hurt others, sometimes without even realizing it. Holding a grudge will not make you feel better, only more stressed.

5. Realize that you can't always make perfect choices.
Think about your goals in life, and set some priorities. For many of us, our number one priority is the people we love. As a vegetarian, you have likely made a lifestyle choice that is different than the rest of your family. There may be times when you feel inclined to give in and eat some meat, poultry, fish, milk or egg in order to avoid offending someone that you care about. If you have made this choice, don't feel guilty about it, for you are following your heart, and that is all any of us can do. On the other hand, if you choose to forgo meat and dairy foods completely, realize that it will have to become a priority. You will often have to plan ahead, to check with restaurants and conferences, to let friends and family know when you will be sharing a meal with them, and to bring appropriate foods along with you much of the time.

6. Become well informed.
If you want to contribute to the vegetarian cause, get well informed about the issues. Read all you can, take courses, go to lectures and listen to all kinds of opinions. Not only will you get a good confidence boost but you'll be able to handle questions and concerns in a clear and logical manner.

FROM MARKET TO MEALS

Your knowledge of foods and nutrition has never been better: you know what nutrients are of greatest concern for vegetarians, and how your food choices affect your health and the world around you. Now comes the real challenge; selecting food from the market and turning it into wonderfully delicious and nutritious vegetarian meals.

This chapter will guide you through the practical aspects of becoming vegetarian. You will learn about what foods to buy, where to buy them and how to incorporate them into your daily meals. As you step boldly into the market place, be undaunted by the new and unfamiliar foods that await you. They are simply adventures waiting to happen.

SHOPPING STRATEGIES

With the utmost confidence, you bound out the front door, armed with your cloth shopping bags, determined to fill them to the brim with wholesome foods that will help transform you into a real vegetarian.

Alas, you return home with little more than oatmeal, peanut butter and a few fresh vegetables. Shopping for healthy foods is not as simple as you might imagine. An incredible array of products awaits you; many masquerade as nutrition powerhouses. Take the time to learn all you can about the foods available to you.

Become an expert label reader and find out more about organically grown foods.

Making Labels Work for You

A food label can be your best ally – if you know how to use it. It pays to invest a little time into understanding label lingo and what a food producer can do with it. There are three different places on a label that will give you information about the nutritional contents of a product – the *nutrition claims*, the *nutrition information* and the *ingredient list*.

1. NUTRITION CLAIMS

Nutrition claims are used to highlight the desirable nutrition features of a product. They usually appear on the front of a package. There are strict regulations set out by governments which control nutrition claims. For example, in Canada, if a product claims to be "low-fat" and "cholesterol-free," it must contain 3 g fat per serving or less, and 3 mg cholesterol per 100 g, or less. When a nutrition claim is made, further details regarding the specific nutrient or nutrients must be provided under the "nutrition information."

Food producers can use nutrition claims in ways that can be very confusing to consumers. For example, the label on a jar of peanut butter may read "cholesterol-free," leading people to believe that other brands of peanut butter contain significant amounts of cholesterol. In fact, no peanut butter (or any other plant foods) contains significant amounts of cholesterol.

2. NUTRITION INFORMATION

The nutrition information section of a label details the nutritional value of the product as it is sold, rather than after it has been prepared. (Although sometimes both are given.) The nutrition information is generally given per typical serving. It includes energy (or calories), protein, fat (sometimes polyunsaturated, monounsaturated and saturated), carbohydrates (sometimes sugars, starches and fiber), sodium and potassium. Other vitamins and minerals are listed as a percent of the recommended intake.

3. INGREDIENT LIST

All packaged foods in Canada and the United States must provide the ingredients used in the product. Ingredients are listed in order of amount according to weight, with the ingredient present in the largest amount listed first. The ingredient list can answer questions that you might have regarding nutrition claims or nutrition information. For example, a package of commercial cookies may claim: "low in saturated fat," "low in cholesterol" and "no tropical oils." This sounds very good, but if you examine the list of ingredients you see enriched flour (i.e., white flour) and vegetable oil shortening as the first two ingredients. The remaining ingredients include sugar, icing sugar, butter, dried whole egg, sodium bicarbonate and salt. All of a sudden the cookies sound a little less wholesome than what the claims might have led you to believe. When examining an ingredient list, there are a few things you'll want to look for:

- the use of whole grain flours as the principle grain in the product;
- minimal use of saturated fats (shortening, partially hydrogenated oils or tropical oils);
- the use of sweeteners that provide some nutritional value whenever possible (fruit juices, dried fruits or blackstrap molasses);
- short ingredient lists with items that you can recognize (this is not a necessity, but such products are often more wholesome).

Organic Options: Are Organic Foods Really Better?

Organic foods are often more expensive, more difficult to find and less perfect in appearance than regular supermarket foods. All that having been said, organic foods are preferable to the foods that have not been grown organically.

The standards and regulations regarding the use of the term "organic" as applied to a food vary considerably from country to country. In Canada, any food that carries an organic claim such as "organically grown," "certified organic" or any other variation of the word organic must meet standards set out by government and local independent certification agencies. These generally include:

- prohibition of the use of synthetically compounded mineral fertilizers, pesticides and herbicides; plant and animal growth regulators; antibiotics; hormones; preservatives; coloring or other artificial additives; ionizing radiation and recombinant genetic manipulation of plants or animals;
- a minimum three-year transition period for farms that have used traditional farming practices;
- processing, packaging, transportation and storage that ensures maximum nutritional value of the food products;
- maintenance of an accurate and comprehensive auditable record of production and handling to be kept for no less than three years.

Organic farming practices are meant to create ecosystems which are sustainable. This is accomplished by natural weed and pest control, recycling of plant and animal residues, crop selection and rotation, water management, tillage, cultivation and soil conservation. Growing food organically makes sense from an environmental and ecological perspective, and thus such foods are highly recommended. Recent research suggests that organic foods may also offer some nutritional advantages over conventionally grown foods, but more studies are needed to confirm these findings. It is not always possible or preferable to buy organic. You'll need to take cost, quality and convenience into account. If you have a good source of organic food close by, the decision is much easier.

Your choice of food can affect your life in many ways. It also has an impact on your environment and those who grow, process and sell the food. As you attempt to make the best possible food choices, remember:

• *Keep your foods simple and wholesome.* The closer a food is to its natural state, the greater your chances of getting what nature intended you to get. Ideally we'd grow all our own food, grind our grains and bake our bread. More commonly, we rush in the door at 6:00 p.m. and look around for something that we can throw together in under 30 minutes. With good planning, we can combine homemade foods with some convenient and wholesome commercial products.

• *Whenever possible, buy locally grown foods.* Not only will you be supporting your local farmer but you'll be making a positive choice for the environment. The farther a food is transported, the greater the energy that is used in getting it to your table.

• *Take the time to read food labels.* The label on a food product can tell you a lot about a product, so it pays to take the time to look it over.

• *Don't forget your shopping list.* A shopping list (see over) can make life a whole lot easier. If it's your first time trying something, buy only enough to make the desired recipe, or you may just find yourself with several pounds of something that you dislike. The list on page 198 provides you with the basics you'll need to get your pantry ready for some delightful vegetarian cooking.

WHERE TO SHOP

There are many places to shop, each with its own strengths and weaknesses. If you like shopping at a large supermarket, you can get almost everything you need there. If you are not a supermarket fan, you may never have to step into one again, particularly if you live in a city where there are all kinds of other stores to choose from.

SUPERMARKETS

Supermarkets have large produce sections, often with a substantial selection of organically grown products. Some of the large stores carry vegetarian frozen convenience foods, tofu patties, and dehydrated instant falafel, hummus and beans. Most stores carry bulk dry goods including whole grain flours, many grains, nuts, seeds (including flax) and spices. The items that supermarkets

Basic Shopping List

Grain Products

- ☐ Flours (wholewheat and others)
- ☐ Brown rice
- ☐ Dry cereal
- ☐ Whole grain breads
- ☐ Whole grain crackers, rye crisps
- ☐ Oatmeal
- ☐ Mixed grain cereals
- ☐ Pasta
- ☐ Wheat germ
- ☐ Other grains, as desired
- ☐ Popcorn

Vegetables and Fruits

- ☐ Fresh greens
- ☐ Garlic and onions
- ☐ Seasonal vegetables
- ☐ Seasonal fruits
- ☐ Tomato sauce or paste, and canned tomatoes
- ☐ Canned fruits
- ☐ Dried fruits
- ☐ Frozen vegetables
- ☐ Frozen fruit products

Beans & Bean Products

- ☐ Dried legumes (navy beans, garbanzos, pinto beans, kidney beans, lentils, split peas)
- ☐ Canned legumes
- ☐ Tofu, tempeh
- ☐ Instant dried legume dishes (e.g., hummus, soups)

Nuts, Seeds and Butters

- ☐ Nuts (almonds, walnuts, pecans, peanuts and raw cashews)
- ☐ Nut butters (almond, peanut, etc.)
- ☐ Seeds (sesame, pumpkin, sunflower and flax)
- ☐ Seed butters (tahini)

Meat Analogues

- ☐ Vegetarian patties
- ☐ Other meat substitutes (tofu wieners, seitan, lunch slices, sausages, loaves, etc.)

Non-dairy or Dairy Products

- ☐ Milks (non-dairy milk, low-fat dairy milks)
- ☐ Cheese (non-dairy or dairy)
- ☐ Yogurt (soy or dairy)

Sweeteners

- ☐ Blackstrap molasses
- ☐ Maple syrup
- ☐ Other sweeteners (e.g., date sugar, Sucanat, rice syrup, brown or white sugar)

Beverages

- ☐ Cereal grain beverages
- ☐ Fruit and vegetable juices
- ☐ Leaf and herbal teas
- ☐ Organic coffee

Miscellaneous

- ☐ Nutritional yeast (Red Star brand T-6635+)
- ☐ Seaweed
- ☐ Miso
- ☐ Eggs

Fats and Oils

- ☐ Oil (unrefined oils such as extra virgin olive, flax, canola or safflower oil)
- ☐ Soy spread, butter or soft margarine
- ☐ Tofunaise or mayonnaise

Seasonings and Condiments

- ☐ Bottled sauces (teriyaki, tamari, soy sauce, etc.)
- ☐ Vegetable broth powder or cubes or chicken style seasoning
- ☐ Vinegar (rice vinegar or apple cider vinegar), lemon juice
- ☐ Instant vegetarian gravy and sauce mixes

Herbs and Spices

- ☐ Basil, oregano
- ☐ Salt, pepper
- ☐ Sage, savory, thyme
- ☐ Chili powder
- ☐ Cinnamon, allspice, nutmeg
- ☐ Cumin, curry
- ☐ Dry mustard (Dijon type)
- ☐ Parsley
- ☐ Ginger

often do not carry are the less common grains such as quinoa, spelt and amaranth, certain legumes, a variety of non-dairy milks and yogurts, organic juices, non-wheat pastas, and other specialty items such as nut and seed butters.

FARMERS MARKETS

If you are lucky enough to have a farmers market nearby, do take advantage of it. Our experience has been that farmers markets tend to undercut regular supermarket prices by at least 30 percent on most items. When you find a good market, you will never look back. The produce is mostly local, the goods are fresh, and the variety is often great. You'll also find produce that you don't normally see at the grocery store, including greens such as collards and kale. Don't hesitate to ask the manager about getting in special foods or purchasing in uncommonly small or large quantities. They are usually quite happy to accommodate you.

NATURAL FOOD STORES

Natural food stores can be a wonderful source of wholesome food items, many of which have been grown without the use of pesticides and herbicides and are certified organic. The trick is to locate one that emphasizes food, not supplements. Try to find a store that sells produce, bulk foods, fresh tofu, nut butters, frozen, canned and dried convenience foods and non-dairy milks. Many of these shops frequently specialize in vegetarian foods and foods for people with allergies. They often carry items that are not generally available in supermarkets: less common grains such as kamut, spelt and quinoa; unrefined vegetable and seed oils; non-dairy alternatives such as soy yogurts and cheeses; snack foods made without hydrogenated fats and convenience foods that are free of animal products. Many larger stores carry wonderful baked goods too.

ETHNIC SHOPS

Most cities have some ethnic grocery stores, and the larger cities have ethnic stores of almost every kind. When you find a good one, it's like finding a treasure chest. Oriental stores carry a wonderful selection of tofu, greens, seaweed and oriental sauces. Some of these items cost only a fraction of what you would pay at a health food or grocery store. Greek stores carry the best tahini in town, as well as a good assortment of legumes, olives, olive oil, Mediterranean herbs and pita bread. Indian stores offer numerous flours, legumes, grains and mixed spices; their curry pastes are great for spicing up vegetable or lentil dishes in one step. Many ethnic stores also carry delicious vegetarian convenience foods.

CO-OPS AND BUYING CLUBS

Food co-ops are grocery stores that are owned and operated by members. This reduces overhead costs, so that foods tend to be cheaper than at normal grocery stores. Members enjoy special discounts and share in profits (often profits go back into the store for maintenance or expansion). Food co-ops are generally oriented towards vegetarian foods. If you do not have a food co-op nearby, you can form a buying club. Simply organize a few friends together and purchase directly from a wholesaler. Most warehouses have minimum orders, so you'll likely have to round up at least four or five people to get a buying club going.

BAKERIES

If you don't make your own bread, you may want to find a bakery that specializes in whole grain products. Many ethnic bakeries sell hearty rye and wheat breads. High-quality baked goods are also available at other stores: be sure to read the label or ask the baker what the ingredients are.

STORAGE TIPS

Now that you've arrived home with loads of wonderfully nourishing vegetarian food, you'll need to know how to care for it. In storing your food, there are three primary objectives:

1. *To keep food fresh and appealing.*
2. *To prevent spoilage, mold, rancidity or infestations with bugs.*
3. *To keep nutrients in.*

Appropriate food storage is especially important when your diet is based on whole foods, as these foods are far more susceptible to rancidity and bug infestations than their refined counterparts. Items with little nutritional value, such as white sugar and white flour, are of little interest to pests and will keep in your pantry for months.

Whole foods come protected by nature. Take grains, for example. Intact wheat berries keep for a couple of years stored in a cool, dry place in a tightly covered container. Grind the berries into flour, and the storage time is reduced to a couple of months. Whole nuts in the shell are far better keepers than shelled nuts, which in turn keep better than chopped nuts. Fresh fruits come packaged in their skin. Remove that and the fruit quickly perishes. It is also important to note that foods containing natural fats, such as wheat germ and nuts, will go rancid much more quickly than containing little fat, such as wheat bran. These higher fat foods should therefore be stored in the refrigerator or freezer. Table 12.1 provides a guideline for food storage.

Table 11.1 Food Storage

Store in a cool, dry place	*Store in the refrigerator*	*Store in the freezer*
• whole grains and pasta • legumes • dry cereals • bread (keeps 3-4 days at room temperature) • crackers and other dry goods • onions, garlic, potatoes and tomatoes (unless very ripe) • dried fruits, unripe fruits and bananas • honey and molasses • milk powder • olive and sesame oil • spices and nutritional yeast	• nuts, seeds and their butters (These also freeze well.) • dairy and non-dairy milks, yogurts and cheeses • vegetables, ripe fruit and their juices • opened condiments and sauces, mayonnaise, tofu-naise and maple syrup • whole grain flours • active dry yeast • cold pressed oils • tofu • fresh pasta • fresh herbs and ginger	• ground flax seed • wheat germ • frozen patties, loaves, vegetables, fruit juices, etc. • fresh herbs (Freeze in a plastic bag, and crumble in the bag for instant use.) • breads (Keep out only small amounts of bread.)

When you get into whole foods cooking, you often end up with such a wide variety of items in your cupboards that it can be a real challenge to find the ingredients needed for a recipe.

The best solution we've found is mason jars or other canning jars with metal catches. Buy two or three dozen jars and label them. Arrange the jars on an open shelf, if possible, or keep them in your pantry. This will make your life a lot less stressful when it comes to meal preparation and baking. For bulkier items, such as flour, you can use larger canisters or buckets. Keep spices in small tightly closed containers, preferably away from the warm stove area.

Many foods are best stored in the refrigerator as they go rancid quickly at room temperature. The refrigerator tends to dry things out, so keep foods covered. Lettuce and other greens keep especially well in plastic containers with tight-fitting lids. Buy only as much produce as you can use up in a week.

Whole grain flours are best stored in the refrigerator. Breads dry out quickly, so freeze what you won't use up within a few days.

A freezer can be a real asset. It allows you to preserve in-season fruits and vegetables, stock up on bulk frozen foods and purchase large quantities of perishables such as nuts and dried fruits.

MAKING THE MOST OF YOUR MEALS

Preparing wonderful vegetarian meals can be a source of great pleasure. The principles are much the same as they are when preparing any meal. Begin with the freshest ingredients you can buy. Fresh herbs and garlic are preferable to dried whenever they are available. Don't overcook foods, especially vegetables, and select a variety of colors and textures in the foods you prepare. Finally, take the time to make your dishes look appealing: a sprig of fresh parsley, an edible flower or slice of fresh lemon adds a special touch without taking much time.

Whether it's breakfast, lunch, dinner or snacks, you'll want your food to be interesting, tasty and nutritious. Don't fall into the rut of eating the same foods day in and day out. Experiment with all kinds of tastes, including those with which you aren't so familiar. The following pages will guide you through your meals and snacks with all sorts of useful suggestions for making the most of your food.

BREAKFAST: A GREAT WAY TO START YOUR DAY!

Let's face it, most of us don't set aside a great deal of time for the morning meal. Indeed, many people don't set aside any time at all. Including breakfast in your daily plan has a number of advantages. Studies have shown that those people who eat a good breakfast work better, play better and have an overall better sense of well being.

This first meal after an 8 to 14 hour fast will refuel your body, giving it the energy it needs to carry out your daily tasks. A healthful vegetarian breakfast can provide close to a third of your daily nutrients, and generally a sizable portion of fiber as well. The best way to get out of the habit of missing breakfast is to make it a priority in your morning. In less than ten minutes, you can be enjoying a delicious meal that will brighten your whole day.

Breakfast is probably the meal that changes the least when you become a vegetarian. Think about our traditional breakfast foods: cereal, toast, pancakes, French toast and eggs. Sure, they are accompanied by meat on occasion, but it's just a side dish and can be easily eliminated. For the lacto-ovo vegetarian, breakfast is a breeze. The one possible pitfall is overdoing the eggs, cheese and other high-fat dairy products. Make whole grains the basis of your breakfast, and reserve the high-fat, high-cholesterol foods for the occasional meal. For the vegan, traditional breakfasts can still work well, excluding the eggs of course. The idea is to become familiar with all of the replacements there are for animal foods. You'll be amazed at how great muffins and pancakes can taste without a speck of milk or egg (see recipes in Chapter 12).

Putting It Together

Coffee and a donut just don't add up to a nourishing morning meal. These foods do little to contribute to your overall nutrient needs. To ensure that your breakfast is all that it can be, follow this simple guideline:

> **Include something from at least three of the four food groups in the vegetarian food guide.**

By selecting nutritious foods from the food guide you can't go wrong. Remember to use whole grain breads and cereals. Look for at least four grams of fiber per serving in your cereals and avoid the presweetened varieties, which derive 40–60 percent of their calories from sugar. Try to include a vitamin C-rich fruit or juice such as a few strawberries on your cereal or a fresh grapefruit. It's also a good idea to choose something to boost your protein, such as nuts or nut butter, tofu, soy milk, cow's milk, cheese or eggs. These foods can help to ward off mid-morning hunger pangs and keep you alert.

The Vegan Breakfast

If you are a recent vegan or a vegetarian trying to reduce your intake of eggs and dairy products, you'll be pleased to know that there are simple ways of replacing both of these animal foods without forgoing your traditional favorites:

• Try different kinds of non-dairy beverages made from soy, tofu, nuts and grains, until you find one that you and your family enjoy. Some are available in powder form and others are reconstituted, ready for use. Their nutritional content varies considerably, so read the label. These milks can be used as a direct substitute for cow's milk. You might want to try making your own nut or soy milk (most vegan cookbooks have recipes for these types of milks).

• Opt for non-dairy cheeses.

• Scramble some tofu (see recipe, page 214). It's an ideal replacement for scrambled eggs.

• Use ground flax seed, a commercial egg replacer, tofu or soy flour as a replacement for eggs in pancakes, muffins and other baked goods.

LET'S DO LUNCH

Whether you have a row of brown bags to fill for hungry family members, are bored of peanut butter sandwiches day in and day out, or are faced with frequent business lunches, there are many things that you can do to make your lunch a little more interesting.

Business or Restaurant Lunch

As North America becomes increasingly health conscious, it is easier to find appealing vegetarian meals in restaurants. Even the well established family restaurants are offering veggie-burgers or meatless pasta dishes. If you are at the mercy of the nearest cafeteria, lunch wagon or fast-food establishment, you may want to consider bagging at least a part of your meal. Bring some hummus and pita, and buy a salad to go with it.

Ethnic Restaurant	*Vegan Choices*	*Vegetarian Choices (additional options)*
Middle Eastern	Falafel Baba ghanoush Meatless stuffed grape leaves Hummus and pita	Eggplant moussaka Greek salad or spinach pie
Mexican	Beans and tortillas Burritos, tacos, enchiladas	Any of the vegan choices with cheese (check for use of lard)
Italian	Pasta and tomato sauce Pasta primavera Pasta with pesto	Pasta with alfredo sauce or other cream sauce Eggplant parmigana
Indian	Bean and vegetable curries with chapatis or other bread	Raita (yogurt)
Chinese	Rice, and noodle dishes Vegetable dishes with nuts, tofu and gluten products Tofu dishes	Stir-fries with egg Egg foo yong
Japanese	Tofu in sauces Miso soups with noodles Vegetarian sushi Vegetable stir-fries	Same as vegan

Those who are living in larger cities and have the opportunity to take some time for lunch are in for a real treat. Delis will make delicious sandwiches to order and offer a variety of pasta or potato salads or nori rolls. However, your best bet for a delicious vegetarian lunch is often the closest ethnic restaurant.

Bag Lunches

If you stick to traditional bag lunch ideas, you may think that becoming vegetarian leaves you with little more than cheese or peanut butter sandwiches. After a year or so, lunch can seem pretty unappealing. The key to enticing vegetarian bag lunches is to move away from the traditional, and experiment a little. Even sandwiches can be interesting if you use your imagination. Start with fresh, thick slices of whole grain bread, rolls, pita bread or bagels. Fill them with hummus and sprouts; thin slices of soy cheese, avocado slices and lettuce; veggie-burgers, green onions, tomatoes and pickles; or tofu salad, olives and red peppers. Consider the variety of "sandwiches" used around the world. The Japanese have nori rolls, the Chinese, rice rolls and the Mexicans, tortillas. All of these make a nice change from traditional Western-style sandwiches. For safety, put a cold pack (freezer pack) or a frozen food item such as a muffin or some frozen juice in your lunch bag.

If you aren't big on sandwiches, pack along something else. Bring rice and leftover vegetable or legume dishes for lunch. Carry soup, stew or chili in a thermos. Include a muffin or some cornbread and a piece of fruit. There are plenty of appetizing alternatives from the plant world, so be creative.

Sandwich and Bag Lunch Ideas

Bread	Sandwich filling	Vegetables	Dessert
Multigrain bun	Almond butter or tahini with banana, blackstrap molasses or preserves	Carrot and green pepper sticks	Cranberry muffin
German rye bread	Tofu bologna and tofunaise	Sprouts and tomato	Homemade granola bar
Whole wheat pita bread	Hummus, falafel or veggie patty	Tabbouleh salad	Oatmeal cookies
Pita bread pizza	Dairy or tofu cheese	Pizza toppings	Pear
Rice rolls	Tofu, green onion, grated carrot and soy sauce	(in roll)	Fruit leather
12-grain bread	Cashew or peanut butter	Cherry tomatoes and celery	Yogurt (soy or dairy)
Nori rolls	Rice, vegetables and tofu with tamari	(in roll)	Molasses cookies
Whole wheat cinnamon bagel	Carrot-tahini filling	Waldorf salad (walnuts, apples)	Trail mix
Sourdough whole wheat roll	Bean salad	Vegetable salad	Carrot loaf
Tortilla	Refried beans	Chopped tomatoes, lettuce, green onion	Grapes

WHAT'S FOR DINNER?

The difficulty with dinner is that it is traditionally centered around meat. That presents a bit of a challenge for the new vegetarian. To make dinner meals both simple and enjoyable, here are a couple of options:

1. MODIFY TRADITIONAL STYLE MEALS

Simply replace the meat in traditional meals with beans, meat analogues, tofu burgers or wieners, nut loaves, homemade or commercial patties or textured vegetable protein. You can still have all the regular trimmings like mashed potatoes and gravy, corn on the cob, dressing and vegetables.

2. GO WITH ETHNIC OPTIONS

Borrow some ideas from the cultures that rarely use meat, or use it in very small quantity. Try Mexican, Lebanese, Indian, Chinese or African dishes.

When you first start out preparing vegetarian dinners, it's probably easiest to use traditional style meals most of the time, and slowly start to incorporate ethnic dishes into your repertoire. Before you know it, you'll be preparing interesting meals from around the world. Of course, you may have the advantage of coming from a culture that generally uses very little meat; if that's the case, your task will be much easier.

If you're concerned about the time it takes to cook vegetarian meals, relax. They needn't take any longer than meat meals to prepare.

Tools for Fixing Fast Dinners

Whether you like to prepare things from scratch or prefer to rely on ready-made convenience foods, there are many things that you can do to make your life easier and your meals tastier.

When you want to "make it from scratch" but need your meals ready fast, the best way is to master the art of planning ahead. Here are a few guidelines to get you started:

1. Decide on your menu in advance.
If you plan ahead, you can soak beans or grains, simmer a hearty soup, stew, chili or spaghetti sauce all day in a crock pot, or take the necessary items for dinner from the freezer in plenty of time.

2. Cook in double or triple batches.
Whether you are on your own or cooking for a family, making double or triple

batches means that you'll be able to enjoy an evening or weekend off some-where down the road. You can save leftovers for the next day (yes, it is all right to serve the same food two days in a row), or freeze a batch for later use. Cook grains, beans and pasta in large quantity too. Package them in meal-sized por-tions and freeze, or plan a couple of different meals using them as a base. For example, you may make a vegetable and cashew stir-fry and brown rice for supper one day, and then some curried tofu and rice the next day.

3. Make up large quantities of baking mixes.
You can pre-mix flour and other dry ingredients to use in baked goods, pan-cakes, muffins and cookie recipes. Simply freeze or refrigerate and use as need-ed. To make the recipe, just add the liquid ingredients.

Vegetarians, and particularly vegans, can't often rely on local fast food restaurants for a quick dinner. The answer is to create your own versions of speedy favorites. You'll need to stock your pantry and freezer well. If you haven't tried any of the vegetarian convenience foods that are on the market, you're in for a pleasant sur-prise. You can have burgers, burritos, hot dogs or pizza ready in minutes. Here are some basic standbys that will help you to create great meals in a flash:

Beans and other legumes
Many kinds of canned lentils and beans are available either plain or dressed up with different sauces. These can go into soups, canned spaghetti sauce, chili or casseroles for a fast dinner. Firmer beans such as garbanzos can also be thrown into a quick stir-fry. Freeze-dried beans such as refried beans and bean soups are particularly useful for backpacking or camping.

Tofu
Tofu is a wonderful convenience food that can be made into a meal in min-utes. There's a choice of different textures, from soft to extra-firm. Some tofu is packaged in tetra-pack containers so that refrigeration isn't necessary. Tofu can be frozen and thawed to obtain a pleasant, chewy consistency. It can be scrambled, stir-fried, baked, made into patties, sandwich fillings, desserts, pud-dings, cakes, mayonnaise and creams.

Quick whole grains and mixes
Quick-cooking wild or brown rice, millet and pastas are now available in most stores. Bulgur, couscous and whole wheat ramen noodles can be softened with boiling water and be added to sautéed vegetables. Whole grain pancake mixes can be turned into dumplings or hot biscuits.

Wheat gluten products (chai or seitan)

The concentrated protein in wheat flour is kneaded, seasoned and cooked to produce seitan or "wheat meat." Its chewy texture resembles beef or chicken, thus it is suitable for use in stews, soups and casseroles.

Seasonings

Flavor your foods with salsa, tamari, miso, nutritional yeast, seaweed powder, garlic powder, lemon juice (try the frozen variety), seasoned vinegars, canned tomatoes and instant vegetable broth powders.

Frozen foods

There are wonderful discoveries to be made in the frozen section of health food stores and supermarkets. In addition to frozen bread dough, pizza crust and vegetables, there are a number of vegetarian entrées now available. Some favorites include:

- Pizza (including soy cheese pizza) and burritos
- Greek foods (spanakopita, tyropita)
- Veggie pies and pockets
- TV dinners (pasta with sauces, cabbage rolls and perogies)
- Burgers, patties and wieners

SNACKS

For most North Americans, snacks are an important part of life. The first snack of the day often comes during our coffee break or recess. Then there's the after work or after school snack, and finally the bedtime snack (or non-stop evening munching). For many people, snacks make up about a quarter of the daily calories. If these calories come from junk food, we get short-changed on nutrients.

The answer is not necessarily to eliminate snacks from our daily diet. In fact, eating snacks between meals, rather than eating only three big meals a day, can be beneficial for the vegetarian. This practice can help to increase mineral absorption, and keep blood sugar even. Snacks are especially important for children with small stomachs who can't get enough calories in meals alone, and for those who are underweight. Instead of omitting the snack, we need to focus on choosing the right kinds of snacks. Simply follow the golden rule of snacking for the vegetarian and you can't go wrong:

Select your snack from the food groups of the vegetarian food guide. If it's not a part of the guide, it's not a healthy snack.

This golden rule is made even better by using the following guidelines:

- *Select snacks that aren't too high in concentrated sugars.* Some high-sugar snacks can be quite nutritious, but they can also contribute to cavities. A good example is dried fruits. When these are eaten along with nuts or cheese, which can protect against dental decay, they seem to be less damaging. It's a good idea to brush your teeth after eating sweet foods, or eat them with meals.
- *Choose a variety of foods from each of the food groups for your snacks.* For example, you could have a muffin for your morning snack, some trail mix on your way home from work, and some soy or dairy yogurt with apple slices before bed.
- *Pick foods that you don't generally include with meals.* For example, if you don't often include fruits at mealtime, be sure to have plenty on hand for snack time.
- *Keep your pantry and refrigerator well stocked with nutritious snack foods.* We tend to eat whatever is handy when we're looking for a snack. If only healthy choices are available, that's what we'll have.
- *If you want a snack while you're away from home, don't go for junk.* Stop at a produce place and buy a pear or apple, at a bakery for a bagel, or at a natural food store for a muffin. Most corner stores carry fresh fruit, yogurt and trail mix, and even vending machines carry fruit juice and nuts. Keep a jackknife with you so that you can make a sandwich or cut up fruit when you need to. Try to remember to bring food from home when you know healthy options will be hard to come by.

Super Snack Suggestions

- Trail mix (use commercial trail mix or make your own)
- Fresh fruit salad or fruit kabobs
- Celery stuffed with nut butter
- Yogurt mixed with cut-up fruit
- Homemade muffins, cookies or loaves
- Whole grain pudding with fruit sauce or canned fruit
- Rye crisps or rice cakes with almond butter and banana slices
- Mini pizza on English muffins or pita bread
- Blender tofu, fruit or yogurt drink
- Frozen juice popsicles
- Raw vegetables with tofu or yogurt dip
- Popcorn topped with grated cheese or seasonings
- Crispy tofu "fingers"
- Hummus and pita bread

- Cold cereal topped with granola, sliced fruit and milk
- Soy nuts
- Bagel with soy cheese or deli slices

RECIPES: SIMPLE TREASURES

elcome to the wonderful, creative realm of vegetarian cooking! These recipes were carefully selected to enhance the nutrition of a plant-based diet and to introduce tasty ways of preparing nutrient dense foods not commonly used in the standard American diet. This is only a sample of the many delightful dishes and new ideas that are available to vegetarian cooks.

Each recipe is suitable for vegans and vegetarians, and important nutritional information is included. The notes on ingredients in the glossary at the back of this book will provide you with information about some of the ingredients used in the recipes and where to purchase them. Enjoy!

GUIDELINES FOR NUTRITIONAL NOTES

The information provided in the written section of the nutritional notes addresses the energy-giving nutrients, protein, carbohydrate and fat, as well as fiber, contents of most dishes. The nutrients highlighted in the box just below provide information regarding minerals and vitamins, including those that are of particular concern to vegetarians. Each nutrient is rated according to the percent of the Canadian Recommended Nutrient Intake (RNI), and is based on the highest recommended intake for both age and sex for each nutrient. The recipes, in many cases, provide a greater percent of nutrient needs than what is reflected by this rating system. For example, we based our calcium ratings on 1100 mg because it is the highest amount recommended for females

19–35 years of age. This is considerably higher than the amount recommended for people in other age and sex categories.

If the recipe meets 5 percent of the Canadian RNI for a nutrient and 10 percent in the case of vitamin C, it is considered a source of that nutrient and is awarded one star. If the recipe meets 15 percent of the RNI and 30 percent in the case of vitamin C, it is considered a good source of that nutrient and is awarded two stars. If a recipe meets 25 percent of the RNI for a nutrient, and 50 percent for vitamin C, it is considered to be an excellent source of that nutrient and is awarded three stars. So if a particular dish is an excellent source of iron, a good source of calcium, and a source of zinc, it would appear in the nutritional notes as follows:

*** IRON   (excellent source)
 ** CALCIUM   (good source)
  * ZINC   (a source)

The nutritional analysis of the recipes has been done using the base ingredients, not the variations given. Optional ingredients are included in the analysis, *unless otherwise specified*. When a choice of milks, sugars or other ingredients are given, the first option is used.

Breakfast

Granola
Scrambled tofu
Fruity whole grain pancakes with jiffy fruit sauce
Whole grain pudding

Spreads and Sandwich Fillings

Corn "butter"
Garlic "butter"
Eggless egg salad
Carrot and tahini sandwich filling
Hazelnut pâté
Quick and delicious hummus

Soups, Salads and Dressings

Green sea soup (split pea)
Non-dairy vegetable cream soup
Garden salad
Sesame tahini salad dressing
Basic flax oil and vinegar dressing
Chinese cabbage (sui choy) salad with Oriental dressing

Greens

> International greens
> Greens and potato

Cooking Grains and Legumes

> Cooking grains
> Perfect pilaf
> Legume wizardry

Entrées

> Chunky red lentil tomato sauce
> Two-bean stew
> Red star tofu fingers
> Crispy tofu fingers
> Vegetable stir-fry
> Millet patties with simple brown gravy
> Creating patties from leftovers

Desserts and Baking

> Fruit and nut muffins
> Carrot cake
> Berry uncheesecake

GRANOLA

The tahini (used instead of oil) and blackstrap molasses (instead of sugar) make this healthy version of granola especially rich in minerals.

5 cups	rolled oats	1.25 L
1 cup	wheat germ	250 mL
1 cup	chopped almonds	250 mL
½ cup	sesame butter (tahini) or almond butter	125 mL
3 tbsp	water	50 mL
¼ cup	liquid sugar	50 mL
	(a combination of blackstrap molasses and maple syrup works especially well)	
1 tsp	vanilla (optional)	5 mL
1 cup	dried fruit	250 mL
	(raisins, apricots, chopped dates)	

In roasting pan or large shallow baking dish, mix together oats, wheat germ and almonds. In small bowl, combine the tahini, water, liquid sugar and vanilla, mixing with fork. Pour over dry ingredients and mix evenly. Roast at 275°F (140°C), covered, for 1 hour, stirring every 15 minutes (move granola that is touching the sides of the pan to center, and press out lumps). Remove from oven, cool, mix in dried fruit and refrigerate in an airtight container.

MAKES 16 SERVINGS, ½ cup (125 mL) each. Per serving: 268 calories; 6 g fiber.

VARIATION: You can substitute wheat, rye, barley, soy flakes or other grains to replace some of the oats, or add 1 cup/250 mL sunflower or pumpkin seeds or coconut, or omit ingredients, according to preferences.

NUTRITIONAL NOTE: This granola provides excellent fiber and half the fat calories compared to the traditional version.

*** MAGNESIUM	*** THIAMIN	*** ZINC
** FOLIC ACID	** IRON	** NIACIN
* RIBOFLAVIN	* VITAMIN B$_6$	

SCRAMBLED TOFU

This dish demonstrates one of the many ways tofu can be used as a convenience food. Whether for a hot breakfast or as a sandwich filling the next day, young children and adults love it.

1 lb	medium-firm tofu made with calcium	500 g
2 tsp	vegetable oil	10 mL
1	large clove garlic, minced	1
2 tbsp	chopped green onion (optional)	25 mL
¼ cup	sliced mushrooms (optional)	50 mL
2 tsp	tamari soy sauce or "chicken style" vegetarian seasoning	10 mL
1 tbsp	nutritional yeast, Red Star T-6635+ (optional)	15 mL
2 tbsp	chopped fresh parsley	25 mL

Drain tofu well (see note). In cast-iron frying pan, sauté vegetables in oil until soft. Add tofu and seasonings. Scramble with fork. Cook on medium heat for 2 to 3 minutes. Sprinkle with parsley and serve immediately.

MAKES 3 SERVINGS. Per serving: 150 calories; 2 g fiber.

NUTRITIONAL NOTE: Red Star T-6635+ nutritional yeast adds B vitamins, including an excellent source of B_{12} for the vegan. One serving of this dish provides 8 grams of soy protein.

✱✱✱ FOLIC ACID	✱✱✱ IRON	✱✱✱ MAGNESIUM
✱✱✱ NIACIN	✱✱✱ RIBOFLAVIN	✱✱✱ VITAMIN B_{12}
✱✱✱ VITAMIN E	✱✱ CALCIUM	✱✱ VITAMIN B_6
✱✱ ZINC	✱ THIAMIN	

REMOVING THE LIQUID FROM MEDIUM-FIRM TOFU

The liquid in tofu can produce too much moisture in the dish, or make the tofu more susceptible to breaking up. To prevent this problem, drain off the liquid before using the tofu. Place the rinsed tofu on a plate. Put another plate or bread board on top. Place a weight on top of the board, such as a can of beans or tomatoes. Allow to sit for at least 15 minutes. Discard excess liquid and pat dry.

FRUITY WHOLE GRAIN PANCAKES

You don't need eggs or cow's milk to make great pancakes. Ground flax seed makes a great egg replacer. Simply grind whole flax seed in a blender and store in your freezer. Use in baking or sprinkle on hot cereal. Load these pancakes up with fruit for a real taste treat. See page 248 for instructions on another way of preparing flax egg replacer.

2 tbsp	vegetable oil	25 mL
1½ cups	milk (non-dairy or dairy)	375 mL
2 tsp	sweetener (e.g., maple syrup, honey) (optional)	10 mL
1 tbsp	ground flax seed (replaces 1 egg)	15 mL
1 cup	whole wheat flour	250 mL

¼ cup	other flour	50 mL
	(e.g., oat, corn, buckwheat, spelt,	
	or more whole wheat)	
¼ cup	wheat germ	50 mL
2 tsp	baking powder	10 mL
2 tsp	cinnamon (optional)	10 mL
1 cup	thinly sliced fruit	250 mL
	(apples, bananas, peaches,	
	blueberries) (optional)	

In large bowl, combine oil, milk, sweetener and ground flax seed (egg replacer). In small bowl or large measuring cup, mix together all dry ingredients very well. Add dry ingredients to milk mixture and stir just to combine. Fold in fruit. (NOTE: If batter is too thick, add ¼ cup/50 mL milk.) Heat non-stick skillet over medium heat (the real key to a great pancake is to make sure the pan is hot before you pour on the batter). Add oil to coat bottom of pan. Pour large spoons of batter onto hot skillet and cook until top begins to bubble. Flip pancake and cook until underside is golden brown. Serve with fruit sauce (given below), fresh fruit slices, and/or maple or fruit syrup.

MAKES 3 SERVINGS. Per serving: 333 calories; 7 g fiber.

NUTRITIONAL NOTE: These hearty pancakes provide over 11 grams of protein per serving. They contain less than 30 percent of calories from fat and a source of omega-3 fatty acids.

✳✳✳ MAGNESIUM	✳✳✳ VITAMIN E	✳✳✳ ZINC
✳✳ CALCIUM	✳✳ FOLIC ACID	✳✳ IRON
✳✳ RIBOFLAVIN	✳✳ THIAMIN	✳ NIACIN
✳ VITAMIN B$_6$		

NOTE: Analysis was done using skim milk (cow's), whole wheat with buckwheat flour added, apples and peaches.

FRUIT SAUCE

Fruit sauces are a refreshing change from sugary syrups. Dream up your own, using whatever fruits you have on hand. Leftovers are wonderful on puddings or cake.

Fruit Sauce in a Jiffy

1	medium banana	1
1	medium orange, peeled, quartered	1
2 tbsp	raisins, apricots or other dried fruit	25 mL
2 cups	fresh or frozen fruit such as blueberries, raspberries or kiwi	500 mL

In blender or food processor, purée banana, orange and raisins until smooth. Pour into medium bowl. Fold in fresh or frozen fruit (thawed).

MAKES ABOUT 6 SERVINGS, ½ cup (125 mL) each. Per serving: 88 calories; 3 g fiber.

NUTRITIONAL NOTE: Fruit sauces are far more nutritious than the sugar-based pancake syrups they replace. They provide antioxidants such as vitamin C and beta-carotene.

*** VITAMIN C	** FOLIC ACID	* IRON
* NIACIN	* THIAMIN	

NOTE: Analysis was done using strawberries.

WHOLE GRAIN PUDDING

This pudding is a great way to use whole grains. Cook overnight in a crockpot for an instant breakfast; leftovers can double as dessert. Try mixing a number of grains together for an interesting combination of flavors and textures. If you soak grains for at least 4 hours the cooking time will be cut in half.

¾ cup	uncooked whole grain	175 mL
	(barley, wheat berries, spelt berries, millet,	
	quinoa, rice or any combination of grains)	
3 cups	boiling water	750 mL
1 to 2 tbsp	maple syrup, honey or sugar	15 to 25 mL
	(optional)	
¼ tsp	salt	1 mL
½ tsp	each cinnamon, cloves, nutmeg or allspice	2 mL
½ cup	raisins or other dried fruit	125 mL
½ cup	milk (non-dairy or dairy)	125 mL

Combine grains and water and cook in a crockpot on low overnight, on high for about 4 hours, or on stove for about 2 hours (add extra water if necessary). Stir in all other ingredients and cook for ½ hour more. Serve hot or cold. Great topped with crunchy granola, fresh fruit, fruit sauce, and/or milk (non-dairy or dairy).

MAKES 4 SERVINGS, 1 cup (250 mL) each. Per serving: 214 calories; 5 g fiber.

NUTRITIONAL NOTE: The nutritional content of this pudding varies according to the grains used in its preparation. To boost its nutritional value, use some quinoa (be sure to rinse it well), or amaranth with the other grains. Less than 5 percent of the calories in this recipe come from fat.

✳✳ THIAMIN	✳ CALCIUM	✳ IRON
✳ MAGNESIUM	✳ NIACIN	✳ RIBOFLAVIN
✳ VITAMIN E	✳ ZINC	

NOTE: Analysis was done using millet, wheat berries and barley.

CORN "BUTTER"

If you'd like to cut down on margarine or butter, here's a great substitute. It works well on bread, muffins and even corn on the cob. These "butter" recipes came from Phil and Eileen Brewer, who operate Silver Hills Guest House in Lumby, B.C.

1 cup	boiling water	250 mL
1 tsp	salt	5 mL
¼ cup	cornmeal	50 mL
1 tsp	agar-agar powder★	5 mL
¼ cup	cold water	50 mL
1 cup	boiling water	250 mL
¼ cup	raw cashews	50 mL
2 tsp	lemon juice	10 mL
2 tbsp	finely grated carrot	25 mL

In medium saucepan, stir corn meal and salt into the boiling water. Continue to stir and cook over low heat for 2 to 3 minutes until thickened. In blender, soak agar-agar in the cold water for a few minutes. Pour the 1 cup of boiling water over agar-agar, and blend to dissolve. Add remaining ingredients and liquefy thoroughly until smooth as cream. Cool and refrigerate.

MAKES 1½ CUPS (375 mL).

★ Emes Kosher-Jel, made from seaweed, is also suitable for vegetarians.

GARLIC "BUTTER"

Try this garlic spread on sliced bread and broil until golden brown. It also doubles as a dip for raw vegetables, or as a topping for baked potatoes or pasta.

¾ cup	boiling water	175 mL
3 tbsp	cornmeal	50 mL
1 cup	water	250 mL
½ cup	raw cashews	125 mL
2 to 4	cloves garlic	2 to 4
1 tbsp	nutritional yeast	15 mL
1 tbsp	onion flakes	15 mL
4 tsp	lemon juice	20 mL
1 tsp	salt	5 mL
½ cup	sesame seeds	125 mL
½ tsp	marjoram (optional)	2 mL
½ tsp	dill weed (optional)	2 mL

In small saucepan, stir cornmeal into the boiling water. On low heat, stir and cook for 2 to 3 minutes until thick. In blender, liquefy the cooked warm cornmeal and all but the last three ingredients until very smooth. Briefly blend in the sesame seeds and herbs. Add a little more lemon juice for a slightly thinner spread ideal for a dip or a topping.

MAKES 2½ CUPS (625 mL).

EGGLESS EGG SALAD

This tasty sandwich filling is a snap to make. The Red Star T-6635+ brand nutritional yeast provides an excellent source of vitamin B$_{12}$.

½ cup	medium tofu, drained (see page 215)	125 mL
2 tsp	tofunaise or mayonnaise	10 mL
1 tsp	tamari soy sauce	5 mL

Optional ingredients (include one or more of the following ingredients as desired):

1 tsp	nutritional yeast (Red Star T-6635+)	5 mL
1 tbsp	finely diced green onion	15 mL
1 tbsp	finely diced celery	15 mL
1 tbsp	minced fresh parsley	15 mL
3	olives, diced	3
1 tsp	each sesame seeds, sunflower and Dijon mustard	5 mL

Salt, pepper, turmeric or other seasonings, as desired.

Crumble tofu with fork. Stir in tofunaise and soy sauce. Stir in optional ingredients as desired. Use as sandwich filling or cracker spread. Add lettuce and tomatoes, or stuff pita bread and top it with sprouts.

MAKES FILLING FOR 2 SANDWICHES. Per serving: 108 calories.

NUTRITIONAL NOTE: This filling is a source of essential fatty acids and provides 5 g of high-quality protein per serving without cholesterol.

** IRON *** VITAMIN E ** MAGNESIUM
* FOLIC ACID * CALCIUM * THIAMIN
* ZINC

NOTE: Analysis was done using optional ingredients excluding nutritional yeast.

CARROT AND TAHINI SANDWICH FILLING

This filling has a tuna-like texture. For the best effect be sure to grate the carrots on the fine part of your grater. Tahini is a very nutritious and tasty seed butter. Flavors can vary, so you may need to try a few brands before finding one you are completely happy with. If you're lucky enough to have a Greek or Lebanese store nearby, you'll find some great tahini at a very reasonable price.

1	medium carrot, finely grated	1
1 to 2 tbsp	tahini sesame butter	15 to 25 mL
1 tsp	tofunaise or mayonnaise	5 mL
1 tsp	nutritional yeast (optional)	5 mL
1 tbsp	diced onion (optional)	15 mL
1 tbsp	diced celery (optional)	15 mL
	Salt and pepper, to taste	

In small bowl, combine all ingredients. Use as sandwich filling or spread. Store in airtight container in refrigerator.

MAKES FILLING FOR 1 SANDWICH. Per serving: 139 calories; 2 g fiber.

VARIATION: Omit salt. Add 1 tsp (5 mL) each kelp powder and lemon juice.

NUTRITIONAL NOTE: Using Red Star T-6635+ nutritional yeast boosts the B vitamin content, including vitamin B_{12}. The seaweed (kelp powder) variation adds a variety of trace minerals.

*** MAGNESIUM	*** VITAMIN A	*** VITAMIN E
** THIAMIN	** ZINC	* FOLIC ACID
* IRON	* NIACIN	* VITAMIN B_6

NOTE: Analysis was done using 1 tbsp (15 mL) tahini and optional ingredients excluding nutritional yeast.

HAZELNUT PÂTÉ

This is an innovative way to take advantage of the full flavor of hazelnuts and mushrooms. It's popular with vegetarians and non-vegetarians alike. Serve on crackers or use as a sandwich filling.

1 cup	raw hazelnuts or filberts	250 mL
½	medium onion, sliced	½
1 cup	mushrooms, sliced	250 mL
2	cloves garlic, sliced	2
1 tsp	olive oil (optional)	5 mL
1 tbsp	sliced black olives (optional)	15 mL
¼ cup	fresh parsley	50 mL
1 tbsp	tamari soy sauce	15 mL
	Your favorite seasoning (Spike, Mrs. Dash)	
	Salt and pepper, to taste	

Roast hazelnuts in microwave oven for 3 to 4 minutes on medium-low heat. Sauté onion, mushrooms and garlic in oil or cover and cook in microwave without oil for about 3 to 4 minutes until soft. In food processor, purée cooked vegetables. Add nuts and all other ingredients, blend until very smooth. Add a little lemon juice if the mixture is too thick. This pâté freezes well.

MAKES 8 SERVINGS, ¼ cup (50 mL) each. Per serving: 113 calories; 2 g fiber.

NUTRITIONAL NOTE: The hazelnuts provide a very good source of monounsaturated fatty acids and no cholesterol.

** MAGNESIUM	** RIBOFLAVIN	* FOLIC ACID
* IRON	* NIACIN	* THIAMIN
* VITAMIN B₆	* ZINC	

QUICK AND DELICIOUS HUMMUS

Hummus is a chick-pea (garbanzo bean) pâté of Middle Eastern origin. This rich spread can be used as the protein part of the meal in a sandwich filling or as an appetizer or dip served with pita bread or raw vegetables. Using more or less garlic and herbs will give the flavor you desire.

¼ cup	tahini	50 mL
⅓ cup	lemon juice (freshly squeezed or frozen)	75 mL
2 to 4	medium garlic cloves	2 to 4
19 oz can	garbanzo beans	540 mL can
	(or 2 cups/500 mL cooked)	

Optional Ingredients

½ tsp	ground cumin	2 mL
1 tbsp	tamari soy sauce	15 mL
3 tbsp	chopped fresh parsley or cilantro	50 mL

Place tahini, lemon juice and garlic in food processor. Blend until smooth. Drain beans, reserving liquid. Add beans and other optional ingredients, if desired. Blend until mixture is creamy. Add 2 to 4 tbsp (25 to 50 mL) bean liquid or more lemon juice to thin out mixture, especially if it is to be used as a dip. This hummus freezes well.

MAKES 4 SERVINGS, ½ cup (125 mL) each. Per serving: 322 calories; 10 g fiber.

VARIATION: Add extra lemon juice, tamari, garlic, oil, or herbs such as basil, thyme and oregano. Grated carrot can be added for a different texture.

NUTRITIONAL NOTE: Each serving provides an excellent source of soluble fiber.

*** FOLIC ACID	*** MAGNESIUM	*** ZINC
** IRON	** VITAMIN E	* CALCIUM
* NIACIN	* RIBOFLAVIN	* VITAMIN B₆
* VITAMIN C		

GREEN SEA SOUP

Simple! You don't need soup bones for great flavor.

This soup freezes so well, you may want to make a double batch and freeze portions for days when you don't feel like cooking.

1½ cups	dry split peas	375 mL
5 cups	water	1.25 L
1 to 2	bay leaves	1 to 2
1 tsp	salt	5 mL
1 to 2	cloves garlic, minced	1 to 2
1	stalk celery, chopped	1
1	large carrot, sliced	1
1	leek, sliced (1 cup/250 mL)	1
1 tsp	each marjoram, basil and cumin	5 mL
2 tbsp	dry hijiki or wakame seaweed (optional)	25 mL

Combine all ingredients in cast-iron Dutch oven, bring to boil and simmer together for 3 to 4 hours (this develops the flavor).

MAKES 6 SERVINGS, 1 cup (250 mL) each. 192 calories; 4 g fiber.

NUTRITIONAL NOTE: One serving provides 14 g of protein with less than 1 g of fat! Quite a contrast to the traditional high-fat version.

*** FOLIC ACID	*** IRON	*** MAGNESIUM
*** THIAMIN	** NIACIN	** ZINC
* CALCIUM	* RIBOFLAVIN	* VITAMIN B$_6$

NOTE: Analysis was done using hijiki.

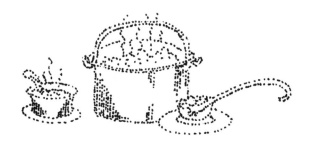

NON-DAIRY VEGETABLE CREAM SOUP

Broccoli, carrots or leeks are excellent choices for this recipe, but use any combination. Prepare it as a thick soup for a meal with some whole grain bread on chilly days or as a thinner version to introduce an elegant meal.

3 cups	fresh vegetables	750 mL
	(Choose from carrot, broccoli, celery, kale, turnip, parsley, etc.)	
2 cups	water or vegetable broth	500 mL
2 to 3	medium potatoes, quartered	2 to 3
1 cup	chopped onion or leek	250 mL
2 tsp	light miso or vegetable powder	10 mL
1 tsp	marjoram or thyme	5 mL
¼ cup	raw cashews	50 mL
¼ cup	chopped fresh parsley	50 mL
	Freshly ground pepper, to taste	

Cook vegetables in water until soft. In food processor, purée vegetables with all other ingredients except parsley. Garnish with parsley.

MAKES ABOUT 5 SERVINGS, 1 cup (250 mL) each. Per serving: 79 calories; 4 g fiber.

VARIATIONS: Garlic Soup: Replace onion or leek with 3 medium cloves garlic and use ⅓ cup (75 mL) non-dairy or dairy milk powder instead of the cashews.

Creamy Leek Soup: Omit all vegetables except potato and leek. Use 2 cups (500 mL) potato and 3 cups (750 mL) chopped leeks. Omit marjoram and use a little grated nutmeg.

NUTRITIONAL NOTE: One serving of this soup provides an excellent source of dietary fiber and less than 2 g of fat.

✳✳✳ VITAMIN A	✳✳✳ VITAMIN C	✳✳ FOLIC ACID
✳✳ IRON	✳✳ MAGNESIUM	✳ RIBOFLAVIN
✳ THIAMIN	✳ VITAMIN B$_6$	✳ ZINC

NOTE: Analysis was done using carrots, broccoli, kale, and turnip.

GARDEN SALAD

For visual appeal, arrange your salad in an interesting bowl or spread it on a platter. To a base of romaine lettuce, add any of the following ingredients (you may like to vary the quantities). The secret to making sturdy greens such as kale appealing in salads is to slice them fine. Salads without dressing keep for 2 days, refrigerated and covered with a damp tea towel. As well as delicious new flavors, your salad will provide calcium, and an abundance of other minerals and vitamins.

2 cups	romaine lettuce	500 mL
2 cups	high-calcium greens (kale, sui choy or collard), sliced matchstick thin	500 mL
½ cup	any of the following: sharp greens (mustard, watercress, radish), sliced matchstick thin; alfalfa sprouts; cucumber, cubed; orange sections; flower petals; (chive flowers, kale flowers, nasturtium, pansy); peppers (red, yellow and green), sliced	125 mL
¼ cup	any of the following: almonds, sliced and toasted; chopped green onion; olives; kohlrabi, chopped; pumpkin or sunflower seeds; pine nuts; radishes, sliced	50 mL
2 tbsp	orange zest (small strips of organic orange rind)	25 mL

Wash greens well. Tear or chop into bite-sized pieces. To prepare greens like kale, remove rib before slicing. Add other ingredients and toss. The sesame tahini dressing following goes particularly well with this salad.

MAKES 5 SERVINGS, 2 cups (500 mL) each. Per serving: 72 calories; 3 g fiber.

NUTRITIONAL NOTE: The dark greens in this salad provide a source of essential omega-3 fatty acids. Each serving provides 4 g protein, and using the tahini salad dressing will add more calcium.

*** FOLIC ACID	*** VITAMIN A	*** VITAMIN C
** MAGNESIUM	* CALCIUM	* IRON
* NIACIN	* RIBOFLAVIN	* THIAMIN
* VITAMIN B$_6$	* ZINC	

NOTE: Analysis was done using kale, mustard greens, alfalfa sprouts, cucumber, almonds and green onion, without dressing.

SESAME TAHINI SALAD DRESSING

Tahini (sesame seed butter) is a calcium powerhouse. This has half the calories of regular salad dressings, and provides small but significant amounts of vitamins and minerals.

¼ cup	lemon juice	50 mL
½ cup	tahini	125 mL
1 tsp	Dijon mustard	5 mL
1 to 3	garlic cloves, chopped	1 to 3
2 tbsp	tamari soy sauce	25 mL
½ tsp	pepper, or to taste	2 mL
½ cup	water	125 mL

Combine all ingredients in blender; purée. You may want to vary the amount of water slightly.

MAKES 1¾ CUPS (325 mL). Per serving (2 tbsp/25 mL): 76 calories.

VARIATIONS: Replace half of the tahini with ¼ cup (50 mL) olive or flax seed oil. OR Add ½ tsp (2 mL) sesame oil or 1 tbsp (15 mL) toasted sesame seeds for a different flavor. OR Add 1 tbsp (15 mL) chopped fresh herbs.

* CALCIUM	* FOLIC ACID	* MAGNESIUMI
* NIACIN	* THIAMIN	* ZINC

BASIC FLAX OIL AND VINEGAR DRESSING

The flax oil in this recipe gives a pleasant nutty flavor and provides an excellent source of omega-3 polyunsaturated fatty acids.

½ cup	flax seed oil	125 mL
3 tbsp	lemon juice, rice or cider vinegar	50 mL
3 tbsp	water	50 mL
2 to 3	medium cloves garlic	2 to 3
½ tsp	sweetener (maple syrup, honey)	2 mL
1 tsp	Dijon mustard	5 mL

Optional

1 tsp	light miso	5 mL
1 tsp	tamari soy sauce	5 mL
½ tsp	ground cumin or curry powder	2 mL

Purée in blender until smooth. Cover and refrigerate for up to 1 week.

MAKES ABOUT ¾ CUP (175 mL). Per serving (1 tbsp/15 mL): 30 calories.

VARIATION: Add 2 tbsp (25 mL) chopped fresh or 1 tsp (5 mL) dried herbs.

NUTRITIONAL NOTE: A 2 tbsp (25 mL) serving provides an outstanding source of alpha linolenic acid and vitamin E.

✱✱✱ VITAMIN E

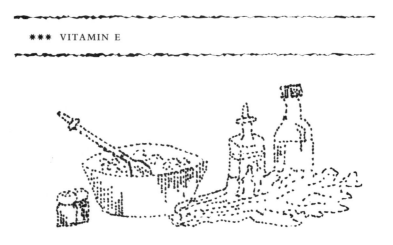

CHINESE CABBAGE (SUI CHOY) SALAD

Sui choy may be sliced very thinly and used in place of lettuce on sandwiches, or the smaller leaves may be sliced down the center of the blade and used on a vegetable platter.

3 cups	sliced Chinese cabbage (sui choy)	750 mL
½ cup	shredded purple cabbage	125 mL
½ cup	grated carrot	125 mL
¼ cup	chopped fresh parsley or cilantro	50 mL
1 cup	bean sprouts	250 mL
3 tbsp	sliced almonds or sunflower seeds	50 mL
1	green onion, chopped	1
4 oz pkg	instant Rahmen Japanese noodle soup (no MSG) (optional)	120 g pkg

In large bowl, combine all ingredients except noodles. Slightly crush noodles in soup package. Save seasoning package for making dressing. Before serving, add noodles and Oriental dressing. Toss lightly.

Oriental Dressing:

1 pkg	soup seasoning (mushroom) or miso	1 pkg
½ tsp	sesame oil	2 mL
2 tbsp	water	25 mL
1 tbsp	rice or berry vinegar	15 mL
1 tsp	tamari soy sauce	5 mL
1 tsp	freshly grated ginger	5 mL
2 tsp	vegetable oil (optional)	10 mL

In jar with tight-fitting lid, combine all ingredients. Shake until well mixed. Pour over salad just before serving.

TIP: Fresh parsley and cilantro can be frozen in plastic bags. When you need some, crush the bag slightly and your minced parsley is ready!

MAKES 6 SERVINGS, 1 cup (250 mL) each. Per serving: 63 calories; 2 g fiber.

NUTRITIONAL NOTE: This salad with the low-fat dressing provides a variety of nutrients including calcium from the almonds and sui choy.

*** VITAMIN A　*** VITAMIN C　** FOLIC ACID

** MAGNESIUM　* RIBOFLAVIN

* VITAMIN B$_6$

NOTE: Analysis done using 1 serving of salad including the dressing.

INTERNATIONAL GREENS

The vegetarian food guide recommends eating greens several times a week. This is easy if you have simple and delicious ways of preparing them. This recipe provides wonderful seasoning options from around the world.

Basic ingredients for all recipes:

2 lb (8 cups)	greens	1 kg (2 L)
	(collards, kale or Chinese greens)	
3	cloves garlic, minced	3
2 tsp	olive oil	10 mL
1	lemon, cut into wedges	1
	Salt and freshly ground pepper, to taste	

Then add one of the following seasoning combinations to the basic recipe:

Middle Eastern

1 tsp	cumin	5 mL
2 tsp	paprika (optional)	10 mL
½ cup	chopped fresh parsley	125 mL
¼ cup	chopped fresh cilantro	50 mL

Far Eastern

2 tbsp	tamari soy sauce	25 mL
2 tsp	freshly grated ginger	10 mL

African

1	medium onion, chopped	1
1 tsp	each cumin and coriander	5 mL
pinch	cayenne (optional)	pinch
2 tbsp	each peanut butter and water (combine, add when greens are almost cooked)	25 mL
1	tomato, cubed (add at the end of cooking)	1

Mediterranean

¼ cup	fresh basil (or 1 tsp/5 mL dried)	50 mL
¼ cup	fresh oregano (or 1 tsp/5 mL dried)	50 mL
½ cup	chopped fresh parsley (or 2 tsp/10 mL dried)	125 mL

East Indian

| 1 to 2 tbsp | mild curry paste | 15 to 25 mL |
| 1 tbsp | water | 15 mL |

Wash greens well. Remove tough ribs. Slice greens in slivers or small cubes. Heat oil in very large skillet or Dutch oven. Add garlic and seasoning combination of your choice. Cook for about 1 minute, stirring well, then add greens and mix. Cover, lower heat and simmer for 5 to 15 minutes or until tender. Serve hot with fresh lemon wedges. Squeeze lemon liberally over greens. Season with salt and pepper.

MAKES 4 TO 5 SERVINGS, 1 cup (250 mL) each. (In cooking, greens shrink to about ⅓ the fresh amount.) Per serving: 70 calories; 3 g fiber.

NUTRITIONAL NOTE: Dark greens are elite among many vegetables because of their high nutrient content including omega-3 fatty acids and calcium.

✳✳✳ RIBOFLAVIN	✳✳✳ VITAMIN A	✳✳✳ VITAMIN C
✳✳ VITAMIN B₆	✳ CALCIUM	✳ FOLIC ACID
✳ IRON	✳ MAGNESIUM	✳ NIACIN
✳ ZINC		

GREENS AND POTATOES

Buy fresh young greens and slice them very thinly so cooking time is reduced. Serve this dish as a vegetable, or add cooked lima or garbanzo beans and serve as a main course. A wonderful soup can be made with leftovers puréed in the blender with additional milk and seasonings.

6 cups (1½ lb.)	**kale or collard greens**	1.5 L (750g)
2 medium	**peeled or scrubbed potatoes**	2 medium
1 cup	**chopped leek or onion**	250 mL
½ cup	**milk (non-dairy or dairy)**	125 mL
¼ cup	**chopped fresh parsley**	50 mL
	Salt and pepper, to taste	
	Tomato wedges or grated cheese	
	(soy or dairy) for garnish (optional)	

Wash greens and remove tough stems and ribs. Chop greens and quarter potatoes. In large microwave baking dish with lid, place potatoes and leeks on one side and sliced greens on the other. Cover and microwave on high for about 10 minutes or until tender. With a fork, mash potato with leek and kale. Add milk, parsley, salt and pepper, mixing well. Cover, cook on medium or low heat for about 10 minutes. Garnish with tomato wedges or grated cheese.

MAKES 4 SERVINGS, 1 cup (250 mL) each. Per serving: 186 calories; 4 g fiber.

VARIATION: This recipe can also be made on the stove top.

NUTRITIONAL NOTE: Kale and collard greens are both good sources of essential omega-3 fatty acids. Each serving provides 8 g of protein.

✳✳✳ VITAMIN C	✳✳✳ VITAMIN A	✳✳ FOLIC ACID
✳✳ MAGNESIUM	✳ CALCIUM	✳ IRON
✳ NIACIN	✳ RIBOFLAVIN	✳ THIAMIN
✳ VITAMIN E	✳ ZINC	

NOTE: Analysis was done using soy milk and dairy cheese garnish. Calcium levels would be substantially higher if fortified soy milk was used.

GREAT GRAINS

The use of a wide variety of whole grains is essential to a well-balanced vegetarian diet as indicated in the vegetarian food guide. They are high in complex carbohydrate, B vitamins, protein and trace minerals. There are many ways to cook grains: simmered in liquid until tender, pressure cooked, or baked. Whatever you choose, remember to use a pot large enough to allow for the expansion of the grain. Millet and barley expand to 4 times their original size, while other grains usually expand 2 to 3 times.

Cooking Whole Grains in Under 30 Minutes

Sometimes people don't use whole grains, assuming they take too long – 45 minutes to 1 hour to cook. But if you put the grains to soak earlier in the day, the cooking time can be cut in half. This method may be used for cooking whole grains such as pot barley, brown rice and whole grain berries (rye, wheat, spelt, kamut and oat groats). Cooking in a cast-iron pot will increase the dietary iron. Soak the grains overnight or during the day in the correct amount of water needed for cooking. When you are ready to cook them, cover and bring to a rapid boil. Stir, cover, and reduce heat to a simmer. Cook without lifting the lid for 20 to 30 minutes (it takes longer for larger grains). Now that the initial cooking is complete, you can add cooked or raw vegetables, fruit, nuts, and additional seasoning.

Cooking Grains in the Microwave Oven

You will be surprised how easy it is to cook grains in the microwave, especially if you have one with programmed cooking stages. Use a large glass casserole with a lid. Measure out the correct amount of water and add your grain. Cover and bring to a rapid boil. Reduce to simmer and cook for the suggested time. If you are using programmed cooking stages, simply set the time for boiling on high heat, then the time for simmering on low heat. If you have soaked the grain for a few hours, cooking will take half the time.

Below is a table with cooking directions for specific grains without presoaking.

Cooking Times and Directions for One Cup of
Whole Grains Without Presoaking

Grains are cooked by combining the grain with the measured amount of water, bringing to a rapid boil, covering and simmering for the recommended time.

Grain (1 cup)	Water (in cups)	Time★ (minutes)	Special Directions
Amaranth	2½	20 to 25	Toast in heavy skillet. Add water, bring to boil, cover, simmer.
Barley			
brown	3 to 4	50 to 55	
pot	2 to 3	40 to 45	
pearl	1 to 2	35 to 40	
Buckwheat groats,			
kasha	2	15 to 20	
Millet	3 to 4	20 to 30	★★
Oats, whole (groats)	3 to 4	45 to 60	
Quinoa	2	15 to 20	Rinse well in fine strainer to remove the bitter resin.
Rice, brown			
long/short grain	2	45	
brown basmati			
or wehani	2	45	
Rice, white	1 to 2	25 to 30	
Rice, wild	3	60	
Rye, triticale	4	60	
Wheat			
whole berries	3 to 4	60	
bulgur	2	15 to 20	
cracked wheat	2	30 to 35	

★ Cooking time will be longer if you have hard water.

★★ Cook the millet for 30 minutes and allow it to sit, covered, for 10 to 15 minutes or more for a fluffy product.

PERFECT PILAF

Pilafs are quick and easy to make. Leftover grains come alive and freshly cooked plain grain dishes flourish with color, flavors and nutrition.

Starting with Uncooked Grains

Lightly sauté a medium onion or some garlic in a little oil. Add any seasonings, cashews, cubes of tofu, or chopped vegetables such as mushrooms. Stir briefly and add grain and required liquid. Stir, cover and cook for the suggested time. Before serving, add a few more vegetables such as peas, chopped sweet red pepper or grated carrot. Cover and simmer for a few minutes to heat everything. Garnish platter with additional vegetables, fruits or nuts.

Reviving Leftover Grains

Sauté onions and garlic with desired spices in a little oil. Add cooked grain and chopped colorful vegetables, such as carrots, mushrooms or okra, cooking until almost soft on medium heat so that all the flavors mix well. Place on platter and garnish with chopped nuts or cherry tomatoes, fruits or parsley.

Seasoning Ideas

ORIENTAL: Soy sauce, seaweed powder, ground sesame seeds, grated ginger. Use all or any combination.

MEDITERRANEAN: Chopped fresh parsley, marjoram, sweet peppers, oregano, basil.

ASIAN: Curry powder or ground cumin with chopped cilantro, hot or sweet peppers, green onion and orange sections.

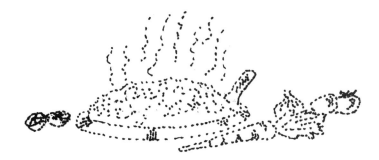

LEGUME WIZARDRY

One important secret of vegetarian cooking is stocking your freezer with a wide variety of cooked legumes to use for quick food preparation. These include adzuki beans for pasta sauce, chick-peas for hummus or a stir-fry, kidney beans for a big batch of chili, or several different beans that can be made into a wonderful stew. So whenever you cook beans, make extra, then freeze them in freezer bags or plastic containers for later use.

Cooking Beans in a Snap

Presoaking can be avoided by bringing beans to a boil, cooling and soaking for one hour. Then cook as usual. Don't add salt, tomatoes, or other highly acidic foods to beans until they are tender or they will not soften and become digestible. Very hard water (high in minerals) will increase bean cooking time.

There are two categories of legumes, each requiring a different cooking method. Presoaking is not required with the first category ("Group 1"); however, it always speeds up cooking time.

Group 1 Legumes	Cooking Time	Legume:Water Ratio
Lentils, red	25 to 35 minutes	1:2 cups (500 mL)
Lentils, brown or green	45 to 60 minutes	1:2 or 2½ cups (500–625 mL)
Mung beans	40 to 50 minutes	1:2 or 2½ cups (500–625 mL)
Split peas	30 to 50 minutes	1:2½ cups (625 mL)

Group 2 – All other beans, such as adzuki, kidney, lima, pinto, garbanzo and black beans. These beans are slower to cook; presoaking is recommended.

Presoaking Method:
1. Sort beans carefully to remove any small stones. Soak beans overnight with three times the volume of water.
2. Discard water and rinse beans thoroughly. Cover with fresh, unsalted water and boil hard for 1 minute. You may wish to add fennel seeds or kombu seaweed to reduce the gas produced during digestion. Cover and simmer for 1 to 3 hours. Add more water, if necessary, to make sure beans are covered in water as they are cooking. The cooked beans should be very soft. If you can mash these beans with your tongue against the roof of your mouth, you know that they have optimum digestibility.

3. Add seasonings and continue to cook for 10 minutes more. These cooked beans are ready for eating as they are, or you can use them in recipes.

4. If your next step is to bake the cooked beans in tomato sauce, cover beans with 2 inches (5 cm) of liquid and replenish this as it evaporates. Cover during cooking to minimize evaporation.

Cooking Beans in a Slow Cooker

Many people prefer to cook beans all day or overnight in a slow cooker. For every cup (250 mL) of dry beans, add 3 cups (750 mL) of water. You may also add bay leaves, peppercorns, or your favorite herbs. Cover, turn on the slow cooker, and by breakfast or dinner your beans will be perfect. Remember to add tomatoes and salt near the end of cooking time.

CHUNKY RED LENTIL TOMATO SAUCE

Red lentils are the fastest cooking of all dried legumes. This sauce can be prepared in about 20 minutes and simmered in a crockpot all day or cooked on the top of the stove for about 1 hour. "Chunky" refers to the vegetables; you can use those listed here, or select others. The lentils almost dissolve into the sauce, and add protein. Use more or less lentils, depending on your taste preferences.

1	onion, diced	1
2 to 3	cloves garlic, minced	2 to 3
1	large carrot, sliced diagonally	1
1	stalk broccoli, chopped	1
1 cup	sliced mushrooms (fresh or canned)	250 mL
½ cup	diced sweet green pepper	125 mL
1	small zucchini, sliced or grated	1
28 oz can	stewed tomatoes, whole or diced	796 mL can
28 oz can	prepared tomato sauce	796 mL can
1 cup	water	250 mL
½ to 1 cup	uncooked red lentils	125 to 250 mL
2 tbsp	each fresh basil and oregano (or 2 tsp/10 mL dried)	25 mL

Place all ingredients in crockpot or saucepan. Stir. If using stove top method, bring ingredients to boil, then turn heat down and simmer sauce for 1 hour or more. If using crockpot, cook on low for 6 to 8 hours, or on high for about 4 hours. Serve with your favorite pasta, or spaghetti squash.

TIP: Be adventurous with pasta! Try quinoa, spelt, kamut, vegetable or other varieties. Fresh pastas make a meal extra special.

MAKES 8 SERVINGS. Per serving: 135 calories; 6 g fiber.

VARIATIONS: Try other vegetables in this recipe: chopped cauliflower, celery, spinach or kale work well. For an extra-fast sauce, use precooked lentils, and sauté vegetables in 1 tbsp (15 mL) olive oil until tender. Add tomatoes and tomato sauce, and cook for 15 to 20 minutes.

NUTRITIONAL NOTE: This spaghetti sauce is packed with nutrients yet derives only 4 percent of its calories from fat.

✳✳✳ FOLIC ACID	✳✳✳ VITAMIN A	✳✳✳ VITAMIN C
✳✳ IRON	✳✳ MAGNESIUM	✳✳ THIAMIN
✳✳ VITAMIN B$_6$	✳✳ VITAMIN E	✳ CALCIUM
✳ NIACIN	✳ RIBOFLAVIN	✳ ZINC

NOTE: Analysis was done using ¾ cup (175 mL) dried lentils.

TWO-BEAN STEW

Any two kinds of cooked beans, your choice of cooked vegetables, dumplings or a slice of good bread make this flavorful stew a quick, nutritious meal. We like to make it with new potatoes, sweet carrots, peas, turnip and cabbage. If you want to freeze leftovers, omit the potatoes.

2 19 oz cans	beans (or 4 cups/1 L cooked)	2 540 mL cans
	(chick-peas, kidney, lima, etc.)	
1 cup	water or vegetable broth	250 mL
2	medium scrubbed potatoes, chopped	2
2	medium carrots, chopped	2
2	medium onions, chopped	2
2 cups	other vegetables, chopped	500 mL
	(turnip, cabbage, celery, kohlrabi, okra, etc.)	

2 tbsp	tamari soy sauce	25 mL
2 to 3	bay leaves	2 to 3
2 tsp	each thyme, marjoram and garlic powder	10 mL
1 to 2	tomatoes or sweet red pepper, chopped (optional)	1 to 2
½ cup	flour	125 mL
¾ cup	water	175 mL
½ cup	minced fresh parsley or frozen green peas	125 mL
	Salt and pepper, to taste	

In large Dutch oven or heavy saucepan, place drained liquid from beans. Set beans aside. Add water, cover and bring to boil. Add vegetables, soy sauce and herbs. Cover, bring to boil, reduce heat and simmer for about 8 minutes, or until vegetables are still a little crunchy. Add beans and tomatoes to cooked vegetables. Cover, and bring to boil. Combine flour and water in jar with tight fitting lid. Shake well, then slowly add mixture to hot stew, stirring while it thickens. Add parsley, cover, reduce heat, and simmer for 3 to 4 minutes. Adjust seasonings to taste.

MAKES 6 HEARTY SERVINGS, 1½ cups (375 mL) each. Per serving: 303 calories; 10 g fiber.

VARIATION: For a very quick dinner, substitute 4 cups (1 L) frozen vegetables for fresh vegetables. For additional minerals, 1 to 2 tsp (5 to 10 mL) kelp powder may be added.

Dumplings: 1 cup (250 mL) whole wheat flour, 1 tsp (5 mL) baking powder, ¼ tsp (1 mL) salt, ⅓ cup (75 mL) milk (non-dairy or dairy), 1 tbsp (15 mL) vegetable oil (optional), ½ tsp (2 mL) dill weed (optional). Mix flour, baking powder and salt thoroughly. Add remaining ingredients, stirring lightly just to mix. Using a tablespoon, place small mounds of batter the size of a walnut over thickened stew. Cover, cook on low heat without peeking, for 15 minutes.

NUTRITIONAL NOTE: A 1½ cup (375 mL) serving of this stew provides an abundance of nutrients including 15 g of protein with less than 3 g of fat and no cholesterol.

*** FOLIC ACID	*** MAGNESIUM	*** IRON
*** VITAMIN A	*** VITAMIN C	*** ZINC
*** THIAMIN	** VITAMIN B$_6$	* CALCIUM
* NIACIN	* RIBOFLAVIN	

NOTE: Analysis was done using chick-peas and red kidney beans.

CRISPY TOFU FINGERS

These two recipes have great track records for turning people (including children) on to tofu. They're super simple too! Tofu fingers can be used as the protein part of a dinner, as appetizers, or in sandwiches. When you go out for dinner with a non-vegetarian group, and want to take along the ingredients for your "meat alternate," these simple recipes work well. Some people like tofu moist; others like it crisp, so experiment with the cooking time.

1 tsp	vegetable oil (or spray)	5 mL
12 oz	extra firm tofu	350 g
½ cup	thick sauce (vegetarian oyster-style sauce,	125 mL
	sweet and sour sauce, BBQ sauce or	
	other favorite thick sauce)	
	Salt, garlic powder or other seasonings, as desired	

Coat cookie sheet with oil. Slice tofu lengthwise, about ¼ in (5 mm) thick, and pat dry. Put sauce in dish, dip each piece of tofu into sauce, coating it well. Place tofu on cookie sheet in single layer (pieces can be touching, but should not overlap). Sprinkle with seasoning. Bake at 350°F (180°C) for 20 to 30 minutes, depending on how crispy you like your tofu.

MAKES 3 SERVINGS.

See Nutritional Note and analysis following Red Star Tofu Fingers for nutritional details.

RED STAR TOFU FINGERS

Tofu is a wonderfully versatile food. It can be used in everything from dips to dessert. It doesn't have an overbearing taste, so you can flavor it however you like. Tofu is nutritious and easy to digest. It's inexpensive too!

2 tbsp	tamari soy sauce	25 mL
½ cup	Red Star T-6635+ nutritional yeast	125 mL
1 tsp	seasoning (garlic powder, curry, Mrs. Dash, Spike, paprika or other)	5 mL
12 oz	extra firm tofu, cut into ¼ in (5 mm) slices	375 g
1 tsp	vegetable oil (or spray)	5 mL

Into small bowl pour tamari. In another small bowl, mix together yeast and seasoning. Dip tofu slices into tamari, then into seasoned yeast. Place tofu slices on baking sheet, lightly wiped or sprayed with oil. Bake at 350°F (180°C) for 20 minutes. Or fry coated tofu in a little oil until both sides are browned.

MAKES 3 SERVINGS. Per serving: 230 calories.

NUTRITIONAL NOTE: Although other brands of nutritional yeast powder or flakes taste just the same, the brand Red Star T6635+ is a reliable source of vitamin B_{12} for vegans. Tofu, with its low fiber content, helps to balance the higher fiber foods found in many vegetarian diets.

✱✱✱ CALCIUM	✱✱✱ FOLIC ACID	✱✱✱ IRON
✱✱✱ MAGNESIUM	✱✱✱ NIACIN	✱✱✱ RIBOFLAVIN
✱✱✱ THIAMIN	✱✱✱ VITAMIN B_{12}	✱✱✱ ZINC
✱✱ VITAMIN B_6		

VEGETABLE STIR-FRY

If you're getting tired of your same old stir-fries, the two easy but interesting combinations here will wake up your taste buds! The first seasoning mixture adds a sweet and gingery taste; the second is more exotic. Hijiki, a seaweed high in calcium, is included as an optional ingredient; this is a good way to introduce seaweed into your menus.

Basic recipe:

1 tbsp	vegetable oil	15 mL
1	medium onion, sliced	1
2	medium carrots, sliced diagonally	2
3 cups	broccoli florets and peeled and sliced stems	750 mL
1½ cups	chick-peas, firm tofu, tempeh or seitan pieces	375 mL
2 tbsp	dry hijiki seaweed (optional)	25 mL
⅓ cup	very hot water (optional)	75 mL

Then add seasoning mixture no. 1 or no. 2 to the basic recipe.

Seasoning mixture no. 1

2 tbsp	tamari soy sauce	25 mL
1 tbsp	freshly grated ginger	15 mL
1 tbsp	rice syrup or honey	15 mL

OR

Seasoning mixture no. 2

2 to 3 tbsp	tamari soy sauce	25 to 50 mL
2 to 3 tsp	rice vinegar or white wine vinegar	10 to 15 mL
1 tsp	ground cumin	5 mL
2	cloves garlic, minced	2
1 tsp	minced or freshly grated ginger	5 mL
2 tbsp	fresh cilantro (optional)	25 mL

If you are using hijiki, combine it with hot water in small bowl. Set aside to soak for 15 minutes. In another bowl, combine ingredients for seasoning mixture no. 1 or no. 2 and pour it over the chick-peas, tofu, seitan or tempeh. Heat oil in wok or deep cast-iron skillet over high temperature. Sauté onion until golden brown. Add carrots and cook until tender-crisp. Add remaining ingredients including seasoning mixture. Cook an additional 2 to 3 minutes. Serve with brown rice, noodles, other grains or pasta.

MAKES 3 SERVINGS, 2 cups (500 mL) each. Per serving: 272 calories; 7 g fiber.

VARIATIONS: Use 1 tsp (5 mL) sesame oil as part of the oil. OR Add 1 cup (250 mL) green beans, cauliflower or okra at the same time as carrots. OR Add 1 cup (250 mL) snow peas, sweet red, yellow or green peppers, mushrooms, mung bean sprouts, bok choy or sui choy, or ½ cup (125 mL) green onions at the same time as broccoli. OR Add ¼ cup (50 mL) cashew nuts.

NUTRITIONAL NOTE: Each serving of this stir-fry provides 12 g protein and only 7 g fat.

✴✴✴ FOLIC ACID	✴✴✴ IRON	✴✴✴ MAGNESIUM
✴✴✴ VITAMIN A	✴✴✴ VITAMIN C	✴✴ CALCIUM
✴✴ NIACIN	✴✴ THIAMIN	✴✴ VITAMIN B$_6$
✴✴ ZINC	✴ RIBOFLAVIN	

NOTE: Analysis was done using chick-peas.

MILLET PATTIES

Cooked millet is moist and has a slightly buttery sweet flavor, apparent in these patties. They are great with gravy for dinner or in a bun or sandwich for lunch.

1 cup	dry millet	250 mL
2½ cups	boiling water	625 mL
¼ cup	finely chopped onion	50 mL
¼ cup	whole wheat flour or gluten flour	50 mL
2 tbsp	tamari soy sauce	25 mL
1 tbsp	Red Star T-6635+ nutritional yeast	15 mL
½ tsp	garlic powder	2 mL
1 tsp	oregano or thyme	5 mL
8 oz	medium-firm tofu made with calcium (optional)	250 g
2 tbsp	ground sunflower seeds, almonds or cashews (optional)	25 mL

Cook millet in water, covered, for 45 minutes; allow to cool. Add remaining ingredients and form into patties or balls. Bake at 325°F (160°C) on greased baking sheet until browned, 30 to 45 minutes. Or, fry in small amount of oil until golden on both sides. Place in casserole, cover with gravy. Bake in oven for about 10 minutes more.

MAKES ABOUT 6 PATTIES, 3 oz (80 g) each. Per patty: 112 calories; 3 g fiber.

NUTRITIONAL NOTE: One patty is a good source of B vitamins, with 10 g of protein, and only 5 g of fat.

✱✱✱ IRON	✱✱✱ MAGNESIUM	✱✱✱ NIACIN
✱✱✱ RIBOFLAVIN	✱✱✱ THIAMIN	✱✱✱ VITAMIN E
✱✱✱ ZINC	✱✱ CALCIUM	✱✱ FOLIC ACID
✱✱ VITAMIN B_6	✱✱ VITAMIN B_{12}	

SIMPLE BROWN GRAVY

This savory gravy is delicious over stuffed squash, mashed potatoes or brown rice.

¼ cup	flour	50 mL
½ cup	cold water	125 mL
1½ cups	boiling water	375 mL
	(vegetable water can also be used)	
1 tbsp	each dark miso and tamari soy sauce	15 mL
	OR	
2 tsp	each nutritional yeast and	10 mL
	vegetarian or chicken-style seasoning	
¼ tsp	each rosemary, thyme, sage	1 mL
1	bay leaf	1
1 tsp	garlic powder	5 mL
	Salt and pepper, to taste	

Put flour and cold water in jar. Put lid on jar and shake until smooth liquid is formed. In small saucepan, make broth with boiling water and all other ingredients. Stir in flour mixture. Cook, stirring, 2 to 3 minutes over medium heat until mixture thickens. Serve hot with loaves or patties.

MAKES 2 CUPS (500 mL).

VARIATION: For a mushroom or onion gravy, sauté ½ cup (125 mL) of finely chopped onions or mushrooms (or both) in 1 tsp (5 mL) oil. Add to broth, and proceed as directed above.

HOW TO MAKE PATTIES FROM LEFTOVERS

Once you learn the secret of what holds a patty together, you can experiment with ethnic seasonings. Select from the following lists of leftovers, moisture and texture ingredients and seasonings. Patties can be fried in a little oil, baked on a greased cookie sheet or frozen for later use.

Leftovers

Start with 1 to 2 cups (125 to 250 mL) of any cooked grains such as rice, millet, bulgar wheat or porridge as your base. Then add one of the following binding ingredients:

½ cup	**mashed or raw grated potato**	125 mL
2 to 3 tbsp	**oatmeal, gluten flour or whole wheat flour**	25 to 50 mL
½ to 1 cup	**crumbled tofu**	125 to 250 mL
1	**egg**	1
½ cup	**ground nuts such as walnuts, filberts or pecans**	125 mL

Use one or more of these moisture and texture ingredients:

¼ cup	**grated carrot**	50 mL
¼ cup	**chopped water chestnuts**	50 mL
¼ cup	**chopped mushrooms, sautéed, onions or celery**	50 mL

Seasonings

Here are some exotic ways of flavoring your patty.

Mexican

Choose one or more of these seasonings.
- 3 tbsp (50 mL) salsa
- 1 to 2 tsp (5 to 10 mL) chili powder
- 2 tbsp (25 mL) cilantro

Asian

Choose one of the following:
- 1 to 2 tsp (5 to 10 mL) mild curry paste
- 1 tsp (5 mL) ground cumin
- ½ tsp (2 mL) coriander
- 2 tsp (10 mL) masala powder

Mediterranean

Choose one or more of the following:
- 1 tsp (5 mL) dill weed, basil, thyme or oregano
- 1 tbsp (15 mL) lemon juice
- 1 tsp (5 mL) sesame tahini

Savory

Add one or more of the following:
- 1 tsp (5 mL) marjoram
- 1 tsp (5 mL) nutritional yeast flakes
- 1 tsp (5 mL) kelp powder

FRUIT AND NUT MUFFINS

Don't let the list of ingredients fool you. These muffins are very simple to make. They are heavier than the "cake muffins" many people have become accustomed to, but much more satisfying, and delicious. If you use mashed banana or grated apple in the recipe you may wish to reduce the sweeteners.

2 cups	whole wheat flour	500 mL
1 cup	wheat germ or oat bran (or a combination)	250 mL
2 tsp	baking powder	10 mL
½ tsp	baking soda	2 mL
2 tsp	cinnamon	10 mL
1 tsp	allspice	5 mL
1 cup	mashed bananas, pumpkin, grated apple, carrot or zucchini	250 mL
⅓ cup	vegetable oil	75 mL
1 cup	milk (non-dairy or dairy)	250 mL
1	flax egg replacer (see next page) or egg	1
¼ cup	blackstrap molasses	50 mL
¼ cup	liquid sugar (maple syrup or honey)	50 mL
½ cup	raisins or dates (optional)	125 mL
½ cup	chopped walnuts or pecans (optional) (¾ cup/175 mL each of raisins and nuts can be used, if desired)	125 mL

In large bowl, combine all dry ingredients except raisins and nuts. In small bowl, stir together wet ingredients including the flax egg replacer. Add wet to dry ingredients and stir until just blended. Add raisins and nuts. Fill 12 greased muffin tins (vegetable or lecithin spray works well). The trick to big, moist muffins is to load tins right to the top. Bake at 375°F (190°C) for about 15 to 20 minutes or until done.

MAKES 12 LARGE MUFFINS. Per muffin: 268 calories; 5 g fiber.

NUTRITIONAL NOTE: These muffins are nutritional powerhouses, and served with some fresh fruit, they make a great breakfast or substantial snack. Each muffin packs over 6 g of protein.

✱✱✱ MAGNESIUM	✱✱ FOLIC ACID	✱✱ IRON
✱✱ THIAMIN	✱✱ ZINC	✱✱ VITAMIN B$_6$
✱✱✱ VITAMIN E	✱ NIACIN	

NOTE: Analysis was done using ground flax, banana and soy milk. If fortified soy milk or cow's milk were used, the calcium content would be considerably higher.

FLAX EGG REPLACER FOR ONE EGG

This flax egg substitute works well in pancakes, cookies, cakes and muffins. It helps to produce a moist, light product and provides essential omega-3 fatty acids. You can buy flax seed already ground, or grind 1 cup (250 mL) of seeds in a blender and store in freezer.

1 tbsp	ground flax seed	15 mL
	(grind 2 cups/500 mL flax seeds in blender and store the remainder in freezer)	
3 tbsp	water	50 mL

Mix flax and water in small bowl. Let sit 2 to 3 minutes. Egg replacer is ready when thick.

MAKES THE EQUIVALENT OF ONE EGG.

NOTE: In some recipes, ground flax seed may be added directly to wet ingredients.

CARROT CAKE

This hearty cake makes a great addition to any lunch box.

½ cup	vegetable oil	125 mL
⅔ cup	maple syrup or honey	150 mL
1½ cups	finely grated carrots	375 mL
½ cup	milk (non-dairy or dairy)	125 mL
1 tbsp	lemon juice	15 mL
2 tbsp	ground flax seed egg replacer or 2 eggs	25 mL
2 cups	whole wheat flour	500 mL
2 tsp	baking powder	10 mL
½ tsp	each baking soda and salt	2 mL
1 tsp	each cinnamon, allspice and ginger	5 mL
½ cup	chopped walnuts or pecans	125 mL
1 cup	raisins	250 mL

In large bowl, stir together first 6 ingredients. In small bowl, combine all other ingredients. Add dry ingredients to wet. Pour into greased bundt pan or a 9 x 9 in. (23 x 23 cm) cake pan and bake at 350°F (180°C) for 50 to 60 minutes.

MAKES 12 SERVINGS. Per serving: 174 calories; 4 g fiber.

VARIATION: To reduce the fat content of this cake, use only ¼ cup (50 mL) oil and increase the milk to ¾ cup (175 mL).

NUTRITIONAL NOTE: This carrot cake puts many other cakes to shame in its nutritional value. All the wholesome ingredients used in making it add up to a little boost in B vitamins, iron and many other minerals. As an added bonus, it's about half the calories of traditional carrot cakes.

** MAGNESIUM	* FOLIC ACID	* IRON
* NIACIN	* ZINC	* RIBOFLAVIN
*** VITAMIN A	* THIAMIN	*** VITAMIN E
* VITAMIN B₆		

BERRY UNCHEESECAKE

Virginia McDougal, an experimental cook from Oregon, developed the filling for this special recipe. The beautiful appearance of this dessert will make it a conversation piece at festive occasions. For those with soy or dairy allergies, this dessert will be a treat.

Oatmeal Cinnamon Crust

1 cup	oatmeal	250 mL
½ cup	whole wheat flour	125 mL
½ cup	finely ground almonds, walnuts or sesame seeds	125 mL
1 tsp	cinnamon	5 mL
¼ tsp	salt	1 mL
1 tsp	vanilla	5 mL
3 tbsp	liquid sugar (maple syrup or honey)	50 mL
¼ cup	vegetable oil	50 mL
1 tbsp	concentrated orange juice	15 mL

Filling

½ cup	millet, uncooked	125 mL
2 cups	water	500 mL
½ tsp	salt	2 mL
⅓ cup	unsalted cashews	75 mL
⅓ cup	lemon juice	75 mL
1 tsp	grated lemon rind	5 mL
⅓ cup	maple syrup or honey	75 mL
1 tsp	vanilla	5 mL
1 tsp	lemon extract (optional)	5 mL

Topping

2 to 3 cups	berries or sliced fruit (strawberries, kiwis, peaches, plums, etc.)	500 to 750 mL

2 to 3 tbsp	**all-fruit jelly or jam, melted**	25 to 50 mL
	(optional)	
1 drop	**almond extract (optional)**	1 drop

Crust: In large bowl, combine dry ingredients. Mix well. In smaller bowl combine wet ingredients. Carefully add wet to dry ingredients without over-mixing. Press firmly into sides and bottom of a 9 or 10 in (23 or 25 cm) pie plate. Bake in 350°F (180°C) oven for 9 to 12 minutes or until lightly browned. Cool before filling.

Filling: In saucepan, place millet, water and salt. Bring to boil, cover and simmer for about 45 minutes, until water is absorbed and millet is soft. Meanwhile, in blender or food processor, add all remaining ingredients. Purée for about 1 minute, until perfectly smooth. Scrape down sides, if necessary. When cooked millet is still warm, add it to blender mixture. Process for about 1 minute, until creamy and smooth. You may have to stop blender and push mixture down with a rubber spatula and stir to blend. Pour into cooked pie shell. Chill.

Topping: Arrange fruit over filling and serve, or prepare a glaze as follows: Add almond extract to melted jelly. Brush fruit with melted jelly. Chill.

TIP: Press crust into plate with your hands inside a plastic bag. No mess!

MAKES 8 TO 10 SERVINGS. Per serving: 190 calories; 4 g fiber.

NUTRITIONAL NOTE: One serving of this delicious pie provides 4 g of protein with less than half the fat of a traditional cheesecake.

** MAGNESIUM	** VITAMIN C	** VITAMIN E
* IRON	* NIACIN	* RIBOFLAVIN
* THIAMIN	* VITAMIN A	* ZINC

NOTE: Analysis was done using ⅛ of a pie with strawberries.

APPENDIX 1: GLOSSARY

Adzuki beans: Small, dark-red, mild-tasting beans, which cook quicker than most other beans. Available in Oriental groceries and natural food stores.

Agar-agar: A clear, flavorless substance from some red seaweeds. It is freeze-dried, sold in sticks, flakes or powder and used like gelatin. Use 1/4 less agar-agar when substituting in place of gelatin. Available in both natural food stores and Oriental markets.

Amaranth: Ancient Aztec grain with a buckwheat flavor. Available at natural food stores and Oriental markets.

Atherosclerosis: A buildup of fatty material (plaque) in the arteries, including those surrounding the heart.

Baba ghanoush: A Middle-Eastern appetizer spread made of eggplant, tahini, garlic and spices; often served with pita bread.

Black turtle beans: Small, black, oval-shaped beans that are a staple in South America and used widely in China. Available dried or canned in natural food stores and many supermarkets.

Blackstrap molasses: A dark, strong-tasting liquid by-product of sugar refining. It contains significant amounts of minerals, calcium and iron. Other types of molasses have very low mineral content compared to blackstrap molasses.

Buckwheat: Technically not a grain, but a member of the rhubarb family; buckwheat is gluten free, and therefore excellent for those who have wheat allergies. It can be purchased as kasha, flour or groats.

Bulgar: Cracked wheat that has been hulled and parboiled. Available in coarse or fine-ground varieties.

Cilantro: The fresh leaves of the coriander plant. It also is called Chinese or Mexican parsley.

Control group: In a scientific study, this group goes untreated or receives a placebo treatment while the experimental group receives the treatment. This allows the researchers to better determine the effects of the treatment.

Couscous: Crushed, steamed and dried durum wheat, popular in Moroccan and other Middle Eastern dishes. Available in refined or whole wheat varieties.

Dulse: A purple-red soft textured seaweed, with a unique spicy flavor used in soups, condiments. It is high in minerals, such as iron, potassium, magnesium, iodine and phosphorus.

Egg replacer: A substitute for eggs in cooked and baked foods. Some examples are ground flaxseed, arrowroot powder and tofu. Available in natural food stores and supermarkets.

Falafel: A spicy chick-pea pattie that originated in the Middle East. Also often made into balls and served in pita bread with lettuce, tomatoes, onions and a creamy dressing.

Flaxseed (linseed): A small brown seed that is high in the omega-3 fatty acid, alpha linolenic acid, and the mineral boron. For maximum benefits, grind and use on cereals or in baking as an egg replacer. Also available in oil form. Once the seed coat has been broken, it becomes rancid very quickly, so it must be frozen or kept refrigerated.

Garbanzo beans (Chick-peas): Round, light-brown beans with a nutty flavor. Traditionally used in Middle-Eastern dishes such as hummus and falafel.

Gram: A unit for measuring weight. Commonly abbreviated as g (28 g = 1 oz).

Hijiki: A black string-like seaweed that expands to five times its dry volume. It should be soaked for about ten minutes before using. Available in Oriental and health food stores. It is a good source of calcium.

Hummus: A Middle-Eastern spread or dip made of chick-peas, tahini, lemon juice, garlic and seasonings.

Hydrogenated fat: A process in which hydrogen is added to liquid vegetable oil changing it into a solid margarine or shortening. The fat that is formed is more saturated and contains trans fatty acids, which can raise cholesterol.

Kamut: An ancient, grain that is related to the wheat family. It can be used in place of wheat in cooking and baking.

Kelp powder: A delicate-flavored, salty-tasting brown seaweed that is ground into a powder. It adds flavor and minerals, such as calcium and iron, to many foods. To increase minerals in your diet, add it to the ingredients for making such foods as breads, muffins, stews and omit the salt. Available in Oriental markets and natural food stores.

Kohlrabi: A root vegetable related to the cabbage family, similar in shape to a turnip but with a light green skin. It can be steamed, stir-fried or eaten raw with a dip.

Leek: A mild onion-garlic-flavored vegetable that resembles a giant green onion.

Legume: A family of plants whose seeds are in pods (e.g., beans, peas, lentils and peanuts). Most legumes are low in fat, and high in protein, minerals and fiber.

Meat analogues: Products made to resemble meat in taste, and nutritional composition. They are often made with wheat gluten or soy protein.

Mg/dl: Milligrams per deciliter (1/1,000 of a gram per 1/10 of a liter).

Microgram: 1/1,000,000 of a gram. Commonly abbreviated mcg or µg.

Milligram: 1/1,000 of a gram. Commonly abbreviated mg.

Millet: A tiny, round, golden grain that becomes light and fluffy when cooked. Popular in India and Africa. It is very low in gluten, making it an ideal grain for those with sensitivity to gluten. Available in natural food stores, many specialty groceries and some supermarkets.

Miso: A salty paste made from cooked, aged soybeans and sometimes grains such as barley and rice. Thick and spreadable, it's used for flavoring and soup bases. Comes in several varieties; darker varieties tend to be stronger flavored and saltier than lighter varieties. Available in natural food stores and some Oriental grocery stores.

Mmol/l: A unit of measure expressing the amount of a given substance in millimoles (mmol) or 1/1000 of a mole per liter of fluid.

Non-dairy "milks": Any "milk" liquid that is made from plant foods such as nuts, seeds, grains and soybeans. Unless they are fortified, the calcium content is lower than that of cow's milk. They can be substituted for cow's milk in most recipes but must **never** be used in place of infant formula.

Nori: Thin, crispy sheets of pressed seaweed usually crumbled as a garnish or rolled around rice for sushi. It is also known as dried laver. Available in both natural food stores and Oriental markets.

Nut butters: Spreads made from finely ground nuts or seeds such as cashews, peanuts, almonds and sesame.

Nut "milks": Non-dairy beverages, such as almond milk, made by puréeing nuts with water in a blender. The calcium content of nut "milks" is considerably lower than cow's milk unless they are fortified. These beverages can be useful for people who are allergic to cow's milk or soy milk. However, they are not suitable for use as infant formula or as the primary milk for children under the age of six.

Nutrients: Chemical substances in food that nourish the body. Classified as protein, fats, carbohydrates, vitamins, minerals and water.

Nutritional yeast: A dietary supplement and condiment, rich in B vitamins, that has a distinct cheese-like flavor and a pleasant aroma. Although there are many brands of nutritional yeast powder or flakes, the Red Star T6635+, because it is grown on a B_{12} medium, is a reliable source of vitamin B_{12} for vegans. Nutritional yeasts are not leavening yeasts used in making bread. Available in natural food stores and some groceries stores.

Okra: Green, finger-like vegetable pods that have a slippery texture when cooked. Used in soups and stews and may be oven-fried; a source of calcium.

Omnivore: A person who eats plants and animals.

Organic food: Foods that have been grown without the use of synthetic fertilizers, pesticides, herbicides or fungicides. Certification codes vary from region to region.

Placebo: A fake harmless supplement or substance given to the control group in a scientific study.

Quinoa: (pronounced keen-wa) An ancient grain of the Incas, quinoa is nicknamed the "supergrain" because it contains more high-quality protein than any other grain. This round, sand-colored, quick-cooking grain has a light texture and a mild, nutty taste. Wash well before cooking to remove a natural strong-tasting resin. It is very low in gluten, which makes it a good substitute for those who have wheat allergies.

Rice "milk": "Milk" made by puréeing rice and water and straining it. Although it can be used by those who have a sensitivity to cow's milk or soy milk, it is lower in protein, calcium and fat. Thus it is not suitable for use as an infant formula, or as a primary milk for children under the age of six.

Rutabaga: A large, yellow-fleshed root vegetable with a sweet flavor. It can be cooked like a potato, added to winter stews, or eaten raw.

Seed butters: Spreads made from finely ground nuts or seeds such as cashews, peanuts, almonds and sesame.

Seitan: A chewy, high-protein food made to resemble meat in taste and texture by boiling or baking flavored wheat gluten.

Soybean: A legume which has a higher percent of protein and fat compared to the others, making it more versatile. Can be made into products such as tofu, miso, tempeh, soy milk, soy sauce, soy flour, soy grits, meat analogues and textured vegetable protein.

Soy milk: A non-dairy milky liquid made from soybeans. As of this printing, the soy milk in Canada is not fortified, so the calcium content is very low compared to cow's milk. Therefore it should not be used as an infant formula. In the United States, some soy milks are fortified with calcium, vitamin D and other nutrients.

Spelt: A Middle-Eastern grain related to wheat.

Sui choy: A crunchy, mild Chinese cabbage. It has pale oblong white stems with pale green top leaves. Rich in calcium.

Tahini: A thick, smooth paste made of raw, ground sesame seeds. Available in natural food stores, Middle Eastern or gourmet groceries, and some supermarkets. Rich in calcium.

Tamari: A type of soy sauce naturally fermented from soybeans.

Tempeh: A high-protein, highly digestible, cultured food made from soybeans and sometimes grains. Available in Oriental grocery stores and natural food stores.

Textured vegetable protein (TVP): A fibrous-textured soy product that resembles meat. Available dried in granules, chunks or flakes at natural food stores.

Tofu (soybean curd): A highly versatile soy product made from the milk of soybeans and coagulated with nigari or calcium salts. Available in many textures from soft to extra firm. Medium firm tofu when made with calcium salts provides an excellent source of calcium, while the extra firm one made with nigari provides higher levels of zinc and iron.

Triticale: A hybrid grain developed by crossing wheat with rye, thus producing a grain that is higher in protein. It is often sold in flakes or flour rather than as a whole grain.

Triglyceride: The chemical structure of fats and oils in the body and in food. It is composed of three fatty acids bonded to glycerol.

Wakame: A brown seaweed with a mild flavor. Used in soups and stir-fries. Rich in minerals such as calcium.

Appendix 2: Nutrition Recommendations

Table 1 – *Estimated Safe and Adequate Daily Dietary Intakes of Selected Vitamins and Minerals.[a] Food and Nutrition Board, National Academy of Sciences, U.S.*

Category	Age (years)	Vitamins	
		Biotin (µg)	Pantothenic Acid (mg)
Infants	0–0.5	10	2
	0.5–1	15	3
Children and adolescents	1–3	20	3
	4–6	25	3–4
	7–10	30	4–5
	11 +	30–100	4–7
Adults		30–100	4–7

Category	Age (years)	Trace Elements[b]				
		Copper (mg)	Man-ganese (mg)	Fluoride (mg)	Chromium (µg)	Molybdenum (µg)
Infants	0–0.5	0.4–0.6	0.3–0.6	0.1–0.5	10–40	15–30
	0.5–1	0.6–0.7	0.6–1.0	0.2–1.0	20–60	20–40
Children and adolescents	1–3	0.7–1.0	1.0–1.5	0.5–1.5	20–80	25–50
	4–6	1.0–1.5	1.5–2.0	1.0–2.5	30–120	30–75
	7–10	1.0–2.0	2.0–3.0	1.5–2.5	50–200	50–150
	11 +	1.5–2.5	2.0–5.0	1.5–2.5	50–200	75–250
Adults		1.5–3.0	2.0–5.0	1.5–4.0	50–200	75–250

[a] Because there is less information on which to base allowances, these figures are not given in the main table of RDA and are provided here in the form of ranges of recommended intakes.

[b] Since the toxic levels for many trace elements may be only several times usual intakes, the upper levels for the trace elements given in this table should not be habitually exceeded.

All tables reprinted with permission.

Table 2 – Summary of Examples of Recommended Nutrients Based on Energy and Expressed as Daily Rates*

Age	Sex	Energy kcal	Thiamin mg	Riboflavin mg	Niacin NE[b]	n-3 PUFA[a] g	n-6 PUFA g
Months							
0-4	Both	600	0.3	0.3	4	0.5	3
5-12	Both	900	0.4	0.5	7	0.5	3
Years							
1	Both	1100	0.5	0.6	8	0.6	4
2-3	Both	1300	0.6	0.7	9	0.7	4
4-6	Both	1800	0.7	0.9	13	1.0	6
7-9	M	2200	0.9	1.1	16	1.2	7
	F	1900	0.8	1.0	14	1.0	6
10-12	M	2500	1.0	1.3	18	1.4	8
	F	2200	0.9	1.1	16	1.2	7
13-15	M	2800	1.1	1.4	20	1.5	9
	F	2200	0.9	1.1	16	1.2	7
16-18	M	3200	1.3	1.6	23	1.8	11
	F	2100	0.8	1.1	15	1.2	7
19-24	M	3000	1.2	1.5	22	1.6	10
	F	2100	0.8	1.1	15	1.2	7
25-49	M	2700	1.1	1.4	19	1.5	9
	F	1900	0.8[c]	1.0[c]	14[c]	1.1[c]	7[c]
50-74	M	2300	0.9	1.2	16	1.3	8
	F	1800	0.8[c]	1.0[c]	14[c]	1.1[c]	7[c]
75+	M	2000	0.8	1.0	14	1.1	7
	F[d]	1700	0.8[c]	1.0[c]	14[c]	1.1[c]	7[c]
Pregnancy (additional)							
1st Trimester		100	0.1	0.1	1	0.05	0.3
2nd Trimester		300	0.1	0.3	2	0.16	0.9
3rd Trimester		300	0.1	0.3	2	0.16	0.9
Lactation (additional)		450	0.2	0.4	3	0.25	1.5

a. PUFA, polyunsaturated fatty acids
b. Niacin Equivalents
c. Level below which intake should not fall
d. Assumes moderate (more than average) physical activity

Source: Health and Welfare Canada, Nutrition Recommendations: The Report of the Scientific Review Committee, Ottawa, Supply and Services Canada, 1990.

Table 3 – Summary of Examples of Recommended Nutrients Based on Age and Body Weight Expressed as Daily Rates*

Age	Sex	Weight kg	Protein g	Vit A RE[a]	Vit D µg	Vit E mg	Vit C mg	Folate µg	Vit B12 µg	Calcium mg	Phosphorus mg	Magnesium mg	Iron mg	Iodine µg	Zinc mg
Months															
0-4	Both	6.0	12[b]	400	10	3	20	25	0.3	250[c]	150	20	0.3[d]	30	2[d]
5-12	Both	9.0	12	400	10	3	20	40	0.4	400	200	32	7	40	3
Years															
1	Both	11	13	400	10	3	20	40	0.5	500	300	40	6	55	4
2-3	Both	14	16	400	5	4	20	50	0.6	550	350	50	6	65	4
4-6	Both	18	19	500	5	5	25	70	0.8	600	400	65	8	85	5
7-9	M	25	26	700	2.5	7	25	90	1.0	700	500	100	8	110	7
	F	25	26	700	2.5	6	25	90	1.0	700	500	100	8	95	7
10-12	M	34	34	800	2.5	8	25	120	1.0	900	700	130	8	125	9
	F	36	36	800	2.5	7	25	130	1.0	1100	800	135	8	110	9
13-15	M	50	49	900	2.5	9	30[e]	175	1.0	1100	900	185	10	160	12
	F	48	46	800	2.5	7	30[e]	170	1.0	1000	850	180	13	160	9
16-18	M	62	58	1000	2.5	10	40[e]	220	1.0	900	1000	230	10	160	12
	F	53	47	800	2.5	7	30[e]	190	1.0	700	850	200	12	160	9
19-24	M	71	61	1000	2.5	10	40[e]	220	1.0	800	1000	240	9	160	12
	F	58	50	800	2.5	7	30[e]	180	1.0	700	850	200	13	160	9
25-49	M	74	64	1000	2.5	9	40[e]	230	1.0	800	1000	250	9	160	12
	F	59	51	800	2.5	6	30[e]	185	1.0	700	850	200	13	160	9
50-74	M	73	63	1000	5	7	40[e]	230	1.0	800	1000	250	9	160	12
	F	63	54	800	5	6	30[e]	195	1.0	800	850	210	9	160	9
75+	M	69	59	1000	5	6	40[e]	215	1.0	800	1000	230	8	160	12
	F	64	55	800	5	5	30[e]	200	1.0	800	850	210	8	160	9
Pregnancy (additional)															
1st Trimester			5	0	2.5	2	0	200	0.2	500	200	15	0	25	6
2nd Trimester			15	0	2.5	2	10	200	0.2	500	200	45	5	25	6
3rd Trimester			24	0	2.5	2	10	200	0.2	500	200	45	10	25	6
Lactation (additional)			22	400	2.5	3	25	100	0.2	500	200	65	0	50	6

a. Retinol Equivalents
b. Protein is assumed to be from breast milk and must be adjusted for infant formula.
c. Infant formula with high phosphorus should contain 375 mg calcium.
d. Breast milk is assumed to be the source of the mineral.
e. Smokers should increase vitamin C by 50%.

Source: Health and Welfare Canada, Nutrition Recommendations: The Report of the Scientific Review Committee, Ottawa, Supply and Services Canada, 1990.

Table 4 – Food and Nutrition Board, National Academy of Sciences – National Research Council Recommended Dietary Allowances,[a] Revised 1989

Category	Age (years) or Condition	Weight[b] (kg)	(lb)	Height[b] (cm)	(in)	Protein (g)	Fat-Soluble Vitamins Vita-min A (μg RE)[c]	Vita-min D[d] (μg)	Vita-min E (mg α-TE)[e]	Vita-min K (μg)	Water-Soluble Vitamins Vita-min C (mg)	Thia-min (mg)	Ribo-flavin (mg)	Niacin (mg NE)[f]	Vita-min B6 (mg)	Fo-late (μg)	Vitamin B12 (μg)	Minerals Cal-cium (mg)	Phos-phorus (mg)	Mag-nesium (mg)	Iron (mg)	Zinc (mg)	Iodine (μg)	Sele-nium (μg)
Infants	0.0–0.5	6	13	60	24	13	375	7.5	3	5	30	0.3	0.4	5	0.3	25	0.3	400	300	40	6	5	40	10
	0.5–1.0	9	20	71	28	14	375	10	4	10	35	0.4	0.5	6	0.6	35	0.5	600	500	60	10	5	50	15
Children	1–3	13	29	90	35	16	400	10	6	15	40	0.7	0.8	9	1.0	50	0.7	800	800	80	10	10	70	20
	4–6	20	44	112	44	24	500	10	7	20	45	0.9	1.1	12	1.1	75	1.0	800	800	120	10	10	90	20
	7–10	28	62	132	52	28	700	10	7	30	45	1.0	1.2	13	1.4	100	1.4	800	800	170	10	10	120	30
Males	11–14	45	99	157	62	45	1,000	10	10	45	50	1.3	1.5	17	1.7	150	2.0	1,200	1,200	270	12	15	150	40
	15–18	66	145	176	69	59	1,000	10	10	65	60	1.5	1.8	20	2.0	200	2.0	1,200	1,200	400	12	15	150	50
	19–24	72	160	177	70	58	1,000	10	10	70	60	1.5	1.7	19	2.0	200	2.0	1,200	1,200	350	10	15	150	70
	25–50	79	174	176	70	63	1,000	5	10	80	60	1.5	1.7	19	2.0	200	2.0	800	800	350	10	15	150	70
	51+	77	170	173	68	63	1,000	5	10	80	60	1.2	1.4	15	2.0	200	2.0	800	800	350	10	15	150	70
Females	11–14	46	101	157	62	46	800	10	8	45	50	1.1	1.3	15	1.4	150	2.0	1,200	1,200	280	15	12	150	45
	15–18	55	120	163	64	44	800	10	8	55	60	1.1	1.3	15	1.5	180	2.0	1,200	1,200	300	15	12	150	50
	19–24	58	128	164	65	46	800	10	8	60	60	1.1	1.3	15	1.6	180	2.0	1,200	1,200	280	15	12	150	55
	25–50	63	138	163	64	50	800	5	8	65	60	1.1	1.3	15	1.6	180	2.0	800	800	280	15	12	150	55
	51+	65	143	160	63	50	800	5	8	65	60	1.0	1.2	13	1.6	180	2.0	800	800	280	10	12	150	55
Pregnant						60	800	10	10	65	70	1.5	1.6	17	2.2	400	2.2	1,200	1,200	300	30	15	175	65
Lactating	1st 6 months					65	1,300	10	12	65	95	1.6	1.8	20	2.1	280	2.6	1,200	1,200	355	15	19	200	75
	2nd 6 months					62	1,200	10	11	65	90	1.6	1.7	20	2.1	260	2.6	1,200	1,200	340	15	16	200	75

[a] The allowances, expressed as average daily intakes over time, are intended to provide for individual variations among most normal persons as they live in the United States under usual environmental stresses. Diets should be based on a variety of common foods in order to provide other nutrients for which human requirements have been less well defined. See text for detailed discussion of allowances and of nutrients not tabulated.

[b] Weights and heights of Reference Adults are actual medians for the U.S. population of the designated age, as reported by NHANES II. The median weights and heights of those under 19 years of age were taken from Hamill et al. (1979) (see pages 16–17). The use of these figures does not imply that the height-to-weight ratios are ideal.

[c] Retinol equivalents. 1 retinol equivalent = 1 μg retinol or 6 μg β-carotene. See text for calculation of vitamin A activity of diets as retinol equivalents.

[d] As cholecalciferol. 10 μg cholecalciferol = 400 IU of vitamin D.

[e] α-Tocopherol equivalents. 1 mg d-α tocopherol = 1 α-TE. See text for variation in allowances and calculation of vitamin E activity of the diet as α-tocopherol equivalents.

[f] 1 NE (niacin equivalent) is equal to 1 mg of niacin or 60 mg of dietary tryptophan.

INDEX